W9-ASJ-372

DATE DUE

DATE DUE			
JAN 0 3 1998			
NOV 2 2 1998			
DEC 1 6 1999			
OCT 0 8 2012			

The Supreme Court

Sixth Edition

Lawrence Baum
Ohio State University

CQ PRESS

A Division of Congressional Quarterly Inc.
Washington, D.C.

Printed in the United States of America

Cover design: Debra Naylor

Library of Congress Cataloging-in-Publication Data

Baum, Lawrence
    The Supreme Court / Lawrence Baum. -- 6th ed.
        p.   cm.
    Includes bibliographical references and index.
    ISBN 1-56802-321-9 (cloth : alk. paper). -- ISBN 1-56802-320-0
(paper : alk. paper)
    1. United States. Supreme Court. 2. Constitutional law--United
States. 3. Courts of last resort--United States. 4. Judicial
review--United States.   I. Title.
KF8742.B35 1998
347.73'26--dc21   97-38477
                                                                                        CIP

To Joel Grossman

Contents

Preface

E very June, the Supreme Court becomes a focus of national attention. As its annual term nears an end, the Court hands down major decisions that garner newspaper headlines. In June of 1997, for instance, the Court addressed such issues as the right to assisted suicide and the power of Congress to regulate material on the Internet.

From time to time, a retirement from the Court is announced. Such an announcement marks the beginning of a political process that continues until the Senate confirms a new justice. The process of selecting a Supreme Court justice always receives considerable publicity, and it is sometimes the subject of great public interest.

The attention that the Court receives reflects a widespread belief that it has a substantial impact on the nation and its people. That belief is well founded. Although the extent of its influence is debated, the Court certainly affects major aspects of national life, ranging from the power of organized labor to the use of capital punishment.

And yet the Supreme Court is not well understood. Even those who care the most about the Court's decisions often have only a limited sense of how and why the Court reaches those decisions. While public understanding of the presidency and Congress is far from perfect, people know more about the other branches of government than they do about the Supreme Court.

This book represents an effort to improve knowledge of the Court, to provide an understanding of how the Court operates, and to offer explanations for its behavior. The book is intended to serve as a short but comprehensive guide to the Court, for both those who already know a good deal about it and those who have a more limited sense of it.

The first chapter of the book serves as an introduction. It discusses the Supreme Court's role in general terms, examines the Court's place in the judicial system, analyzes the Court as an institution, and presents a brief summary of its history.

Each of the other chapters deals with an important aspect of the Court. Chapter 2 focuses on the justices: their selection, their backgrounds and careers, and the circumstances under which they leave the Court. Chapter 3 discusses how cases reach the Court and why some are chosen for full decisions.

Chapter 4 looks at decision making in the cases that the Court accepts for full decisions. After outlining the Court's decision-making procedures, I turn to the chapter's primary concern: the factors that influence the Court's choices among alternative decisions and policies. Chapter 5 deals with the kinds of issues on which the Court concentrates, the policies it supports, and the extent of its activism in policy making. I give special attention to changes in the Court's role as a policy maker and the sources of those changes.

The final chapter examines the ways in which other government policy makers respond to the Court as well as the Court's impact on American society as a whole. The chapter concludes with a summary of the Court's significance as a force in American life.

This edition of the book reflects the contributions that many people made to earlier editions. In revising the book for this edition, I benefited from information provided by the Office of the Solicitor General in the Justice Department and the Public Information Office of the Supreme Court. Richard Pacelle generously compiled and shared with me information on the Court's agenda in the 1990s.

As always, the people at CQ Press facilitated my efforts with their good work. I appreciate the assistance of copy editor Tracy Villano. And I am grateful to Brenda Carter, acquisitions editor for the Press, for her help and support over several editions of this book.

This book is dedicated to Joel Grossman. As a teacher, he inspired my interest in studying the courts. As an advisor and professional colleague, he has given me good counsel and needed encouragement. His own teaching and scholarship have set a standard of excellence for me. This book, and all my work, reflect his help over the years.

Chapter 1

The Court

E arly in 1996, Senator Bob Dole was the leading candi- date for the Republican presidential nomination. Emerg- ing from the large group of challengers to Dole was Patrick Buchanan, who won the important New Hampshire primary election. One of Buchanan's major themes was an attack on fed- eral courts—particularly the Supreme Court—as unduly lib- eral. Buchanan frequently attacked "ultra-liberal" justice Ruth Bader Ginsburg by name, and he cited what he saw as the disas- trous effects of the Supreme Court's decisions.[1]

Later in the campaign, Dole criticized President Clinton's appointees to the federal courts, including the Supreme Court. Clinton's "appointees to the Supreme Court," said Dole, "have been among the most willing to use technicalities to overturn death sentences for proven murderers." In contrast, Dole said, he would "appoint justices to the Supreme Court who know how to read and respect the clear language of the Constitution as it is written."[2]

Along with Dole and Buchanan, the third Republican can- didate to survive the early primary elections was Steve Forbes, a magazine publisher who had never run for office. Forbes's unexpectedly strong campaign was made possible by his ex- penditure of more than thirty million dollars of his own money. The Federal Election Campaign Act (FECA) of 1974 had set strict limits on self-financing of campaigns for president and Congress, but in *Buckley v. Valeo* (1976), the Supreme Court ruled that those limits violated the First Amendment rights of candidates.

1

In the general election, Clinton and Dole both accepted federal money to fund their campaigns. Under the FECA, their acceptance of that money limited severely the amount of additional money that they could spend. But in *Buckley v. Valeo* and later decisions, the Court struck down limits on campaign money spent independently of the candidate's campaign. One of those later decisions, issued in June 1996, held that a limit on spending in Senate elections by state political parties violated the First Amendment.[3] Seemingly freed from legal restraints by those decisions, the Republican and Democratic parties spent campaign money lavishly in 1996, thereby rendering the limits on spending by candidates nearly irrelevant.

The central theme of Dole's campaign against Clinton was the "character issue," the argument that Clinton did not meet the moral and ethical standards expected of a president. Paula Jones, an Arkansas state employee when Clinton was governor, had sued Clinton for sexual harassment. Clinton's lawyers argued that under the constitutional separation of powers, the lawsuit could not proceed while Clinton was president. A federal court of appeals had ruled against Clinton on this issue, but in June 1996 the Supreme Court accepted the case for consideration.[4] By doing so, the Court ensured that there would be no further action in the case—and no further embarrassments from it for the president—until after the November election.

Taken by itself, the Supreme Court's impact on the 1996 presidential election is striking. Yet we are accustomed to the Court's prominence in the political process. In some presidential and congressional elections, past and future appointments of justices have become major campaign issues. The Court has shaped national and state politics through its decisions on the form of legislative districts, and its decision in *U.S. Term Limits v. Thornton* (1995) allowed several dozen members of Congress to remain in office by disallowing state-imposed term limits on Congress. In an earlier era, the Court's ruling in *United States v. Nixon* (1974) forced President Nixon to give tape recordings of some of his conversations to a federal court and thereby ensured that he would leave office.

The Supreme Court's impact extends far beyond the political process, reaching issues that affect the nation in fundamental ways. The Court's decisions in *Roe v. Wade* (1973) and *Planned*

Parenthood v. Casey (1992) are the most important government policies on abortion. Supreme Court decisions establish rules for use of the death penalty, for religious observances in public schools, and for regulation of the environment. These and other decisions have aroused great controversy, but most people on both sides of these issues would agree that the Court plays a central role in American life.

For this reason, those who seek to understand government and politics in the United States must inquire into the Supreme Court. Who are the people who serve on it, and how do they get there? What determines which cases and issues the Court decides? In resolving the cases before it, how does the Court choose between alternative decisions? In what policy areas is it active, and what kinds of policies does it make? Finally, what happens to the Court's decisions after they are handed down, and what impact do they actually have?

This book is intended to contribute to an understanding of the Supreme Court by answering these questions. Each question is the subject of one of the book's chapters. Chapter 1 introduces the Court and provides background information for the remainder of the book.

A Perspective on the Court

The Court in Law and Politics

The Supreme Court as a Legal Institution. The Supreme Court is, first of all, a court—the highest court in the federal judicial system. Like other courts, it has a specified *jurisdiction,* the power to hear and decide particular kinds of cases. And, like other courts, it can decide legal issues only in those cases that are brought to it. Although the Supreme Court differs from every other court in the United States, its behavior and its position in the political system are influenced by the fact that it *is* a court.

Perhaps most important, the Supreme Court makes decisions within a legal framework. While Congress simply writes new law, the policy choices that the Court faces are framed as interpretations of existing law. In this respect the Court operates within a constraint from which legislators are free.

In another respect, however, the Supreme Court's identity as a court reduces the constraints on it. The widespread belief that courts should be insulated from the political process has given the Court a certain degree of actual insulation. The lifetime appointments of Supreme Court justices allow them some freedom from concerns about approval by political leaders and voters. Justices usually stay out of partisan politics, because open involvement in partisan activity is perceived as inappropriate. And because direct contact between lobbyists and justices is generally deemed unacceptable, interest group activity in the Court is basically restricted to the formal channels of legal argument.

The Supreme Court as a Political Institution. The insulation of the Supreme Court from politics should not be exaggerated. People sometimes speak of courts as if they are, or at least ought to be, "nonpolitical." In a literal sense, of course, this is impossible: as part of government, courts are political institutions by definition. What people really mean when they refer to courts as nonpolitical is that courts are separate from the political process and that their decisions are unaffected by nonlegal considerations. This is also impossible—for courts in general and certainly for the Supreme Court.

The Court is political chiefly because it makes important decisions on major issues; people care about those decisions and want to influence them. As a result, appointments to the Court are frequently the subject of political battles. Similarly, interest groups bring cases and present arguments to the Court in an effort to affect what it does. Because members of Congress pay attention to the Court's decisions and hold powers over the Court, the justices may take Congress into account when they decide cases. And their own political values affect the votes they cast and the opinions they write in the Court's decisions.

Thus the Supreme Court should be viewed as both a legal institution and a political institution. What it does and how it operates are influenced by both the political process and the legal system. This ambiguous position makes the Court more complex in some ways than most political institutions; it also makes the Court an interesting case study in political behavior.

The Court as a Policy Maker

This book is concerned with the Supreme Court in general, but I give particular emphasis to the Court's role in the making of public policy—the authoritative rules by which government institutions seek to influence the operation of government and to shape society as a whole. Legislation to provide subsidies for wheat farmers, a judge's ruling in an auto accident case, and a Supreme Court decision laying down rules to govern police procedure are all examples of public policy. The Court may be viewed as part of a policy-making system that includes lower courts as well as the other branches of government.

Policy Making through Legal Interpretation. As I have noted, the Supreme Court makes public policy by interpreting provisions of law. Issues of public policy come to the Court in the form of legal questions that the Court is empowered to resolve. In this respect the Court's policy making differs fundamentally in form from that of Congress.

The Court does not face legal questions in the abstract. Rather, it addresses these questions in the process of settling specific controversies between parties (sometimes called litigants) that bring cases to it. In a sense, then, every decision by the Court has three aspects: it is a judgment about the specific dispute brought to it, an interpretation of the legal issues in that dispute, and a position on the policy questions that are raised by the legal issues.

These three aspects can be illustrated with the Court's decision in a 1996 case, *Board of County Commissioners v. Umbehr.* Keen Umbehr, owner of a waste hauling business, held a contract with a Kansas county to dispose of solid waste. Umbehr strongly criticized the county governing board at its meetings and in local newspapers, and he once ran unsuccessfully for a seat on the Board. In 1991 the Board voted to terminate his contract with the county. A year later he sued the Board in federal court, claiming that it had terminated his contract in retaliation for his criticism in violation of his free speech rights under the First and Fourteenth Amendments to the Constitution. The federal district court in Kansas held that as an independent contractor, Umbehr did not have the same free speech rights that a government employee possesses; on that basis, the court ruled that his claim against the Board need not be considered. The court of appeals for the Tenth Circuit reversed the district court's decision. The Supreme Court accepted the Board's petition to hear the case, and it reached a decision.

With regard to the specific dispute in the case, the Court

affirmed the court of appeals decision and sent the case back—
remanded it—to that court for further action. That action likely
would be a further remand to the district court for the trial that
Umbehr originally had been denied. He might ultimately win
or lose the case, but the Supreme Court's decision meant that
he had a chance to win.

With regard to the legal issue in the *Umbehr* case, the Court
held that the First and Fourteenth Amendments protected
contractors from government retaliation for exercise of their
free speech rights, though that protection had to be balanced
against the interests of a government body that makes a contract. That rule became applicable to any other cases in which
contractors alleged that their contracts had been terminated in
retaliation for what they said or wrote.

Finally, the *Umbehr* decision constituted a significant expansion of free speech rights. In recent years the Court has taken a
mixed position in cases involving freedom of expression, interpreting those rights broadly in some decisions but adopting
narrower interpretations in others. Its protection of the rights
of government contractors shifted the balance a little in favor of
a broad reading of the First Amendment, though future decisions would tell more about where the current Court draws the
line between free speech and government interests that may
weigh against it.

The Court's Significance in Policy Making. Through its individual decisions and lines of decisions, the Supreme Court con-
tributes a great deal to government policy on a variety of important issues. The Court's assumption of this role has been
facilitated by several circumstances. For one thing, as the French
observer Alexis de Tocqueville noted more than a century ago,
"scarcely any political question arises in the United States that
is not resolved, sooner or later, into a judicial question."[5] One
reason that policy disputes tend to reach the courts is the existence of a written Constitution whose provisions offer a basis for
challenging the legality of government actions.

Because so many policy questions come to the courts, the
Supreme Court has the opportunity to rule on a large number
that are significant. Moreover, during much of its history the
Court has welcomed that opportunity, first insisting on its supremacy as legal arbiter and later making frequent use of its

chances to rule on major issues. By doing so, it has made itself the subject of considerable criticism, not only for its specific rulings but for its general activism as a policy maker. The term *judicial activism* is sometimes used to indicate disapproval. "Basically," according to Joel Grossman, "judicial activism is what the other guy does that you don't like."[6] Negative connotations aside, the term can have many meanings. But its key element is that a court makes significant changes in public policy, particularly in policies established by other institutions.[7] In this sense the Court has engaged in a great deal of activism, and not everyone agrees that its activism is legitimate or wise.

At the same time, the Court's role in policy making is limited by three conditions. First, the Court can do only so much with the relatively few decisions that it makes in a year. In the 1993 through 1996 terms, the Court issued decisions with full opinions in fewer than 90 cases each year. In deciding such a small number of cases, the Court addresses only a select group of policy issues. Inevitably, there are whole fields of policy that it barely touches. Even in the areas in which the Court does act, it can deal with only a limited number of the issues that exist at a given time.

Second, the Court exercises considerable judicial restraint, which is the avoidance of activism. This behavior stems in part from judges' training in a legal tradition that emphasizes the value of restraint, and in part from a desire to avoid controversy and attacks on the Court. Judicial restraint is reflected in the Court's refusal to hear some important and controversial cases, such as the legal challenges brought against U.S. participation in the war in Vietnam.[8] It is also reflected in the frequent—though not consistent—practice of deciding cases on relatively narrow grounds where possible.

Third, even a highly activist Court is limited in its impact by the actions of other policy makers. The Court is seldom the final government institution to deal with the policy issues that it addresses. Its rulings usually must be implemented by lower court judges and administrators, who often retain considerable discretion about how they will put a Supreme Court decision into effect. The impact of a decision concerning police searches for evidence depends largely on how police officers react to it. Congress and the president influence the ways in which the

Court's decisions are carried out, and they can overcome its interpretations of federal statutes simply by amending those statutes. In this way Congress has superseded several of the Court's interpretations of civil rights law in recent years. There may be a considerable difference between what the Court rules on an issue and the public policy that ultimately results from government actions on that issue.

For these reasons, those who see the Supreme Court as the dominant force in the U.S. government almost surely are wrong. But if not dominant, the Court is a very important policy maker. Certainly the extent of its role is extraordinary for a court.

The Court in the Judicial System

Structure of the System

The Supreme Court works within a system of courts, and its place in that system structures its role. Strictly speaking, however, it is inaccurate to refer to a single court system in the United States, for there is both a federal court system and a separate court system in each state. The federal system can be distinguished from the state systems in terms of jurisdiction. Most of the jurisdiction of the federal courts can be placed in three categories. First are the criminal and civil cases that arise under federal laws, including the Constitution. A prosecution for bank robbery, which is a violation of federal criminal law, is brought to federal court. So are civil cases based on federal patent and copyright laws.

Second are all cases to which the U.S. government is a party. When the federal government sues an individual to recover what it claims to be owed from a student loan, or when an individual sues the federal government over disputed social security benefits, the case generally goes to federal court.

Third are civil cases involving citizens of different states, if the amount in question is at least $75,000; if this condition is met, either party may bring the case to federal court. If a citizen of New Jersey sues a citizen of Texas for $100,000 as compensation for injuries resulting from an auto accident, the plaintiff (the New Jersey resident) might bring the case to federal court, or the defendant (the Texan) might have the case "removed" from state court to federal court. If neither does so, the case will

FIGURE 1-1
Most Common State Court Structures

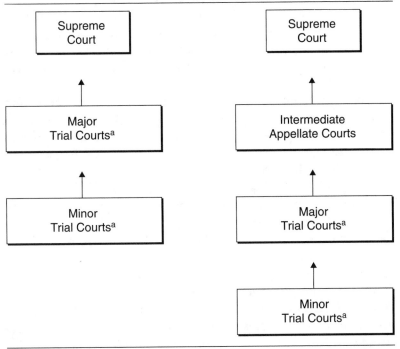

Note: Arrows indicate most common routes of appeals.

[a] In many states, major trial courts or minor trial courts (or both) are composed of two or more different sets of courts. For instance, minor trial courts in California include municipal courts and justice courts.

be heard in state court—generally, in the state where the accident occurred.

Only a small minority of cases fall into these categories. The most common kinds of cases—criminal prosecutions, personal injury suits, divorces, debt collection actions—typically are heard in state court. The trial courts of a single populous state such as Illinois or Florida hear far more cases than do the federal trial courts. But federal cases are more likely than state cases to raise major issues of public policy. If the workload of the federal courts is relatively small, it is hardly unimportant.

State Court Structure. There is considerable variation in the structures of state court systems, but some general patterns exist (see Figure 1-1). Each state system has courts that are primarily *trial courts,* which hear cases initially as they enter the court system, and courts that are primarily *appellate courts,* which review lower court decisions that are appealed to them. Most states have two sets of trial courts, one to handle major cases and the other to deal with minor cases. Major criminal cases usually concern what the law defines as felonies; major civil cases are those involving large sums of money. Most often, appeals from decisions of minor trial courts are heard by major trial courts.

Appellate courts are structured in two ways. In about one-quarter of the states, generally the less populous states, there is a single appellate court—usually called the state supreme court. All appeals from major trial courts go to this supreme court. About three-quarters of the states have a set of intermediate appellate courts below the supreme court. These intermediate courts initially hear most appeals from major trial courts. State supreme courts are required to hear certain appeals brought directly from the trial courts or from the intermediate courts, but for the most part they have discretionary jurisdiction over appeals from the decisions of intermediate courts. The term *discretionary jurisdiction* means simply that a court can choose to hear some appeals and refuse to hear others; cases that a court is required to hear fall under its *mandatory jurisdiction*.

Federal Court Structure. The structure of federal courts is shown in Figure 1-2. At the base of the federal court system are the federal district courts. There are ninety-four district courts in the United States; each state has between one and four, and there is one district court in the District of Columbia and in some of the territories such as Guam. The district courts hear all federal cases at the trial level, with the exception of a few types of cases that are heard in specialized courts.

Above the district courts are the twelve courts of appeals, each of which has jurisdiction over appeals in one of the federal judicial circuits. The District of Columbia constitutes one circuit; each of the other eleven circuits includes three or more states. The Second Circuit, for instance, includes Vermont, New York, and Connecticut. Appeals from the district courts in one circuit generally go to the court of appeals for that circuit, along with appeals from the Tax Court and from some administrative agencies. Patent cases and some claims against the federal government go from the district courts to the specialized Court of Appeals for the Federal Circuit, as do appeals from three

FIGURE 1-2
Basic Structure of the Federal Court System

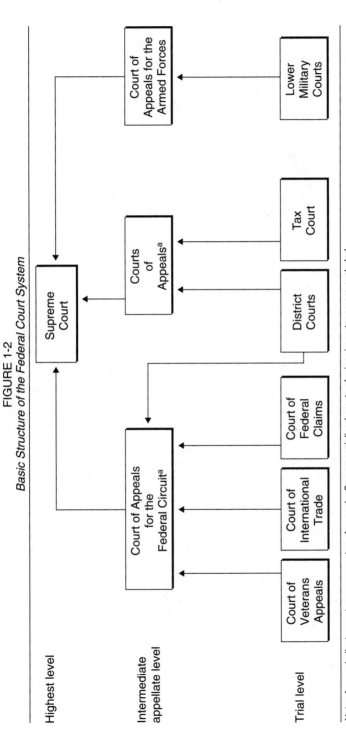

Note: Arrows indicate most common routes of appeals. Some specialized courts of minor importance are excluded.

^a These courts also hear appeals from administrative agencies.

TABLE 1-1
Summary of Supreme Court Jurisdiction

A. Original jurisdiction
   1. Disputes between states[a]
   2. Some types of cases brought by a state
   3. Disputes between a state and the federal government
   4. Cases involving foreign diplomatic personnel

B. Appellate jurisdiction[b]
   1. All decisions of federal courts of appeals and specialized federal
      appellate courts
   2. All decisions of the highest state court with jurisdiction over a case,
      concerning issues of federal law
   3. Decisions of special three-judge federal district courts (mandatory)

[a] It is unclear whether these cases are mandatory, and the Court treats them as discretionary.
[b] Some minor categories are not listed.

specialized trial courts. The Court of Appeals for the Armed Forces hears cases from lower courts in the military system.

The Court's Jurisdiction

The Supreme Court stands at the top of the federal judicial system. Its jurisdiction, summarized in Table 1-1, is of two types. First, the Constitution gives the Court jurisdiction over certain specified classes of cases as a trial court—what is called *original jurisdiction*. Those cases may be brought directly to the Court. The Court's original jurisdiction includes some cases to which a state is a party and cases involving ambassadors. Most cases within the Court's original jurisdiction can be heard alternatively by a district court. Lawsuits between two states can be heard only by the Supreme Court, and these lawsuits—often involving disputed state borders—account for most of the decisions based on the Court's original jurisdiction. The Court frequently refuses to hear cases under its original jurisdiction— even some lawsuits by one state against another. In part for this reason, full decisions in original jurisdiction cases are not plentiful; there have been about 175 such decisions in the Court's entire history.[9] When the Court does accept an original case, it usually appoints a "special master" to gather facts and propose a decision to the Court.

TABLE 1-2
Sources of Supreme Court Cases in Recent Periods
(in percentages)

	Federal courts			State courts
	Courts of appeals	District courts	Specialized courts	
Cases brought to the Court[a]	74.1	0.1	1.9	23.9
Cases heard by the Court[b]	77.6	3.9	5.3	13.2

Note: Original jurisdiction cases are not included.

[a] Cases in which the Court granted or denied hearings, October 7–21, 1996.
[b] Cases in which the Court heard oral argument, 1995 term.

Second, the Court has *appellate jurisdiction* to hear cases brought by parties dissatisfied with certain lower court decisions. In the federal system, such cases can come from the federal courts of appeals and from the two specialized appellate courts. Cases may also come directly from special three-judge district courts that hear a few classes of cases. Most cases that reach the Court from the three-judge district courts concern voting and election issues.

Cases can come to the Supreme Court after decisions by the state supreme courts if they involve claims arising under federal law, including the Constitution. More precisely, a case can come to the Court from the highest state court with the power to hear it—in one instance, from the police court of Louisville, Kentucky.[10] Table 1-2 shows that a substantial majority of the cases that come to the Court, and an even larger majority of the cases that it hears, originated in federal court rather than in state court.

The rule by which state cases come to the Supreme Court may be confusing, because cases arising under federal law ordinarily start in federal court. But cases brought to state courts on the basis of state law sometimes contain issues of federal law as well. This situation is common in criminal cases. A person who is accused of burglary under state law will be tried in a state court. But during the state court proceedings, the defendant may argue that his rights under the Constitution were violated in a police search. The case eventually can be brought to the Supreme Court on that issue. If it is, the Court will have the power to rule only on the federal issue, not on the issues of state law involved in the case. For instance, the Court cannot rule on whether the defendant actually committed the burglary.

Nearly all cases brought to the Court are under its discretionary jurisdiction, so it can choose whether or not to hear them. They come to the Court primarily in the form of petitions for a writ of certiorari, a legal device by which the Court calls up a case for decision from a lower court. Some cases, called appeals, must be heard by the Court. In a series of steps culminating in 1988, Congress converted the Court's jurisdiction from mostly mandatory to almost entirely discretionary. Today, appeals can be brought in only the few small classes of cases that come directly from three-judge district courts.

The Supreme Court hears only a fraction of 1 percent of the cases brought to federal and state courts. As this figure suggests, courts other than the Supreme Court have ample opportunity to make policy on their own. Moreover, their decisions help to determine the ultimate impact of the Court's policies. Important though it is, the Supreme Court is hardly the only court that matters.

A First Look at the Court

The Court's Physical Structure

The Supreme Court did not move into its own building until 1935. During its first decade the Court met first in New York and then in Philadelphia. The Court moved to Washington, D.C., with the rest of the federal government at the beginning of the nineteenth century. For the next 130 years it sat in the Capitol, as a "tenant" of Congress.

The Court's accommodations in the Capitol were not entirely adequate. Among other things, the lack of office space meant that justices did most of their work at home. After an intensive lobbying effort by Chief Justice William Howard Taft, Congress appropriated money for a Supreme Court building in 1929. The five-story structure, completed in 1935, occupies a full square block across from the Capitol. Because the primary material in the impressive building is marble, it has been called a "marble palace."

The building houses all the facilities necessary for the Court's operation. The Court's formal sessions are held in the courtroom on the first floor. The justices sit behind their bench at the front of the courtroom; other participants and spectators sit in sections in the back of the room and along the sides. Behind the courtroom is the conference room, where the justices meet to decide cases. Also near the courtroom are the chambers that contain offices for the associate justices and their staffs. (The chief justice's chambers are attached to the conference room.) Like members of Congress, justices often move into "better" offices as they are vacated by departing colleagues. Clarence Thomas did so when Byron White retired in 1993. Newly appointed justice Ruth Bader Ginsburg then took the unprecedented step of moving into a second-floor office rather than inheriting Thomas's old office, which she thought too small and too dark.[11]

The Court's Personnel

The Justices. Under the Constitution, members of the Supreme Court must be nominated by the president and confirmed by a majority vote in the Senate. The Constitution establishes that they will hold office "during good behavior"— that is, for life unless they relinquish their posts voluntarily or are removed through impeachment proceedings. Beyond these basic rules, such questions as the number of justices, their qualifications, and their duties have been settled by federal statutes and by tradition.

We are accustomed to a Court of nine members, but the number of justices was changed several times during the Court's first century. The Judiciary Act of 1789 provided for six justices. Subsequent statutes changed the number successively to five, six, seven, nine, ten, seven, and nine. The changes were made in part to accommodate the justices' duties in the lower federal courts, in part to serve partisan and policy goals of the president and Congress. The most recent change to nine members was made in 1869; any further changes in size appear quite unlikely.

In 1997 each of the associate justices received a salary of $164,100; the chief justice received $171,500. These salaries may be supplemented by income earned outside the Court, primarily through fees for speeches and lectures, up to a limit of $20,400 a year. Some justices also have considerable personal wealth on which they can draw: Sandra Day O'Connor, John Paul Stevens, Ruth Bader Ginsburg, David Souter, and Stephen Breyer apparently are millionaires, and Antonin Scalia may be as well.[12]

The primary duty of the justices, of course, is to participate in the collective decisions of the Court: determining which cases to hear, deciding cases, and writing and contributing to opinions. Ordinarily, the Court's decisions are made by all nine members, but there are several exceptions.

A justice may decide not to participate in a case because of a perceived conflict of interest; this self-disqualification is called a *recusal*. In a period of two-and-a-half years between 1994 and 1997, there were 192 recusals in the Court's rulings on petitions for hearings and decisions on the merits. While the justices usually give no reasons for recusing themselves, the most common reason clearly is their stock holdings; 158 of the 192 recusals were by Stephen Breyer and Sandra Day O'Connor, both of whom have substantial holdings.[13] Justices sometimes recuse themselves when a relative's law firm participates in a case, and in 1993 seven justices issued a statement describing the rules they would follow in deciding whether such a recusal was appropriate.[14] To take a different kind of example, Clarence Thomas recused himself from *United States v. Virginia* (1996), in which the all-male status of the Virginia Military Institute was challenged, because his son was a student at VMI.

The Court may function with only eight members for some period because a vacancy on the Court has not yet been filled. This last occurred at the beginning of the 1991 term, until Thomas was confirmed to replace Thurgood Marshall. Illness may also leave the Court short-handed, though a justice who misses the oral arguments in a case may still participate in the Court's decision. This was the course that Chief Justice William Rehnquist took after back surgery required him to be absent from arguments at the beginning of the 1995 term.[15]

When only eight justices participate in a decision, the Court may divide 4–4. A tie vote affirms the lower court decision. Ordinarily in this situation the individual votes are not announced and no opinions are written. A recent example was a 1996 case that raised an important issue about the application of copyright law to computer software; Justice Stevens recused himself, and the other eight justices split evenly.[16]

In rare instances, the Court fails to achieve a quorum of six members. In 1995, a federal court of appeals ruled that a 1983 federal statute requiring federal judges to pay social security and Medicare taxes had diminished their salaries in violation of the Constitution. The federal government asked the Court to hear the case. Four of the justices potentially were affected financially by the outcome, so they recused themselves and the Court fell one member short of a quorum.[17] Failure to achieve a quorum, like a tie vote, results in affirmance of lower court decisions.

In addition to their participation in collective decisions, the justices make some decisions individually, as circuit justices. The United States has always been divided into federal judicial circuits. Originally, most appeals within a circuit were heard by ad hoc courts composed of a federal trial judge and two members of the Supreme Court assigned to that area as circuit justices. The circuit duties were arduous, particularly in the days when long-distance travel was very difficult. The justices' "circuit-riding" responsibilities were reduced in several stages and eliminated altogether when Congress created the courts of appeals in 1891.

The twelve judicial circuits continue to have circuit justices assigned to them, with three justices doing double duty. The circuit justices deal with applications for special action, such as a request to stay a lower court decision (prevent it from taking effect) until the Court decides whether to hear a case. Ordinarily, such an application must go first to the circuit justice. That justice may rule on the application as an individual or refer the case to the whole Court. If the circuit justice rejects an application, it can then be made to a second justice. That justice ordinarily refers it to the whole Court.

Some applications for stays concern important issues such as state restrictions on abortion or the drawing of legislative districts. The death penalty is a recurring issue; the Court is confronted with numerous requests to grant or vacate (remove) stays of execution, many of which come very close to the scheduled execution time. Since 1992 the Court has had a law clerk to help it handle these cases.[18] When considered by the full Court, these requests sometimes result in close votes, dissenting opinions, and what one commentator called "hard feelings among the Justices."[19] In *Anderson v. Buell* (1996), for instance, three other justices joined Justice Scalia's strong dissent from the Court's decision not to vacate a stay of execution. Not surprisingly, votes on stays of execution reflect the same perspectives on the death penalty that justices express in the Court's full decisions on the issue.

For the most part, the nine justices are equal in formal power. The exception is the chief justice, who is the formal leader of the Court and of the federal judicial system. The official title, "Chief Justice of the United States," symbolizes the chief's responsibilities for the federal judicial system as a whole. In this role, the chief chairs the Judicial Conference and conveys to Congress the views of the conference on legislative issues. The chief also delivers an annual "state of the judiciary" message, directed primarily at Congress.[20]

Within the Court, the chief justice presides over the Court's public sessions and conferences. The chief also supervises administration of the Court, with the assistance of committees of justices such as the Committee for the Budget and the Cafeteria Committee. One justice (in recent years, Scalia) serves as "social secretary."[21]

For Rehnquist, at least, the chief's special title is important; several years ago he scolded a few attorneys for referring to him as "Justice." In 1995 he began to wear a judicial robe with four gold stripes on each sleeve, one modeled on the costume of the British lord chancellor in a theater production that he had attended. The new robe had the effect, if not the intent, of distinguishing the chief justice from his colleagues.[22] Justice Blackmun sometimes received letters that addressed him as "Chief Justice." "Whenever these come in," he reported, "I send them down the hall" to Rehnquist. "It kind of burns him up a bit."[23]

Busy though they are with their judicial work, the justices engage in a good deal of outside activity. Most common are speeches and lectures at law schools and legal conferences. This activity is heaviest in summer, when the Court's workload is lightest. This work often provides opportunities for paid travel. The justices' 1996 financial disclosures indicated that in the preceding year they had traveled to such places as Barcelona, London, and Beijing.[24]

What the justices say in these settings often conveys a sense of their views on public issues. In a 1996 speech, Chief Justice

Rehnquist argued that impeachment of judges should be based solely on criminal conduct and not on their rulings in cases; some observers inferred that he was responding to presidential candidate Bob Dole's suggestion that a federal judge be impeached for his ruling in a drug case.[25] In a 1995 speech to a conservative legal group, Justice Thomas criticized some developments in legal thought and a specific Supreme Court decision of a past era on the rights of public welfare recipients.[26]

Justices sometimes become involved in the political process more directly, primarily by consulting with presidents. Such consultation troubles some observers of the Court, especially when it might compromise a justice's impartiality. Abe Fortas, appointed by Lyndon Johnson, continued to serve actively as a presidential adviser on a wide range of issues, some of which could have come before the Court. Fortas also disclosed information on the Court's deliberations in two cases to an FBI official.[27] Warren Burger, appointed chief justice by Richard Nixon, later talked with Nixon about pending cases.[28] Since Burger and Nixon, however, it appears that no justice has engaged in that kind of presidential consultation.

Each justice is a powerful figure, with the ability to cast one of nine votes in decisions that have considerable impact on the lives of Americans. Yet few of the justices qualify as famous. In a 1995 survey, 31 percent of the respondents could name Sandra Day O'Connor, the first female justice, and 30 percent named Clarence Thomas, whose 1991 confirmation hearings received enormous publicity. Chief Justice Rehnquist ranked third at 8 percent, and Steven Breyer and John Paul Stevens were recalled by only 1 percent each. Among the respondents, 17 percent could name three justices—compared with 59 percent who could name the Three Stooges.[29]

While the faces of newly seated justices may be familiar initially, public recognition fades quickly. Frequently, justices discover that even visitors to the Court do not recognize them. During a parade of antiabortion marchers in front of the Court, Harry Blackmun—who had written the opinion legalizing abortion in *Roe v. Wade* (1973)—stood nearby and watched without being noticed. Tourists have asked Anthony Kennedy and former justice Lewis Powell to take pictures of them. Another group of tourists waved to John Paul Stevens to move aside so he would not block a picture of the Court building.[30] The justices are certainly not unhappy with their anonymity. Former justice William Brennan was recognized by few people despite his considerable influence on civil liberties law; one biographer noted that "he enjoyed all the benefits of power with none of the annoyances."[31]

Law Clerks and Other Support Staff. The justices are supported by a staff of more than 300 people. A large majority of those staff members carry out custodial and police functions under the supervision of the marshal of the Court. About thirty people work for the clerk of the Court, who is responsible for the clerical processing of all the cases that come to the Court. The reporter of decisions supervises preparation of the official record of the Court's decisions, *United States Reports*. The librarian is in charge of the libraries in the Supreme Court building.

Of all the members of the support staff, the law clerks have the most direct impact on the Court's decisions. Justices can employ four clerks each, though John Paul Stevens and William Rehnquist choose to use only three. (Rehnquist likes to play tennis with his clerks, and one reporter pointed out that his three clerks are "just enough to fill a doubles team."[32]) The clerks typically are recent law school graduates who have compiled exceptional records, generally in prestigious schools; in the 1996 term, two law schools (Harvard and Yale) accounted for half of the clerks.[33] In recent years, nearly all clerks in the Court had previously clerked for judges in lower federal courts.

Clerkships are prized positions, and more than 1,000 people apply for them each year.[34] Many apply to more than one justice. One former clerk reported that "I was selective—I applied to only nine justices."[35] Clerks usually work with a justice for only one year. After leaving the Court, clerks have little difficulty obtaining good positions; indeed, some large law firms pay them "signing bonuses" of $10,000 to $30,000.[36] Many go on to establish distinguished careers. Indeed, William Rehnquist, John Paul Stevens, and Stephen Breyer were once law clerks in the Court.

What clerks do differs from justice to justice. They typically spend much of their time on the petitions for hearings by the Court, digesting information in the petitions and the lower court records and summarizing it for the justices. Clerks also work on cases that have been accepted for decision, analyzing case materials and issues and drafting opinions. Clerks also participate in the informal communication that helps the justices work toward collective decisions.

Law clerks inevitably gain some influence over what the justices do. One recent clerk estimated that "well over half of the text the Court now produces was generated by law clerks" and argued that "delegation of the initial drafting task inevitably entails a substantial transfer of responsibility over the final content of an opinion."[37] The same is true of the law clerks' role in the give-and-take of collective decision making. As a result, some observers see law clerks as highly powerful. Those observers may underestimate the ability of justices to maintain control over their decisions,[38] but clerks unquestionably hold some power.

The Court's Schedule

The Schedule by Year. The Court holds one term each year, lasting from the first Monday in October until the beginning of the succeeding term a year later. The term is designated by the year in which it begins: the 1997 term began in October 1997. Ordinarily, the Court does its collective work from late September to late June. This work begins when the justices meet to dispose of the petitions for hearings that have accumulated during the summer and ends when the Court has issued decisions in all the cases it heard during the term.

Most of the term is divided into sittings of about two weeks, when the Court holds sessions to hear oral arguments in cases and to announce decisions, and recesses of two weeks or longer. The justices meet in conference during the sittings and, less frequently, during recesses. After the Court begins its last sitting in mid-May, it hears no more cases and holds one or more sessions each week to announce decisions.

The Court issues few decisions early in the term, because of the time required after oral arguments to write opinions and reach final positions. The largest number of decisions—more than one-third in the 1996 term—are announced in June, as the justices scramble to finish their work by the end of the term. This deadline creates considerable pressure. Justice Blackmun once said that because of this pressure, "I think we do our cruddiest, our shoddiest work in April, May and June."[39]

When the Court has reached and announced decisions in all the cases it heard during the term, the summer recess begins.

Cases that the Court accepted for hearing but that were not argued during the term are carried over to the next term. In summer the justices generally spend some time away from Washington but continue their work on the petitions for hearings that arrive at the Court. During that time the Court and individual circuit justices respond to applications for special action. When the justices meet at the end of summer to dispose of the accumulated petitions, the cycle begins again.

The Schedule by Week. The schedule of weekly activities, like the annual schedule, is fairly regular. During sittings, the Court generally holds sessions on Monday through Wednesday of two weeks and Monday of the third week. All these sessions can be viewed only by the audience at the Court. Taking a position similar to that of most colleagues, Souter said in 1996 that "the day you see a camera coming into our courtroom, it's going to roll over my dead body."[40]

The sessions generally begin at ten o'clock in the morning. Oral arguments usually are held during each session except on the last Monday of the sitting. They may be preceded by several types of business. On Mondays the Court announces the filing of its order list, which is a report of the Court's decisions on petitions for hearing and other actions taken at its conference on the preceding Friday. Justices announce their opinions in cases that the Court has resolved. New members are admitted to the Supreme Court bar (thus becoming eligible to argue cases before the Court).

The oral arguments consume most of the time during sessions. Most often one hour is allocated for argument in a case, divided equally between the two sides. Thus, if there is a full complement of four cases to hear, the session lasts until about three o'clock in the afternoon, with a one-hour break for lunch. With the reduced numbers of cases accepted by the Court in recent years, however, sessions have become shorter; on average, the Court hears two or three cases on each argument day.

During sittings the Court holds two conferences each week. The Wednesday afternoon conference is devoted to discussion of the cases that were argued on Monday. In a longer conference on Friday, the justices discuss the cases argued on Tuesday and Wednesday, as well as all the other matters that must be taken up by the Court. The most numerous of these matters are the petitions for hearing.

The Court also holds a conference on the last Friday of each recess to deal with the continuing flow of business. The remainder of the justices' time during recess periods is devoted to their individual work: study of petitions for hearing and of cases scheduled for argument, writing of opinions, and reaction to other justices' opinions. That work continues during the sittings.

The Court's History

This book is concerned primarily with the Supreme Court at present and in the recent past. To better understand the current Court, it is useful at this point to examine some relevant highlights of Supreme Court history to provide context for the excursions into history later in the book.

The Court from 1790 to 1865

The Constitution explicitly created the Supreme Court, but it said much less about the Court than about Congress and the president. In the Judiciary Act of 1789, which set up the federal court system, the Court's jurisdiction under the Constitution was used as the basis for granting the Court broad powers. Still, what it would do with its powers was uncertain, in part because their scope was ambiguous.

The Court started slowly, deciding only about fifty cases and making few significant decisions between 1790 and 1799.[41] Several candidates rejected offers of nominations to the Court, and two justices—including Chief Justice John Jay—resigned to take more attractive positions in state government. But the Court's fortunes improved considerably under John Marshall, chief justice from 1801 to 1835. Marshall, who was appointed by President John Adams, dominated the Court to a degree unmatched by any other justice. He used his dominance to advance the policies that he favored and the position of the Court itself.

The Court's key assertion of power under Marshall probably was its decision in *Marbury v. Madison* (1803), in which the Court struck down a federal statute for the first time. In his opinion for the Court, Marshall argued that when a federal law is inconsistent with the Constitution, the Court must uphold the supremacy of the Constitution by declaring the law unconstitutional and refusing to enforce it. A few years later, the Court also claimed the right of judicial review over state acts.

The Court's aggressiveness resulted in denunciations and threats, including an effort by President Thomas Jefferson to have Congress remove at least one justice through impeachment. But Marshall's skill in avoiding confrontation helped to protect the Court from a successful attack. Gradually the powers that he claimed for the Court and the Court's central role in the policy-making process came to be accepted by the other branches of government and by the general public.

This acceptance was tested by the Court's decision in *Scott v. Sandford* (1857), generally known as the *Dred Scott* case. Prior to that decision the Court had overturned only one federal statute, the minor law involved in *Marbury v. Madison.* In *Dred Scott,* however, Marshall's successor, Roger Taney (1836–1864), wrote the Court's opinion holding that Congress had exceeded its constitutional powers in prohibiting slavery in some territories. That decision was intended to resolve the legal controversy over slavery. Instead, the level of controversy increased, and the Court was vilified in the North. The Court's prestige suffered greatly, but the Court and its basic powers survived without serious challenge.[42]

During this period the Court was concerned with more than its own position; it was addressing major issues of public policy. The primary area of its concern was federalism, the legal relationship between the national and state governments. Under Marshall, the Court gave strong support to national powers. Marshall wanted to restrict state policy where that policy interfered with activities of the national government, especially its power to regulate commerce. Under Taney, the Court was not as favorable to the national government. But Taney and his colleagues did not reverse the direction the Court had taken under Marshall. As a result, the constitutional power of the federal government remained strong; the Court had subtly altered the lines between the national government and the state governments in support of the former.

The Court from 1865 to 1937

After the Civil War, the Court increasingly focused on government regulation of the economy. By the late nineteenth century, all levels of government were adopting new laws to regulate business activities. Among them were the federal antitrust laws, state regulations of railroad practices, and federal and state laws concerning employment conditions. Inevitably, much of this legislation was challenged in the courts on constitutional grounds.

Although the Supreme Court upheld a great many government policies regulating business in this period, it gradually became less friendly to those policies. That position was reflected in the development of constitutional doctrines limiting government power to control business activities. Those doctrines were used with increasing frequency to attack regulatory legislation; in the 1920s, the Supreme Court held unconstitutional more than 130 regulatory laws.[43]

In the 1930s, the Supreme Court's attacks on economic regulation brought it into serious conflict with the other branches. President Franklin Roosevelt's New Deal program to combat the Great Depression included sweeping statutes to control the economy, measures that enjoyed widespread support. In a series of decisions in 1935 and 1936 the Court struck down several of these statutes, including laws broadly regulating industry and agriculture, generally by 6–3 and 5–4 margins.[44]

Roosevelt responded in 1937 by proposing legislation under which an extra justice could be added to the Court for every sitting justice over the age of 70. The result would have been to increase the Court's size temporarily to fifteen justices, thus allowing Roosevelt to "pack" the Court with justices favorable to his programs. While this plan was being debated in Congress, however, the Court took away most of the impetus behind it. In a series of decisions in 1937, the Court upheld New Deal legislation and similar state laws by narrow margins, taking positions contrary to its collective views in recent cases.[45] As a result of this shift, which came to be known as "the switch in time that saved nine," the Court-packing plan died.

During the congressional debate, one of the conservative justices retired. Several other justices left the Court in the next few years, giving Roosevelt the ideological control of the Court that he had sought through the Court-packing legislation. The new Court created by his appointments fully accepted the economic regulation that had been viewed unfavorably by its predecessor, giving very broad interpretations to the constitutional powers to tax and to regulate interstate commerce.

The Court from 1937 to the Present

A Shift to Civil Liberties Concerns. Since its retreat in the late 1930s, the Court has continued to uphold major economic policies of the federal government. The Court hears many cases concerning economic regulation, but this field has become less important as part of its work and as a source of major decisions. Instead, the Court's primary emphasis in the current era is on civil liberties. More precisely, the Court gives most attention to the interpretation of legal protections for freedom of expression and freedom of religion, for the procedural rights of criminal defendants and others, and for equal treatment of racial minorities and other disadvantaged groups by the government.

The Court's general position on civil liberties issues has varied a good deal during this period. Changes in the Court's position have reflected changes in its membership. The one constant factor has been the Court's collective interest in addressing civil liberties issues.

Activism in the Warren Court. The Court was most supportive of civil liberties during the 1960s, the latter part of the period in which Earl Warren was chief justice (1953–1969). The policies of the Court during that period are often identified with Warren but other liberal justices played roles of at least equal importance. Especially important were Hugo Black and William Douglas, Roosevelt appointees who served throughout Warren's tenure, and William Brennan, an Eisenhower appointee.

The best-known decision of the Warren era was *Brown v. Board of Education* (1954), in which the Court ordered the desegregation of southern school systems and began the long process of desegregation that continues today. The Court also supported the rights of black Americans in several other policy areas. During the 1960s, the Court expanded the rights of criminal defendants in state trials, most notably in landmark decisions concerning the right to counsel (*Gideon v. Wainwright,* 1963), police search and seizure practices (*Mapp v. Ohio,* 1961), and the questioning of suspects (*Miranda v. Arizona,* 1966). The Court supported freedom of expression by expanding First Amendment rights in several areas, particularly obscenity and libel. In a series of cases beginning with *Baker v. Carr* (1962), the Court required that legislative districts be equal in population.

Partial Retrenchment in the Burger and Rehnquist Courts. When Earl Warren retired in 1969, he was succeeded as chief justice by Warren Burger, President Nixon's first appointee to the Court. Nixon made three more appointments in 1970 and 1971. The Court's membership changed much more slowly after that, but each new justice chosen in the next twenty years was selected by a conservative Republican president—one by Gerald Ford, three by Ronald Reagan, and two by George Bush. In 1986 Reagan named Nixon appointee William Rehnquist, the most conservative member of the Court, to succeed Warren Burger as chief justice. The string of Republican appointments was broken with Bill Clinton's two appointments in 1993 and 1994.

The Republican appointments gradually made the Court's policies more conservative, but not as quickly or as decisively as many observers had expected. As the number of liberal justices declined, the Court's record shifted from support of most civil liberties claims that it considered to a denial of most. The shift was most decisive on issues of criminal procedure, but it occurred in other fields as well. Even in the Rehnquist Court, however, many minor decisions and some major ones supported broad interpretations of civil liberties. The Court was also increasingly conservative on economic issues such as labor relations and environmental protection, but here too the shift was moderate and undramatic.

The Supreme Court's policies continue to evolve in complex ways; recent history has underlined the difficulty of predicting where the Court is going. The Court's history has also taught us that its direction is largely a reflection of its membership, so the selection of justices is a crucial process. I examine that process in the next chapter.

NOTES

1. Joan Biskupic, "GOP Presidential Candidates Stage Full-Court Press Against Justices," *Washington Post,* March 9, 1996, A10.

2. Katharine Q. Seelye, "Dole Criticizes Court Nominees," *New York Times,* April 20, 1996, 7.

3. *Colorado Republican Federal Campaign Committee v. Federal Election Commission* (1996). Full legal citations for the cases mentioned in this book are provided in the Case Index.

4. *Clinton v. Jones* (1996).

5. Alexis de Tocqueville, *Democracy in America,* trans. Henry Reeve, rev. Francis Bowen (New York: Alfred A. Knopf, 1945), 1:280.

6. Richard Willing, "'Activist' Label Actively Applied," *USA Today,* March 10, 1997, 3A.

7. Bradley C. Canon, "A Framework for the Analysis of Judicial Activism," in *Supreme Court Activism and Restraint,* ed. Stephen C. Halpern and Charles M. Lamb (Lexington, Mass.: Lexington Books, 1982), 385–419.

8. *Mora v. McNamara* (1967); *Massachusetts v. Laird* (1970); *Sarnoff v. Shultz* (1972).

9. See Vincent L. McKusick, "Discretionary Gatekeeping: The Supreme Court's Management of Its Original Jurisdiction Docket Since 1961," *Maine Law Review* 45 (1993): 185–242.

10. *Thompson v. City of Louisville* (1960).

11. Claudia MacLachlan, "Ginsburg's New Digs," *National Law Journal,* September 6, 1993, 2.

12. Tony Mauro, "Justices' Private Holdings Can Affect Their Public Duty," *USA Today,* June 2, 1997, 2A.

13. Ibid.,1A.

14. Erwin N. Griswold and Ernest Gellhorn, "High Court Recusal: Just the First Steps," *National Law Journal,* April 11, 1994, A21, A22.

15. Joan Biskupic, "Justices Review Voting Rights Case," *Washington Post,* October 3, 1995, A3.

16. Joan Biskupic, "High Court Split on Computer Copyright," *Washington Post,* January 17, 1996, A3. The case was *Lotus Development Corporation v. Borland International, Inc.* (1996).

17. Linda Greenhouse, "Justices Skeptically Review Law on Cable System Access," *New York Times,* October 8, 1996, A10. The case was *United States v. Hatter* (1996).

18. See Phil McCombs, "The Clerk of Last Appeals," *Washington Post,* February 24, 1996, D1, D2.

19. John C. Jeffries, Jr., *Justice Lewis F. Powell, Jr.* (New York: Charles Scribner's Sons, 1994), 445.

20. See, for example, "Rehnquist's Year in Review," *Legal Times,* January 6, 1997, 16–18.

21. See Bernard Schwartz, *Decision: How the Supreme Court Decides Cases* (New York: Oxford University Press, 1996), 73–74.

22. David Margolick, "Here Comes the Chief Justice (Please Don't Call Him Judge)," *New York Times,* April 26, 1991, B1; Tony Mauro, "High Court Highs and Lows," *Legal Times,* December 18–25, 1995, 20.

23. Reynolds Holding, "Blackmun Says Court Direction Disappointing," *San Francisco Chronicle,* June 10, 1992, A12.

24. Joan Biskupic, "From Moscow to Missoula, Justices' Jaunts Span the Globe," *Washington Post,* August 5, 1996, A17.

25. Linda Greenhouse, "Rehnquist Joins Fray on Rulings, Defending Judicial Independence," *New York Times,* April 10, 1996, A1, A11; Katharine Q.

Seelye, "Dole Rejects Chief Justice's Criticism of Politicians Who Scold Judges for Their Rulings," *New York Times*, April 11, 1996, A12.

26. "Justice Thomas: On Heroes and Victims," *Legal Times*, October 16, 1995, 10, 12–13. The decision was *Goldberg v. Kelly* (1970).

27. James Rowen, "FBI Files Show Justice Violated Court Secrecy," *Milwaukee Journal*, January 21, 1990, 1A, 20A; see also Alexander Charns, *Cloak and Gavel: FBI Wiretaps, Bugs, Informers, and the Supreme Court* (Urbana: University of Illinois Press, 1992).

28. Seymour M. Hersh, "Nixon's Last Cover-Up: The Tapes He Wants the Archives to Suppress," *New Yorker*, December 14, 1992, 81.

29. Joan Biskupic, "Has the Court Lost Its Appeal?" *Washington Post*, October 12, 1995, A23.

30. David G. Savage, *Turning Right: The Making of the Rehnquist Supreme Court* (New York: John Wiley & Sons, 1992), 210, 236; Linda Greenhouse, "Life and Times," *New York Times Magazine*, March 7, 1993, 84.

31. Kim Isaac Eisler, *A Justice for All: William J. Brennan, Jr., and the Decisions That Transformed America* (New York: Simon & Schuster, 1993), 247.

32. Savage, *Turning Right*, 306.

33. Information on the law clerks' backgrounds was provided by the Supreme Court's Public Information Office.

34. Joan Biskupic, "Clerks Gain Status, Clout in the Temple of Justice," *Washington Post*, January 2, 1994, A23.

35. John Greenya, "Super Clerks," *Washington Lawyer* 6 (May–June 1992): 40.

36. See Carrie Johnson, "Snagging Supreme Court Clerks," *Legal Times*, November 25, 1996, 1, 11, 13–14, 16.

37. Sean Donahue, "Behind the Pillars of Justice: Remarks on Law Clerks," *The Long Term View* 3 (Spring 1995): 81–82.

38. See Mark Tushnet, "Thurgood Marshall and the Brethren," *Georgetown Law Journal* 80 (August 1992): 2110–2119.

39. Stuart Taylor, Jr., "Blackmun Provides a Peek at the People under Those Robes," *New York Times*, July 25, 1988, B6.

40. Ronald Goldfarb, "The Invisible Supreme Court," *New York Times*, May 4, 1996, 15.

41. See William R. Casto, *The Supreme Court in the Early Republic: The Chief Justiceships of John Jay and Oliver Ellsworth* (Columbia: University of South Carolina Press, 1995).

42. Robert G. McCloskey, rev. by Sanford Levinson, *The American Supreme Court*, rev. ed. (Chicago: University of Chicago Press, 1994), 64–66.

43. This figure was calculated from data in Congressional Research Service, *The Constitution of the United States of America: Analysis and Interpretation* (Washington, D.C.: Government Printing Office, 1987), 1885–2113.

44. The cases included *Carter v. Carter Coal Co.* (1936), *United States v. Butler* (1936), and *Schechter Poultry Corp. v. United States* (1935).

45. The cases included *National Labor Relations Board v. Jones & Laughlin Steel Corp.* (1937), *Steward Machine Co. v. Davis* (1937), and *West Coast Hotel Co. v. Parrish* (1937).

Chapter 2

The Justices

The course that the Supreme Court takes is a product of many influences, but the dominant influence is its membership. The Court's frequent 6–3 and 5–4 votes are a reminder that different people would decide cases in different ways. They would also differ in the cases they chose to hear and in the rules of law they proclaimed in their opinions. Thus the identity of the people who serve as justices is a matter of fundamental importance for the Court, and the attention given to the selection of new justices is fully merited.

As of mid-1997 there have been 148 nominations to the Supreme Court, and 108 justices have sat on the Court. Four candidates were nominated and confirmed twice, 8 declined appointments or died before beginning service on the Court, and 28 did not secure Senate confirmation.[1] This chapter focuses on the past several decades. (Table 2-1 lists the 50 nominations to the Court since 1920 and the 41 justices chosen since that time.) The chapter's three sections discuss the selection of justices, the characteristics of the people who are selected, and how and why they leave the Court.

The Selection of Justices

Selection of a Supreme Court justice begins with the creation of a vacancy, when a member of the Court dies or steps down from the Court. Inevitably, vacancies occur at an irregular rate. Four justices left the Court in Richard Nixon's first three years in office, and Bill Clinton was able to select two new justices in his first eighteen months in office. In contrast, the absence of vacancies in the four years from 1977 through 1980 made Jimmy Carter the first president in more than a century—and the only president in history who served a full term—not to select any justices.

The formal process for selection of justices is simple. When a vacancy occurs, the president makes a nomination, which must be confirmed by a majority of those voting in the Senate. When the chief justice's position is vacant, the president has two options: to nominate a sitting justice to that position and also nominate a new associate justice, or to nominate a person as chief justice from outside the Court. Presidents usually have taken the latter course, chiefly to have a wider field from which to select the chief. But President Reagan elevated Justice William Rehnquist to the position of chief justice after Warren Burger retired in 1986.

The actual process of selection is far more complicated than the simple formal process suggests. The president and the Senate make their decisions surrounded by individuals and groups who are deeply interested in these decisions, and the process of reaching decisions is quite complex. In examining this process it will be useful first to discuss the roles of unofficial participants in the selection of justices and then to consider how the president and Senate reach their decisions.

Unofficial Participants

Since Supreme Court appointments are so important, a variety of individuals and groups seek to influence the president and Senate. Apart from members of the president's administration, the most important of these participants fall into three categories: the legal community, other interest groups, and potential justices.

The Legal Community. Because the Supreme Court is a court, lawyers have a particular interest in its membership. Because they are lawyers, their views about potential justices may carry particular weight. Occupying a special position is the American Bar Association (ABA), the largest organization of lawyers and the most prominent voice of the legal profession. The ABA seeks to influence the appointments of federal judges through evaluations of the candidates by its fifteen-member "Committee on Federal Judiciary."

TABLE 2-1
Nominations to the Supreme Court since 1921

Name	Nominated by	Replaced	Years served
William Howard Taft (CJ)	Harding	White	1921–30
George Sutherland	Harding	Clarke	1922–38
Pierce Butler	Harding	Day	1923–39
Edward Sanford	Harding	Pitney	1923–30
Harlan Fiske Stone	Coolidge	McKenna	1925–46
Charles Evans Hughes (CJ)	Hoover	Taft	1930–41
John Parker	Hoover	(Sanford)	Defeated for confirmation, 1930
Owen Roberts	Hoover	Sanford	1930–45
Benjamin Cardozo	Hoover	Holmes	1932–38
Hugo Black	F. Roosevelt	Van Devanter	1937–71
Stanley Reed	F. Roosevelt	Sutherland	1938–57
Felix Frankfurter	F. Roosevelt	Cardozo	1939–62
William Douglas	F. Roosevelt	Brandeis	1939–75
Frank Murphy	F. Roosevelt	Butler	1940–49
James Byrnes	F. Roosevelt	McReynolds	1941–42
Harlan Fiske Stone (CJ) [a]	F. Roosevelt	Hughes	1941–46
Robert Jackson	F. Roosevelt	Stone	1941–54
Wiley Rutledge	F. Roosevelt	Byrnes	1943–49
Harold Burton	Truman	Roberts	1945–58
Fred Vinson (CJ)	Truman	Stone	1946–53
Tom Clark	Truman	Murphy	1949–67
Sherman Minton	Truman	Rutledge	1949–56
Earl Warren (CJ)	Eisenhower	Vinson	1953–69
John Harlan	Eisenhower	Jackson	1955–71

Justice	President	Seat	Term/Notes
William Brennan	Eisenhower	Minton	1956–90
Charles Whittaker	Eisenhower	Reed	1957–62
Potter Stewart	Eisenhower	Burton	1958–81
Byron White	Kennedy	Whittaker	1962–93
Arthur Goldberg	Kennedy	Frankfurter	1962–65
Abe Fortas	Johnson	Goldberg	1965–69
Thurgood Marshall	Johnson	Clark	1967–91
Abe Fortas (CJ) [a]	Johnson	(Warren)	Nomination withdrawn, 1968
Homer Thornberry	Johnson	(Fortas)	Nomination became moot, 1968 [b]
Warren Burger (CJ)	Nixon	Warren	1969–86
Clement Haynsworth	Nixon	(Fortas)	Defeated for confirmation, 1969
G. Harrold Carswell	Nixon	(Fortas)	Defeated for confirmation, 1970
Harry Blackmun	Nixon	Fortas	1970–94
Lewis Powell	Nixon	Black	1971–87
William Rehnquist	Nixon	Harlan	1971–
John Paul Stevens	Ford	Douglas	1975–
Sandra Day O'Connor	Reagan	Stewart	1981–
William Rehnquist (CJ) [a]	Reagan	Burger	1986–
Antonin Scalia	Reagan	Rehnquist	1986–
Robert Bork	Reagan	(Powell)	Defeated for confirmation, 1987
Douglas Ginsburg	Reagan	(Powell)	Withdrew before formal nomination, 1987
Anthony Kennedy	Reagan	Powell	1988–
David Souter	Bush	Brennan	1990–
Clarence Thomas	Bush	Marshall	1991–
Ruth Bader Ginsburg	Clinton	White	1993–
Stephen Breyer	Clinton	Blackmun	1994–

[a] Nominated as chief justice while serving as associate justice.

[b] When Fortas's nomination for chief justice was withdrawn, no vacancy for his seat as associate justice existed.

Some presidents—most recently, Gerald Ford—have al-lowed the ABA committee to screen candidates for Supreme Court nominations, giving it essentially a veto over nomi-nations. But the Court's increasing importance to presidents has made them reluctant to give up so much power. Thus the committee has been reduced to investigating and evaluating presidential nominees who await confirmation. In each in-stance, it rates a nominee as "well qualified," "qualified," or "not qualified."

The committee is reluctant to rate nominees as unqualified, and it has never done so. But the extent of its enthusiasm for a nominee can affect the confirmation process. A unanimous rat-ing of "well qualified," one awarded to both Ruth Bader Gins-burg and Stephen Breyer, helps to smooth the path to Senate approval. By the same token, when four committee members rated Robert Bork as "not qualified" in 1987 and two did so for Clarence Thomas in 1991, the prospects for confirmation were weakened.

The ABA committee was once perceived as ideologically con-servative, but—in part because of the votes against Bork, a pres-tigious legal scholar—many conservatives now see it as unduly liberal. For that reason, some Republican senators give little weight to its judgments, and its power over appointments has declined further. Still, at least for now, the ABA remains a ma-jor participant in the process.

Other legal groups and individual lawyers also participate in the selection process. Law professors and other prominent at-torneys often announce their evaluations of nominees the Sen-ate is considering. Such evaluations may have considerable im-pact. The criticism of Nixon's nominees Clement Haynsworth and G. Harrold Carswell by prominent attorneys countered the ABA's official judgment that the two nominees were qualified and thus contributed to their rejection by the Senate.

The lawyers involved in the selection of justices sometimes include sitting members of the Supreme Court. Even though they have a direct interest in determining who their colleagues will be, justices usually stay out of the selection process. When they do participate, most often it is by recommending a poten-tial nominee.

The most active Supreme Court lobbyist in the twentieth century was Chief Justice William Howard Taft. During his tenure as chief justice (1921–1930), Taft, a former president, was not reluctant about tendering his advice to his successors and even campaigning for a candidate. In the past half century, Chief Justice Warren Burger stands out for his involvement in the selection process. He lobbied in the Senate for Haynsworth and Carswell and, a year after his retirement, testified on behalf of Bork. He also sought to influence nominations, suggesting the name of his longtime friend Harry Blackmun to the Nixon administration and recommending Sandra Day O'Connor to the Reagan administration.

Judicial intervention sometimes has a decisive effect. If Burger had not suggested his name, Blackmun might not have been considered for nomination. But justices cannot exert strong pressure on presidents, and their recommendations can be ignored or rejected. The same, of course, is true of intervention by lower court judges. In 1994, about one hundred federal judges wrote to President Clinton to endorse Richard Arnold of the Eighth Circuit Court of Appeals. Clinton was hardly hostile to Judge Arnold, a longtime friend from Arkansas, and he came close to nominating him. But ultimately Clinton decided to nominate Stephen Breyer instead.[2]

Other Interest Groups. Because they have a stake in Supreme Court decisions, many interest groups seek to influence the selection of justices. At the nomination stage, groups that are politically important to the president are in a good position to exert influence. A Democratic president, for instance, generally gives some weight to the views of labor and civil rights groups. Such groups usually can communicate directly with the president or with top presidential advisers, the best way to affect the president's views. They can also make their wishes known publicly. When President Clinton was considering his choice of a nominee to succeed Byron White in 1993, leaders of several women's groups made statements emphasizing their desire to have a woman appointed to the Court. Groups that are opposed to the president ideologically can also try to influence the nomination decision by threatening to fight the confirmation of any nominee whose views they consider too "extreme."

After White's retirement, the leader of one conservative group announced that "if Clinton makes this nomination an ideological battleground, it will turn into a judicial Armageddon."[3]

Once a nomination has been announced, groups often work for or against Senate confirmation. Group opposition to a nominee is more common than support, because groups that favor a nominee may perceive confirmation as certain even if they do nothing.

Significant interest group activity at the confirmation stage can be traced back as far as 1881, but it was fairly limited and sporadic until the late 1960s.[4] In 1968 conservative groups opposed the confirmation of Abe Fortas, President Johnson's nominee for chief justice, while liberal groups worked in support of Fortas. This activity, and Fortas's defeat, initiated an era of more frequent and more intensive interest group involvement in confirmation decisions. Labor and civil rights groups opposed President Nixon's nominations of Clement Haynsworth and G. Harrold Carswell; their efforts made possible the defeats of both nominees. Several liberal groups worked against the elevation of William Rehnquist to chief justice in 1986, helping to build significant opposition, but ultimately Rehnquist was confirmed with about a two-thirds majority.

President Reagan's nomination of Robert Bork in 1987 gave rise to an unprecedented level of group activity.[5] Liberal groups feared that the strongly conservative Bork would move an ideologically divided Court substantially to the right. Accordingly, they devoted considerable effort, and an estimated $12 million to $15 million, to achieving his defeat.[6] Their activities ranged from newspaper advertisements to direct lobbying of senators. Groups favorable to Bork's nomination took action as well. The pro-Bork groups did not mobilize as quickly or as fully as the opposition groups, and the higher level of activity against Bork was an important factor in his defeat for confirmation.[7]

The nomination of Clarence Thomas in 1991 also provoked considerable group activity. Among Thomas's supporters were the United States Chamber of Commerce and Young Americans for Freedom. Opponents included the Leadership Conference on Civil Rights, a coalition of 185 groups concerned with civil rights and civil liberties, and a smaller coalition called the Alliance for Justice; both had played central roles in the opposition to Bork as well. Individual groups such as the AFL-CIO and the National Abortion Rights Action League were also involved. The opposition groups were unable to achieve the same kind of massive campaign against Thomas that they had launched against Bork. But their opposition helped to create concern about Thomas among liberal senators and thereby contributed to the decisions by most Democratic senators to vote against Thomas's confirmation.

Interest groups played a more limited role in the confirmations of Ruth Bader Ginsburg in 1993 and Stephen Breyer in 1994; the numbers of group representatives testifying before the Senate Judiciary Committee hearings on Ginsburg and Breyer were the lowest since the nomination of John Paul Stevens in 1975.[8] In the current era as a whole, however, the level of group involvement in the confirmation process is higher than ever. That change can be explained largely by the increased number of interest groups and the increased intensity of group activity, greater awareness that nominations to the Court are important, and group leaders' learning from past episodes how to participate effectively in the confirmation process.[9] Ideological groups have also found that opposition to controversial nominees is a good way to generate interest in their causes and monetary contributions from their supporters.

Candidates for the Court. One difference between the Supreme Court and the lower federal courts is that people often become members of the Court without taking any actions to obtain their appointments. Because presidents consider Court appointments so important, they look for candidates who best serve presidential goals rather than restricting their choices to candidates who seek the job openly. For this reason most potential justices believe it is counterproductive to conduct campaigns on their own behalf.

Some people do work to obtain appointments, and some of them are successful. According to Justice William Douglas, federal judge Sherman Minton simply asked his close friend Harry Truman for a nomination in 1949; though Truman had agreed to nominate another candidate, he chose Minton instead.[10] A far more elaborate campaign secured a nomination for William Howard Taft, a somewhat reluctant president who really wanted to be chief justice. As president he worked toward his eventual selection by appointing an older chief justice, Edward White, to increase the likelihood of a vacancy in that position in the foreseeable future. White returned the favor by refusing to retire or die, despite his extreme disability, until a Republican replaced President Woodrow Wilson. When White died early in President Warren Harding's term, Taft was appointed to replace him; the appointment came after an intensive campaign by Taft that had begun even before Harding's election. One commentator appropriately described Taft as "virtually appointing himself" chief justice.[11]

In the case of Ruth Bader Ginsburg, it was her husband who did the campaigning. Apparently without his wife's knowledge, Martin Ginsburg mobilized support for her candidacy among legal scholars and members of the women's movement.[12] His activity on her behalf may have been decisive in making Ginsburg a leading candidate and ultimately the successful nominee.

People can increase their chances of winning a nomination without actively campaigning for the Court. The most obvious approach is to take public positions that would appeal to an appointing president. When a federal court of appeals overturned a Louisiana prohibition on abortion in September 1992, Judge Emilio Garza wrote a concurring opinion in which he implied that he would vote to overturn *Roe v. Wade* if given the opportunity. President George Bush had seriously considered nominating Garza to the Supreme Court in 1991. A caustic newspaper editorial charged that Garza had used this opinion "shamelessly" to show his agreement with the Bush administration's position on an issue that had been critical in the selection of nominees to the Court.[13]

Despite the success stories, campaigning for the Court is a chancy matter. There are far more aspiring justices than there are vacancies on the Court, and presidents make their choices for their own reasons. As one observer remarked in 1990, "Trying to get yourself appointed to the court by George Bush is likely to be as successful as trying to kill yourself by getting hit by lightning."[14] And someone who wants to get on the Court cannot control who becomes president. If Judge Garza was trying to appeal to President Bush, his effort became irrelevant when Bush lost his bid for reelection six weeks later.

While some people actively seek appointments to the Court,

others are reluctant to accept them. A number of candidates have declined nominations or taken themselves out of the running when they appeared likely to be nominated. Senator Howard Baker declined a nomination by President Nixon in 1971; reaffirming his lack of interest in a nomination in 1987, he said, "I've seen funeral homes that are livelier than that court."[15] In 1993 and 1994 at least four candidates for nominations to the Court withdrew from consideration. One, Senate Majority Leader George Mitchell, was even offered a nomination.[16]

Among those who accept nominations, some are ambivalent about doing so. After accepting an invitation to interview for a position on the Court, David Souter called Senator Warren Rudman—who had brought about Souter's candidacy for the position—to ask "what have you done to me now?"[17] Lewis Powell withdrew from consideration for a nomination in 1969. Two years later he declined a nomination twice before President Nixon prevailed on him to accept; Powell then came close to backing out before ultimately, and reluctantly, giving a final acceptance.[18]

Such cases are exceptions, however. Whether or not they actively sought a position on the Supreme Court, most of those who are offered a nomination have little difficulty in accepting it. Speaking of William Brennan's appointment in 1956, President Dwight Eisenhower's press secretary reported, "I never saw a man say 'yes' so fast when the President asked him to take the job."[19]

In past eras, nominees typically played little part in the confirmation process. Today, they participate actively in that process. Nominees visit with senators (Clarence Thomas, setting a record, paid "courtesy calls" on more than half of the senators) and testify before the Senate Judiciary Committee.

That testimony presents a challenge to nominees. When there is already substantial opposition to confirmation, nominees try to use their testimony to win the support of wavering senators. Even when confirmation seems assured, nominees seek to avoid saying something that raises doubts about them.

Nominees face their greatest challenge in responding to questions about their views on legal issues. Senators try to determine where a nominee stands on important issues such as

abortion and the death penalty. For their part, nominees prefer
not to make their positions clear, so that they do not "prejudge"
issues that might come before the Court or arouse opposition
from senators who disagree with their positions. Yet nominees
also know that refusal to respond to questions about their views
may anger senators.

Nominees' typical response to this dilemma is to offer some
information about their views but to speak only vaguely about
matters that might create trouble for them. Clarence Thomas
was asked repeatedly and in various ways where he stood on
abortion as a constitutional issue, and he adamantly refused
to indicate his views. In response to questions from Senator
Patrick Leahy of Vermont, Thomas said that he had never "debated the contents" of *Roe v. Wade* and that "I have not made,
Senator, a decision one way or the other" about whether the
case was properly decided.[20]

Robert Bork found himself in a particularly difficult position when he went to the Judiciary Committee. Bork had written about his views on many legal issues, taking positions that
seemed unduly conservative to many senators. In his testimony
he spoke about his views in extraordinary detail, trying to show
that he was more moderate than his writings suggested.

Both the specifics of nominees' testimony and the general
impression they give can make a difference when confirmation
is not assured. Bork's appearance before the committee left no
doubt about his impressive legal skills, but many liberal and
moderate senators remained convinced that he was too conservative—and some felt that he had not been candid about his
views. Thomas's answers to questions about abortion and other
issues also raised doubts in some senators' minds about his candor. Their testimony thereby contributed to Bork's Senate defeat and to the narrowness of Thomas's victory. In contrast,
David Souter's testimony avoided raising concerns about his
views and reassured many senators that he was not strongly conservative; as a result, his confirmation was assured.

The President's Decision

Today, every president understands the importance of Supreme Court nominations. By selecting a single justice, a president can have substantial impact on the course of national pol-

icy for many years. For this reason, presidents give nominations to the Court a high priority, and they usually give nominations a good deal of personal attention.

This does not mean that the president acts alone. In identifying candidates for nomination to the Court and making a final selection, the president receives considerable help from senior officials on the White House staff and in the Justice Department. When Bill Clinton sought a nominee in 1993, he also used a group of seventy-five volunteer lawyers to gather information and prepare lengthy biographies on forty-two candidates.[21]

Presidents and the people who help them to choose nominees must take the confirmation process into account. If presidents could appoint Supreme Court justices without Senate approval, they would simply select the people who best serve their goals. Because Senate approval *is* required, presidents must consider the possibility of a difficult battle to secure confirmation, a battle that the nominee might lose. A tough confirmation battle requires the president to expend valuable political resources, and Senate defeat of a nominee is a defeat for the president as well. The interplay of presidents' goals and the need for confirmation can be seen in the four broad considerations that influence nominations: the "objective" qualifications of potential nominees, their policy preferences, the ability to reward political and personal associates, and the building of political support.

"Objective" Qualifications. Presidents have strong incentives to select Supreme Court nominees who have demonstrated high levels of legal competence and adherence to ethical standards. A candidate who falls short on either of these criteria is vulnerable to opposition and potential defeat in the Senate. Confirmation aside, presidents want to avoid the embarrassment of identification with a justice who proves unfit. Further, most presidents have considerable respect for the Supreme Court and thus want to uphold high standards in selection.

In general, presidents' choices reflect a concern for competence. This does not mean that all nominees are highly skilled in the law, but in only a few cases has the capacity of a nominee to serve on the Court been questionable. One of those few cases was that of G. Harrold Carswell (chosen by Nixon in 1970), whose legal ability was doubted strongly and widely; Carswell was denied confirmation.

The ethical behavior of most nominees has been unexceptionable, at least so far as that behavior was known, but there are some exceptions. Abe Fortas (when nominated to be chief justice), Clement Haynsworth, and Stephen Breyer were attacked for alleged financial conflicts of interest; Fortas was also criticized for continuing to consult with President Johnson while serving as an associate justice. The charges against Fortas and Haynsworth helped bring about their defeats in the Senate. After Douglas Ginsburg was announced as a Reagan nominee, disclosures were made about a financial conflict of interest that may have occurred when he was in the Justice Department and about his past use of marijuana. The latter disclosure was especially damaging, and Ginsburg withdrew his name from consideration. An allegation that Clarence Thomas had sexually harassed an assistant while he was a federal administrator resulted in a special set of Senate hearings on the charge and put his confirmation in jeopardy.

To minimize the possibility of such embarrassments, administrations today give close scrutiny to potential nominees. After its difficulty with Douglas Ginsburg, the Reagan administration wanted to ensure that Anthony Kennedy, its choice as the next nominee, had no problems in his personal life. White House counsel A.B. Culvahouse came to Kennedy with a twenty-one-page list of questions. The FBI, itself embarrassed by its failure to discover Ginsburg's drug use, undertook a massive investigation of its own. Culvahouse stopped Kennedy during a visit to the White House to tell him that the investigation had uncovered a problem: Kennedy's daughter had an unpaid parking ticket. When nothing else turned up, Kennedy was nominated.[22]

Competence and ethics can be considered screening criteria for potential nominees. These criteria may eliminate some people from consideration, but enough candidates survive the screening process to give presidents a wide range of choices for a nomination.

Policy Preferences. By policy preferences, I mean a person's attitudes toward policy issues. These preferences have become increasingly important in nominations to the lower federal courts in recent years. They were always a major consideration in the selection of Supreme Court justices, because the Court's role in policy making was well understood. As noted earlier, presidents recognize that the ability of their appointees to influence the Court's policies is among their major legacies. On leaving the presidency, William Howard Taft reported that he had told his six appointees, "If any of you die, I'll disown you."[23] Thus all presidents seek to put on the Court individuals who share their views on important policy questions.

Presidents differ in the weights they give to the policy preferences of potential nominees. Presidents who seek to usher in a new political era are especially concerned with bringing the Supreme Court more in line with their own positions.[24] This was true of Richard Nixon and Ronald Reagan, who sought to move the country and the Court in a more conservative direction. Presidents with less ambitious policy agendas, such as Harry Truman, have put less emphasis on policy preferences as a basis for their choices. In periods when the Court plays a particularly prominent role in policy making, as it does today, presidents give more weight to the policy positions of potential nominees. In any period, some specific issues may be especially important to presidents and their political allies, as abortion has been in recent years; Bill Clinton indicated that he would not have nominated Ruth Bader Ginsburg if he had not concluded that she took a pro-choice position on abortion.[25]

It is in relation to this criterion that the Senate's role creates the greatest complications. Most Democratic presidents are distinctly liberal, most Republicans distinctly conservative. If a strongly liberal president chose a nominee whose preferences were also strongly liberal, that nominee's views would be somewhat distant from the views of Senate moderates and very distant from the views of many Republican senators. Of course, a strongly conservative president is in a similar situation. Thus most presidents face a dilemma: choose a nominee whose views mirror their own and risk difficulty with confirmation, or choose a more moderate nominee and reduce their ability to reshape the Court.

Presidents react to this dilemma in different ways, giving varying weights to the collective views of the Senate. When President Reagan nominated Robert Bork and President Bush

chose Clarence Thomas even though the Senate had a Democratic majority, they showed a willingness to trigger a Senate
battle and risk a defeat in the interest of putting a strong conservative on the Court. In contrast, Bill Clinton in 1994 chose
not to nominate Interior Secretary Bruce Babbitt after some Republican senators threatened to oppose him because they considered him too liberal and because they disagreed with his
policies concerning federal lands in the West. Even though
Babbitt was unlikely to lose in the Senate, Clinton preferred
to avoid a difficult confirmation process. Instead of Babbitt,
Clinton selected federal judge Stephen Breyer, who was viewed
as more moderate.

It is not always easy for presidents to ascertain the policy preferences of a potential nominee and to determine how those
preferences would be reflected in votes and opinions on the
Supreme Court. This is one reason that every nominee since
1975 has been a lower court judge. As Reagan's attorney general
Edwin Meese said, "You know the judicial philosophy of those
judges because they've had experience and they've written
opinions you can look at."[26] Administrations usually examine a
judge's record with some care. According to one reporter, the
Reagan administration ruled out federal judge Patrick Higgin-
botham of Texas because a footnote in one of his opinions
"could be read as endorsing the *Roe v. Wade* ruling."[27] On the
whole, sitting judges appointed to the Court have been less
likely to disappoint their nominators with their votes and opinions than have other justices.[28]

Whether or not candidates are judges, their views about legal
issues can be gauged from their public expressions or from
their interactions with people whom the president trusts. Sometimes presidents or their representatives question prospective
nominees directly about their views. Sandra Day O'Connor was
questioned by two sets of administration officials and then by
President Reagan himself, with whom she discussed abortion
and other issues.

Here, too, the need for confirmation comes into play. Presidents sometimes choose nominees whose views on major issues
are not very clear to give potential opponents less of a target. In
doing so, however, they run the risk of guessing wrong themselves about a nominee's views. President Bush chose David

Souter in 1990 partly because Souter had a very short record of statements and positions on controversial judicial issues, but people who knew Souter assured Bush that he was suitably conservative. Souter indeed was confirmed easily, but his record as a justice suggests that he was not nearly as conservative as Bush thought.

Souter is not the only justice whose positions on the Court have surprised the appointing president. Dwight Eisenhower was unhappy about the liberalism of two of his appointees, Earl Warren and William Brennan. Indeed, according to a story that is widely circulated but of uncertain accuracy, when Eisenhower was asked if he had made any mistakes as president, he replied, "Yes, two, and they are both sitting on the Supreme Court."[29]

Such disappointments are not rare, but most justices turn out to be ideologically compatible with the presidents who appoint them. And presidents who were especially careful to select compatible justices have suffered relatively few disappointments. Both Franklin Roosevelt and Richard Nixon did rather well in getting what they wanted from the justices they selected. Presidents who emphasized other criteria or chose with less care, such as Truman and Eisenhower, often did less well.

When careful presidents suffer disappointments, it is often because a justice shifts position after reaching the Court. Nixon's one "failure" in this respect was Harry Blackmun, who had a distinctly conservative record in his early years on the Court but gradually adopted more liberal positions. Anthony Kennedy also may have shifted in a liberal direction after reaching the Court—most notably, on abortion. When President Reagan was considering Kennedy, according to one aide, the administration "knew it for a fact" that Kennedy would vote to overturn *Roe v. Wade*. "His clerks had talked to him about it. He is Catholic, too. I can be emphatic about it because we were certain."[30] Indeed, Kennedy joined a 1989 opinion by William Rehnquist that seemed to support the overturning of *Roe* in an appropriate case. But three years later, Kennedy collaborated with two colleagues in an opinion that reaffirmed *Roe* in most respects.[31] Responding to this and other decisions, in 1996 a conservative publication referred to Kennedy as "surely Reagan's biggest disappointment."[32]

In any event, no justice will please the appointing president with every decision. President Clinton's two appointees joined in the unanimous decision in *Clinton v. Jones* (1997) that allowed a lawsuit against him for sexual harassment to go forward, and President Nixon's three appointees joined in the unanimous decision in *United States v. Nixon* (1974) that required him to yield tape recordings of his conversations as president. After learning of the decision, Nixon reportedly "exploded, cursing the man he had named chief justice, reserving a few choice expletives for Blackmun and Powell, his other appointees."[33]

Even though some decisions and some justices fail to meet the appointing president's expectations, the power of appointment is still a potent means by which presidents can shape the Court's policies. I examine the impact of this power more fully in Chapter 5.

Political and Personal Reward. Abe Fortas was one of Lyndon Johnson's closest associates. In 1948 Fortas's legal skills had helped preserve Johnson's victory in a disputed Senate election. As Fortas became an increasingly eminent lawyer, he continued to advise Johnson, who came to rely heavily on his counsel. Not surprisingly, when Johnson had his first opportunity to choose a Supreme Court justice, he chose Fortas. The nomination rewarded someone who had done much for Johnson, even if Fortas was quite reluctant to accept the reward. It also put on the Court someone whose ability and policy views Johnson knew well from personal experience. Three years later, Johnson nominated Fortas for elevation to chief justice. To replace Fortas as associate justice, Johnson selected Homer Thornberry, a federal judge from Texas who was also a close friend of the president.

In choosing Fortas and Thornberry, Johnson was taking a common approach. About 60 percent of the nominees to the Court had known the nominating president personally.[34] Most of Johnson's recent predecessors—Franklin Roosevelt, Truman, and Kennedy—had selected primarily personal acquaintances. For Truman, reward for political associates seemed to be the main criterion for selection.

Some appointments to the Court were direct rewards for political help. Eisenhower selected Earl Warren to serve as chief justice in part because of Warren's crucial support of Eisenhower at the 1952 Republican convention. As governor of California and leader of that state's delegation, Warren had provided needed votes on a preliminary issue, and Eisenhower's success on that issue helped to secure his nomination.

Since the 1968 nominations of Fortas and Thornberry (both of which failed when Fortas's confirmation was blocked), no president has chosen a close associate to serve on the Supreme Court. Only William Rehnquist—an official in the Nixon Justice Department—might qualify as an associate. And Nixon, three months before nominating Rehnquist, recalled his name as "Renchburg."[35] Some other appointees knew the president who selected them, but the relationships were not close.

Perhaps the main reason for the decline in the selection of personal acquaintances is that such nominees are vulnerable—as Fortas was—to charges of "cronyism." Still, future presidents might begin once again to select acquaintances, because the impulse to reward close associates can be strong. In any case, one element of political reward continues to be important: about 90 percent of all nominees to the Court—and all those chosen since 1975—have been members of the president's party. One reason is that lawyers who share the president's policy views are more likely to come from the same party, but there is also a widespread feeling that such an attractive prize should go to one of the party faithful. Nominees who were not members of the president's party were appointed because they appealed to the president in other respects. In the most recent instance, Nixon nominee Lewis Powell was an eminent lawyer who also served the president's goal of putting a southerner on the Court in order to strengthen his electoral support in that region.

Building Political Support. If nominations can reward those who helped the president politically in the past, they can also be used to seek political benefits in the future. Most often, presidents select justices with certain characteristics in order to appeal to leaders and voters who share those characteristics.

For most of the Court's history, the most important characteristic was geography. Presidents sought to provide each region with representation on the Court in order to please a maximum number of voters. Geographical diversity also had practical value. Until 1891 the justices "rode circuit," helping to staff lower federal courts in designated regions of the country, and it made sense to choose justices from the circuits they would represent. But with the end of circuit-riding and a perceived decline in sectional consciousness, geography has become less important to presidents; Nixon's effort to choose a southerner was unusual for the current era.

In the twentieth century, an interest in providing representation for religious and ethnic minority groups has influenced some nominations. It was a bonus for Reagan that Antonin Scalia would be the first justice of Italian ancestry and for Clinton that Ruth Bader Ginsburg would be the first Jewish justice since 1969. But ethnicity and religious affiliations are not viewed as critical. When Clarence Thomas rejoined the Catholic Church in 1996 and gave the Court its first non-Protestant majority, that landmark was noticed but not viewed as highly significant.[36]

In contrast, representation by race and gender has become quite important. President Bush's nomination of Clarence Thomas to succeed Thurgood Marshall reflected the pressure he felt to maintain black representation on the Court. According to one scholar, "gender was the primary and decisive factor" in President Reagan's nomination of Sandra Day O'Connor, at a time when there was a widespread feeling that a woman should be appointed.[37] By nominating Ginsburg, Clinton reaffirmed his support for groups that seek greater representation of women in government—support reflected as well in his appointing a higher proportion of women to lower court judgeships than any prior president.

Important though they are, it is doubtful that Supreme Court nominations have much direct impact on people's votes in presidential elections. It is more likely that nominations help presidents gain support from political leaders and activists, which can improve their electoral prospects indirectly. In any case, making appointments to high positions to appeal to voters is a well-established practice. And in nominating a woman (to take one example), a president may act not just for political advantage but in the belief that the country benefits from female representation on the Court.

Summary. Nominations to the Supreme Court depend on a variety of criteria, and most appointments serve multiple goals. All the considerations discussed here have been important to some nominations, but their importance has changed over time and varies from one nomination to another.

The Court's importance has at least two effects on the criteria for selection of justices. First, it makes presidents weigh all the criteria more carefully than their representatives generally do in making lower court nominations. Second, it leads to an emphasis on the criteria of competence and policy preferences rather than on the "political" considerations of reward and support building. If Supreme Court justices are better jurists than lower court judges, and if their policy preferences are more accurate reflections of their nominators' views, it is largely because presidents have a strong incentive to achieve those results.

Senate Confirmation

Once the president has nominated someone to fill a vacancy on the Supreme Court, the nomination goes to the Senate for confirmation. The nomination is referred to the Judiciary Committee, which gathers extensive information on the nominee, holds hearings at which the nominee and other witnesses testify, and then votes its recommendation for Senate action. After this vote the nomination is referred to the floor, where it is debated and a confirmation vote taken. The length of this process depends primarily on the degree of controversy concerning the nomination, though the general trend in recent years has been toward lengthier consideration of nominees.

The Senate's Role. When the president nominates someone to any position in the executive branch or the judiciary, the presumption typically is in favor of confirming that nominee. That presumption applies to the Supreme Court. But the Senate gives Supreme Court nominations a collective scrutiny that district court nominations seldom receive, and the occasional defeats of nominees are reminders that confirmation is not automatic. Thus the president has good reason to take the Senate's likely reaction into account in making a nomination.

The Senate's Record. As of mid-1997 the Senate had failed to confirm twenty-six nominations to the Supreme Court, either through an adverse vote or through a refusal to act. These twenty-six cases constituted about one-sixth of the nominations that the Senate considered. This proportion of defeats is higher than for any other position to which the president makes appointments. For instance, presidents have made far more nominations of cabinet members, but only nine were defeated.

Presidents in the twentieth century have been more successful with Supreme Court nominations than were presidents in the nineteenth. Since 1900, only five of the sixty nominations considered by the Senate have failed: Hoover's nomination of John Parker in 1930, Johnson's elevation of Abe Fortas to chief justice in 1968 (withdrawn after Fortas's supporters failed to end an anticonfirmation filibuster), Nixon's nominations of Clement Haynsworth in 1969 and G. Harrold Carswell in 1970 (both for the same vacancy), and Reagan's nomination of Robert Bork in 1987. And only two successful nominees were confirmed by less than a two-thirds margin in the Senate.

This record of success is impressive, but it may give a misleading impression of the Senate's approach to nominations—particularly since the late 1940s. During this period the Senate has scrutinized nominations with increasing care, as indicated by such measures as the length of time spent in hearings. And of the twenty-eight nominees considered by the Senate from 1949 through mid-1997, four were defeated, seven received more than ten negative votes, and others faced serious opposition. The Senate votes in this period are shown in Table 2-2. Certainly the Senate has not been inclined to confirm nominees automatically.

Just as clearly, nominees vary a great deal in the number of votes for confirmation that they win. This variation reflects characteristics of nominees and of the situations in which the Senate considers them.[38]

Nominees and Situations. As suggested already, the most important characteristics of nominees in the confirmation process are their perceived ideological positions and qualifications. Nominees who are thought to be highly liberal or highly conservative have greater difficulty than those who seem to be moderate, simply because extremists are more distant ideologically from the average senator.

Nominees who seem less qualified also may arouse opposition. Of course, a perceived absence of excellence in legal skills or ethical standards might cause senators who are otherwise favorable to oppose a nominee. More important, senators who

TABLE 2-2

Senate Votes on Supreme Court Nominations, 1949–1994

Nominee	Year	Vote
Tom Clark	1949	73–8
Sherman Minton	1949	48–16
Earl Warren	1954	NRV[a]
John Harlan	1955	71–11
William Brennan	1957	NRV
Charles Whittaker	1957	NRV
Potter Stewart	1959	70–17
Byron White	1962	NRV
Arthur Goldberg	1962	NRV
Abe Fortas	1965	NRV
Thurgood Marshall	1967	69–11
Abe Fortas[b]	1968	withdrawn[c]
Homer Thornberry	(1968)	no action
Warren Burger	1969	74–3
Clement Haynsworth	1969	45–55
G. Harrold Carswell	1970	45–51
Harry Blackmun	1970	94–0
Lewis Powell	1971	89–1
William Rehnquist	1971	68–26
John Paul Stevens	1975	98–0
Sandra Day O'Connor	1981	99–0
William Rehnquist[b]	1986	65–33
Antonin Scalia	1986	98–0
Robert Bork	1987	42–58
Douglas Ginsburg	(1987)	no action
Anthony Kennedy	1988	97–0
David Souter	1990	90–9
Clarence Thomas	1991	52–48
Ruth Bader Ginsburg	1993	96–3
Stephen Breyer	1994	87–9

Source: Elder Witt, *Congressional Quarterly's Guide to the Supreme Court,* 2d ed. (Washington, D.C.: Congressional Quarterly, 1990), 998, updated by the author.

[a] No recorded vote.

[b] Elevation to chief justice.

[c] Nomination withdrawn after Senate vote failed to end filibuster against nomination; vote was 45–43 to end filibuster, and two-thirds majority was required.

are ideologically distant from a nominee often use questions about a nominee's qualifications as an "objective" justification for opposing the nominee.

Whatever a nominee's personal characteristics, the outcome of the confirmation process is also influenced by several aspects of the situation that exists at the time. One is the president's political strength in the Senate. It helps enormously for the president's party to have a Senate majority; according to one count, presidents with a Senate majority have had 90 percent of their nominees confirmed, as against 61 percent for presidents who faced an opposition majority.[39] One reason for this difference is that senators of the majority party chair the Judiciary Committee and schedule votes on the floor. Another reason is that a Senate controlled by the opposition has more senators who are politically opposed to the president and who are ideologically distant from a nominee.

Presidents with high public approval also have an advantage, because strong public support deters opposition to their nominees. And nominations made late in a president's term are more vulnerable because the president's popularity tends to decline, some presidents are "lame ducks" who will leave office shortly, and partisanship often increases. Nearly half of the nominees selected in the last year of a presidential term were defeated in the Senate.[40]

A second aspect of the situation is the mobilization of activity for and against the nominee. Substantial activity against a nomination on the part of interest groups can overcome the assumption that a nominee will be confirmed and thus cause senators to consider voting against confirmation. It is also important whether some senators decide to play an active role in mustering votes against a nominee and whether the administration mounts a strong effort to secure confirmation.[41]

Finally, the apparent importance of a nomination helps to determine whether senators feel that efforts to defeat the nominee are worthwhile. Probably the key explanation for the intense scrutiny given to recent nominations is the increased prominence of the Supreme Court in the resolution of significant and controversial policy issues. If a nominee has the potential to change the Court's policies substantially, particular importance will be attached to that nomination.

Among recent nominees, David Souter and Clarence Thomas illustrate the importance of personal characteristics. The two were chosen by President Bush a year apart, with the Democrats holding majorities in the Senate. Each would replace a strongly liberal justice and thus change the Court's ideological balance considerably. But Souter won confirmation with only moderate difficulty while Thomas's margin was only four votes. The difference can be explained primarily by two widespread perceptions: that Souter was a moderate conservative and Thomas a strong conservative, and that Souter was well qualified while Thomas's qualifications might be questioned.

Another pair of nominees illustrates the importance of the situation. President Reagan selected Antonin Scalia in 1986 and Robert Bork in 1987. Both were viewed as highly conservative, and both were former legal scholars who were thought to be well qualified for service on the Court. But Scalia was confirmed unanimously while Bork was defeated. One difference was that the Senate in 1986 had a Republican majority, but Bork the next year faced a Democratic majority. Another was that Scalia would replace another strong conservative, while Bork would replace a moderate conservative on a Court with a close ideological balance. Finally, in 1986 liberal senators and interest groups focused their efforts on defeating William Rehnquist, nominated for elevation to chief justice, and largely ignored Scalia. In 1987, in contrast, Senator Edward Kennedy took the lead in opposing Bork and liberal interest groups mounted a massive campaign against him, while the Reagan administration did relatively little to mobilize support for him.

These generalizations can be examined more fully by focusing on the Senate's treatment of nominations from 1968 to 1994. The Senate's actions in this period fall into three categories: confirmations that involved little difficulty, confirmations that were achieved with more difficulty, and defeats of nominees.

The Easy Confirmations. Of the seventeen nominees who were considered by the Senate between 1968 and 1994, nine achieved relatively easy confirmation: Warren Burger, Harry Blackmun, Lewis Powell, John Paul Stevens, Sandra Day O'Connor, Antonin Scalia, Anthony Kennedy, Ruth Bader Ginsburg, and Stephen Breyer. Five of these nominees received no negative votes, Powell received one negative vote, and Burger and Ginsburg each received three. Breyer also fits in this category, even though nine senators voted against his confirmation.

This does not mean that these nominees enjoyed overwhelming support. Certainly liberal Democrats would have preferred nominees less conservative than Burger and Scalia. Anti-abortion groups opposed O'Connor and Ginsburg. But these nominees escaped strong challenges because their objective qualifications seemed unassailable and because there was only limited concern about their ideological positions.

Circumstances favored other nominees besides Scalia. Blackmun probably would have won confirmation easily in any case, but that result was ensured by the Senate's collective desire to avoid a third consecutive battle over a Nixon nomination. Observers disagreed about how liberal Ginsburg was, but her presence on the Court could do no more than moderate its conservative tendencies.

Breyer was something of a special case. His abilities as a lawyer and judge were clear, and he had won the respect of both Democrats and Republicans while serving on the staff of the Senate Judiciary Committee. He seemed less liberal in his views than most Democratic nominees, so he was attractive to many Senate conservatives. In any case, as the successor to Harry Blackmun, he could not move the Court very far in a liberal direction. For these reasons he quickly won widespread support, and indeed he was easily confirmed.

Nine Republican senators voted against confirmation, however. Some said that even Breyer was too liberal for them. Some opponents pointed to his investment in Lloyd's of London, an insurance syndicate, which provided the basis for several charges: lack of prudence in making a risky investment, past participation in some cases despite a seeming financial conflict of interest, and the prospect of frequent recusals by Breyer as a Supreme Court justice to avoid such conflicts. But other senators rejected these arguments, and nobody ever expected that—barring an unexpected and dramatic disclosure—Breyer would be defeated.

The Difficult Confirmations. Some of the successful nominees have been confirmed with difficulty. They include William

Rehnquist, when nominated as associate justice in 1971 and as chief justice in 1986; Clarence Thomas in 1991; and—with somewhat less difficulty—David Souter in 1990. In each instance, the nominee's apparent conservatism aroused opposition from liberal senators and interest groups.

When Rehnquist was first nominated in 1971, the Leadership Conference on Civil Rights led the opposition. Rehnquist's opponents argued that his conservatism on civil liberties was so extreme as to be unacceptable in a Supreme Court justice. But the case against him was weakened by the general perception that he was a highly competent lawyer. The opposition thus had to be based almost entirely on ideological grounds, and even for some liberals those grounds were insufficient to justify a negative vote. Rehnquist was confirmed by a 68–26 vote.

Rehnquist's record as an associate justice was as conservative as had been expected, so his prospective elevation to chief justice in 1986 also aroused strong opposition from liberal interest groups and senators. These opponents sought to gain support by raising questions about Rehnquist's ethical standards. They made several charges, of which the most important was that Rehnquist had sought to intimidate black and Hispanic voters in Arizona during the 1960s. These charges attracted attention but ultimately had little impact. Rehnquist was confirmed by a 65–33 vote; with few exceptions, Northern Democrats voted against him and other senators voted for him.

When David Souter was nominated in 1990, the prospective replacement of liberal William Brennan by a conservative on a closely divided Court helped to arouse the opposition of some liberal senators and interest groups. But Souter's objective qualifications were generally considered quite good. Moreover, his record gave few clues about his views on policy issues. One commentator wrote, "The chief qualification for confirmation was not being Robert Bork."[42] Once Souter had given indications that he was more moderate in views and personal style than Bork, his confirmation was assured; the Senate vote was 90–9.

A year later, Clarence Thomas won confirmation by the smallest margin in the twentieth century. His very conservative record aroused opposition from several liberal interest groups, but initially they had little impact. Thomas benefited from effective support by the Bush administration, and many Democrats favored the continuation of black representation on the Court.

Opposition grew after Thomas testified before the Judiciary Committee. His testimony raised doubts about his candor and abilities, and the committee split 7–7 on whether to recommend his confirmation. Still, as senators announced their positions, Thomas seemed assured of success. The disclosure of Anita Hill's sexual harassment charge against Thomas threatened his confirmation. But after committee hearings on that charge few senators changed their position, and Thomas was confirmed by a 52–48 vote. The vote was primarily along party lines. But Thomas won crucial support from eleven southern Democrats, responding in part to their perception of support for Thomas by black constituents.[43] This response underlines the public visibility of controversial confirmation decisions in the current era.

The Defeats. Of the four confirmation defeats since 1968, three came in a two-year period, 1968–1970. The first was that of Abe Fortas, a sitting justice nominated to be chief justice by President Johnson in 1968. Fortas's strong liberalism on the liberal Warren Court aroused early opposition by conservative senators, and some Republicans wanted to prevent Fortas's confirmation in order to reserve the vacancy for a new president—expected to be Republican—in 1969. These opponents pointed to two activities that raised doubts about Fortas's ethical fitness: his continued consultation with the president about policy matters while a member of the Court, and an arrangement by which he gave nine lectures at American University, in Washington, D.C., for a fee of $15,000 raised from businesses. The Judiciary Committee approved the nomination by a divided vote, but it ran into a filibuster on the Senate floor. A vote to end the filibuster fell fourteen votes short of the two-thirds majority then required; the opposition came almost entirely from Republicans and southern Democrats. At Fortas's request, his nomination was then withdrawn.

In 1969, Fortas resigned from the Court. President Nixon selected Clement Haynsworth, chief judge of a federal court of appeals, to replace him. Haynsworth was opposed by labor groups and the National Association for the Advancement of

Colored People (NAACP), both of which disliked his judicial record. Liberal senators, concerned about this record, sought revenge for Fortas's defeat as well. Haynsworth was also charged with unethical conduct: he had sat in two cases involving subsidiaries of companies in which he owned stock, and in another case he had bought the stock of a corporation in the interval between his court's decision in its favor and the announcement of the decision. These charges aroused additional opposition by Senate moderates. Haynsworth ultimately was defeated by a 45–55 vote, with a large minority of Republicans voting against confirmation.

President Nixon then nominated another court of appeals judge, G. Harrold Carswell. After the fight over Haynsworth, most senators were inclined to support the next nominee. One senator predicted that any new Nixon nominee "will have no trouble getting confirmed unless he has committed murder— recently."[44] But Carswell drew almost immediate opposition from civil rights groups for what they perceived as his hostility to their interests, and their cause gained strength as a result of a series of revelations about Carswell that suggested an active opposition to black civil rights. Carswell was also criticized for his alleged lack of judicial competence. Legal scholars attested to his limited abilities, and data indicated that an unusually high proportion of his decisions had been reversed on appeal. Carswell's supporters were not successful in countering this attack. The nomination was defeated by a 45–51 vote; the lineup was similar to that in the vote on Haynsworth.

Robert Bork's 1987 defeat differed from the three that preceded it in that no serious charges were made about his competence or his ethical standards. But liberals were concerned about his strong conservatism on civil liberties issues and his potential to shift the Court's ideological balance. As noted earlier, Senator Kennedy and liberal interest groups worked hard to secure votes against Bork. Concern about Bork's views was intensified by his testimony before the Senate Judiciary Committee, in which he discussed in detail his positions on issues such as the right to privacy.

This growing concern, combined with the unprecedented level of interest group activity against Bork, made his defeat possible. Also important was President Reagan's political weakness: not only did the Democrats control the Senate, but Reagan's popularity both inside and outside Congress had declined. Even so, a more effective campaign for Bork by the administration might have secured his confirmation. In any event, confirmation was denied by a 42–58 vote. All but eight senators voted along party lines; the overwhelming and unexpected opposition of southern Democrats made the difference in the outcome.

Summary. Since 1968, the Senate has taken a more active role in scrutinizing nominees to the Supreme Court. One spur prompting it to take this active role has been the increasing efforts of interest groups to defeat some nominees. Another spur has been the growing awareness that a single Court appointment can have considerable impact on national policy. In both respects one issue—abortion—has been especially important. As a result of these developments, the confirmation battles over Robert Bork and Clarence Thomas became national spectacles. And even relatively uncontroversial nominations, such as those of David Souter and Ruth Bader Ginsburg, received a good deal of scrutiny.

Even so, the great majority of nominees from 1968 to 1994 still were confirmed—most with little difficulty. One reason for this success is that presidents often sought nominees whom they expect the Senate to accept. More fundamentally, the Senate as a whole still typically began with a presumption in favor of confirming nominees. Because of this presumption, presidents continued to hold most of the power to determine who will sit on the Supreme Court.

This situation is not necessarily permanent. At the end of Bill Clinton's first term and the beginning of his second term, the Republican majority in the Senate strongly resisted confirming nominees to the lower federal courts. In effect, they were seeking to shift the balance of power further in the Senate's favor. Future Clinton nominees to the Supreme Court may face strong opposition from Senate Republicans, or Clinton may choose to select nominees whom the Senate majority views favorably. In response, Democratic senators may be less willing to acquiesce in nominations by future Republican presidents. The roles of the president and Senate in selecting Supreme Court justices should be viewed as dynamic, especially in a period of strong partisan contention.

The Impact of the Selection Process

The process of selecting people to hold a particular office is likely to affect the office itself. Certainly this is true of the Supreme Court.

Most important, the process helps to determine what kinds of people become justices. In the current era, the need for Senate confirmation sometimes deters presidents from nominating lawyers who appear to be strong liberals or strong conservatives, particularly if those people also have substantial records of positions on controversial issues. Professor Laurence Tribe of the Harvard Law School is widely regarded as one of the best constitutional scholars, and he is admired for his skill as an advocate in Supreme Court cases. But there is virtually no chance that Bill Clinton or another Democratic president would nominate Tribe to the Court, because he has taken highly liberal positions on a wide array of issues in his writing. Were he nominated, he likely would suffer the same fate as Robert Bork—and conservatives in and out of the Senate would be delighted to exact that revenge.

Further, the intense scrutiny that nominees now undergo may affect people's willingness to be considered as candidates for nomination. Some nominees have complained about this scrutiny. David Souter told his friend and Senate sponsor Warren Rudman that "if I had known how vicious this process is, I wouldn't have let you propose my nomination."[45] Others may take themselves out of the running because they want to spare themselves and their families what has become a considerable ordeal.[46]

Among those who win confirmation, the experience may shape their behavior as justices. Hugo Black's 1937 confirmation was difficult, largely because of charges that he had been a member of the Ku Klux Klan—charges that he admitted to be true after his confirmation. One commentator concluded that Black "came on the Court determined to prove that he was not a racist member of the Klan,"[47] and in any case he established himself as one of the strongest civil libertarians in the Court's history. In contrast, some commentators have suggested that the bitter fight over confirmation of Clarence Thomas strengthened his resolve to take strongly conservative positions on the Court.[48] Whatever may be true of Black and Thomas, undoubtedly some justices are changed by what they go through to achieve their positions.

Who Is Selected

As a result of the selection process, certain kinds of people are more likely to reach the Supreme Court than others. The characteristics of those who become justices are interesting in themselves, because they tell us something about how people achieve such a lofty position in the American political system. And justices' characteristics can influence their policy choices, the choices that make the Court an important institution.

The kinds of people who become justices can be understood in terms of the paths that they take to the Court. These paths have changed over time. In this section I give particular attention to the period extending from the presidency of Franklin Roosevelt to the present. In that period thirty-three justices were selected. Some characteristics of these justices are listed in Table 2-3. The box on pages 64–65 summarizes the careers of the justices who sat on the Court in 1997.

Career Paths

The Legal Profession. The Constitution does not require that Supreme Court justices be attorneys. In practice, however, this restriction has been absolute. Most of those involved in the selection process assume that only a person with legal training can serve effectively on the Court. If a president nominated a non-lawyer to the Court, this assumption—and the large number of lawyers in the Senate—probably would prevent confirmation.

Thus the willingness and ability to obtain a law degree constitute the first and least flexible requirement for recruitment to the Court. Most of the justices who served during the first century of the Court's history had followed what was then the standard practice—apprenticing under a practicing attorney. In several instances, the practicing attorney was a leading member of the bar.[49] James Byrnes (chosen in 1941) was the last justice to study law through apprenticeship; all his successors have taken what is now the conventional route of law school training. A high proportion of justices have graduated from the more prestigious schools. Of the nine justices sitting in 1997, seven received their law degrees from Harvard, Yale, or Stanford.

High Positions. If legal education is a necessary first step in the paths to the Court, almost equally important as a last step is attaining a high position in government or the legal profession. Obscure private practitioners or state trial judges might be superbly qualified for the Court, but their qualifications would be questioned because of their lowly positions. A high position in government or the legal profession also makes a person more visible to the president and to others involved in the nomination process.

At the time they were selected, the thirty-three justices appointed since 1937 held positions of four types. Ten justices served in the federal executive branch. Seven of the ten, including Chief Justice Rehnquist, served in the Justice Department. (The role of the Justice Department in the selection process helps to explain this large number.) The other three justices served as chair of the Securities and Exchange Commission (Douglas), secretary of the treasury (Vinson), and secretary of labor (Goldberg).

Sixteen of the justices appointed in this period were appellate judges at the time of selection. Fourteen of them served on the federal courts of appeals; the other two (Brennan and O'Connor) served on state courts. Five of the fourteen federal judges (Rutledge, Burger, Scalia, Thomas, and Ginsburg) came from the District of Columbia circuit, which is particularly visible to the president and to other officials in Washington.

Of the other seven justices appointed since 1937, four held high elective office; three were senators (Black, Byrnes, and Burton) and the fourth was governor of California (Warren). The other three held positions outside government. Each had attained extraordinary success and respect—as a legal scholar (Frankfurter), a Washington lawyer (Fortas), and a leader of the legal profession (Powell). Frankfurter and Fortas had also been informal presidential advisers.

The Steps Between. The people who have become Supreme Court justices took a variety of routes from legal education to

TABLE 2-3

Selected Characteristics of Justices Appointed since 1937

Justice	Age[a]	State of residence[b]	Law school	Position at appointment[c]	Years as judge	Elective office[d]	Administrative position[e]
Black	51	Ala.	Alabama	Senator	1	Senate	—
Reed	53	Ky.	Columbia	Solicitor general	0	State leg.	Solicitor general
Frankfurter	56	Mass.	Harvard	Law professor	0	—	Subcabinet
Douglas	40	Wash.	Columbia	Chair, Sec. & Exchange Comm.	0	—	Sec. & Exchange Comm.
Murphy	49	Mich.	Michigan	Attorney general	7	Governor	Attorney general
Byrnes	62	S.C.	None	Senator	0	Senate	—
Jackson	49	N.Y.	Albany	Attorney general	0	—	Attorney general
Rutledge	48	Iowa	Colorado	U.S. Ct. App.	4	—	—
Burton	57	Ohio	Harvard	Senator	0	Senate	—
Vinson	56	Ky.	Centre (Ky.)	Sec. of Treasury	5	House of Rep.	Sec. of Treasury
Clark	49	Texas	Texas	Attorney general	0	—	Attorney general
Minton	58	Ind.	Indiana	U.S. Ct. App.	8	Senate	Asst. to president
Warren	62	Calif.	Calif.	Governor	0	Governor	—
Harlan	55	N.Y.	New York	U.S. Ct. App.	1	—	Asst. U.S. Attorney
Brennan	50	N.J.	Harvard	State Sup. Ct.	7	—	—
Whittaker	56	Mo.	Kansas City	U.S. Ct. App.	3	—	—
Stewart	43	Ohio	Yale	U.S. Ct. App.	4	City council	—
White	44	Colo.	Yale	Dep. atty. general	0	—	Dep. atty. general
Goldberg	54	Ill.	Northwestern	Sec. of labor	0	—	Sec. of labor

Name	Age[a]	State[b]	Law school	[c]		[d]	[e]
Fortas	55	D.C.	Yale	Private practice	0	—	Subcabinet
Marshall	59	N.Y.	Howard	Solicitor general	4	—	Solicitor general
Burger	61	Minn.	St. Paul	U.S. Ct. App.	13	—	Asst. atty. general
Blackmun	61	Minn.	Harvard	U.S. Ct. App.	11	—	—
Powell	64	Va.	Wash. & Lee	Private practice	0	—	State Bd. of Education
Rehnquist	47	Ariz.	Stanford	Asst. atty. general	0	—	Asst. atty. general
Stevens	55	Ill.	Northwestern	U.S. Ct. App.	5	—	—
O'Connor	51	Ariz.	Stanford	State Ct. App.	6	State leg.	State asst. atty. general
Scalia	50	D.C.	Harvard	U.S. Ct. App.	4	—	Asst. atty. general
Kennedy	51	Calif.	Harvard	U.S. Ct. App.	11	—	—
Souter	51	N.H.	Harvard	U.S. Ct. App.	12	—	State atty. general
Thomas	43	D.C.	Yale	U.S. Ct. App.	1	—	Equal Empl. Opp. Comm.
Ginsburg	60	D.C.	Harvard, Columbia	U.S. Ct. App.	13	—	—
Breyer	56	Mass.	Harvard	U.S. Ct. App.	13	—	—

Sources: Leon Friedman and Fred L. Israel, *The Justices of the United States Supreme Court 1789–1969: Their Lives and Major Opinions* (New York: R. R. Bowker Co., 1969; 1978 supplement); Harold W. Chase and Craig R. Ducat, *Constitutional Interpretation*, 2d ed. (St. Paul: West, 1979), 1361–1376; Joan Biskupic and Elder Witt, *Guide to the U.S. Supreme Court*, 3d ed. (Washington, D.C.: Congressional Quarterly, 1997), 930–962.

a Age at time of appointment.
b Primary state of residence before selection.
c In this and following columns, positions are federal except where noted otherwise.
d Highest office.
e Highest appointive administrative position. Minor positions omitted.

Careers of the Supreme Court . . .

William H. Rehnquist   (born 1924)
Law degree, Stanford University, 1952
Supreme Court law clerk, 1952–1953
Private law practice, 1953–1969
U.S. Justice Department, 1969–1971
Appointed to Supreme Court, 1971
Appointed chief justice, 1986

John Paul Stevens   (born 1920)
Law degree, Northwestern University, 1947
Supreme Court law clerk, 1947–1948
Private law practice, 1949–1970
Judge, U.S. Court of Appeals, 1970–1975
Appointed to Supreme Court, 1975

Sandra Day O'Connor   (born 1930)
Law degree, Stanford University, 1952
Deputy county attorney, 1952–1953
Civilian attorney, U.S. Army, 1954–1957
Private law practice, volunteer work, family
  responsibilities, 1957–1965
Assistant state attorney general, 1965–1969
Arizona legislator, 1969–1975
Arizona trial judge, 1975–1979
Judge, Arizona Court of Appeals, 1979–1981
Appointed to Supreme Court, 1981

Antonin Scalia   (born 1936)
Law degree, Harvard University, 1960
Private law practice, 1960–1967
Law school teaching, 1967–1971
Legal positions in federal government, 1971–1977
Law school teaching, 1977–1982
Judge, U.S. Court of Appeals, 1982–1986
Appointed to Supreme Court, 1986

Anthony M. Kennedy   (born 1936)
Law degree, Harvard University, 1961
Private law practice, 1961–1975
Judge, U.S. Court of Appeals, 1975–1988
Appointed to Supreme Court, 1988

David H. Souter   (born 1939)
Law degree, Harvard University, 1966
Private law practice, 1966–1968

...Justices (1997)

David H. Souter   (continued)

New Hampshire attorney general's office,
   1968–1978
Attorney General, New Hampshire, 1976–1978
Judge, New Hampshire trial court, 1978–1983
Justice, New Hampshire Supreme Court,
   1983–1990
Judge, U.S. Court of Appeals, 1990
Appointed to Supreme Court, 1990

Clarence Thomas   (born 1948)

Law degree, Yale University, 1974
Missouri attorney general's office, 1974–1977
Attorney for Monsanto Company, 1977–1979
Legislative assistant to a U.S. senator,
   1979–1981
Assistant U.S. secretary of education, 1981–1982
Chair, U.S. Equal Employment Opportunity
   Commission, 1982–1990
Judge, U.S. Court of Appeals, 1990–1991
Appointed to Supreme Court, 1991

Ruth Bader Ginsburg   (born 1933)

Law degree, Columbia University, 1959
Federal district court law clerk, 1959–1961
Law school research position, 1961–1963
Law school teaching, 1963–1980
Judge, U.S. Court of Appeals, 1980–1993
Appointed to Supreme Court, 1993

Stephen G. Breyer   (born 1938)

Law degree, Harvard University, 1964
Supreme Court law clerk, 1964–1965
U.S. Justice Department, 1965–1967
Law school teaching, 1967–1980
Staff, U.S. Senate Judiciary Committee,
   1974–1975, 1979–1980
Judge, U.S. Court of Appeals, 1980–1994
Appointed to Supreme Court, 1994

Source: Based chiefly on information in Kenneth Jost, *The Supreme Court Yearbook 1995–1996* (Washington, D.C.: Congressional Quarterly, 1996), 305–321.

Note: With the exception of Justice Breyer's Senate staff service, only the primary position held by a future justice during each career stage is listed.

the high positions that made them credible candidates for the Court. Frankfurter, Fortas, and Powell illustrate one simple route: entry into legal practice or academia, followed by a gradual rise to high standing in the legal profession. Some justices took a similar route through public office. Earl Warren held a series of appointive and elective offices, culminating in his California governorship. David Souter worked for ten years in the New Hampshire attorney general's office, the last two years as attorney general. He then spent twelve years in the New Hampshire judiciary before his appointment in 1990 to a federal court of appeals. Clarence Thomas held a series of nonelected positions in government, culminating in positions as chair of the federal Equal Employment Opportunity Commission and then as judge on a federal court of appeals.

In the current era, the most common route is through private practice or law teaching, often combined with some time in government, before appointment to a high judicial or administrative position. William Rehnquist practiced law in Arizona until President Nixon appointed him assistant attorney general. Antonin Scalia, Stephen Breyer, and Ruth Bader Ginsburg were all law professors; Scalia and Breyer also had held government positions during their careers. Each was appointed to a federal court of appeals. John Paul Stevens and Anthony Kennedy went from law practice to a court of appeals appointment. People who take this route often achieve considerable prestige in practice or teaching, prestige that assists them in winning appointment to a high position.

The path that Sandra Day O'Connor took was unusual. She spent time in private practice and government legal positions, with some career interruptions for family reasons, before becoming an Arizona state senator and majority leader of the senate. O'Connor left the legislature for a trial judgeship. Her promotion to the state court of appeals through a gubernatorial appointment put her in a position to be considered for the Supreme Court.

O'Connor's career underlines the multiplicity of paths to the Court. Justices have brought to the Court a broad range of career experiences. What they have shared is their credential as lawyers and their success in reaching the higher levels of the legal profession or in government that make them candidates for nomination to the Court.

Implications of the Career Paths

The paths to the Supreme Court help to explain some significant characteristics of the justices. They also underline the role of chance in determining who becomes a justice.

Age. Young people are not appointed to the Supreme Court. Most of the justices selected in the twentieth century were in their fifties when they joined the Court; of the remainder, most were over the age of 60. William Douglas was the youngest appointee, at age 40; only three other appointees—Potter Stewart, Byron White, and Clarence Thomas—were under 45.

In one sense, this pattern is surprising. We might expect presidents to select relatively young candidates in order to maximize the length of time "their" justices would serve. In this way, presidents could increase their indirect influence on the Court's future policies. The main reason they do not do so is the time required to achieve the high positions that most justices hold when they are selected and to attain the eminence that makes one a serious candidate for selection.

Within this constraint, most recent presidents have sought to select justices who are relatively young. Thomas was 43 when selected; the other four Reagan and Bush appointees were all aged 50 or 51. This pattern reflects strong presidential interest in the Court's future direction. In this respect Clinton's selection of 60-year-old Ruth Bader Ginsburg—the oldest appointee in more than twenty years—stands out.

Class, Race, and Gender. The Supreme Court's membership has been quite unrepresentative of the general population in terms of social class; most justices grew up in families that were relatively well off. One study found that one-third of the justices were from the upper class and one-quarter were from the upper middle class. Only one-quarter were from the lower middle class or below.[50]

In the past half century, an unusually high percentage of appointees to the Court have had lower-status backgrounds; this is especially true of Democrats. Still, the recent justices as a group grew up in better than average circumstances. The 1997 Court included one justice from the upper class (John Paul Stevens), four from the upper middle class, three from the middle class, and one (Clarence Thomas) whose family was impoverished.

The predominance of higher-status backgrounds can be explained by the career paths that most justices take. First and most important, a justice must obtain a legal education. To do so is easiest for individuals of high status, because of the cost of legal training and the education that necessarily precedes it. Second, individuals of high status have a variety of advantages in their posteducational careers. Those who can afford to attend elite law schools, for instance, have the easiest time obtaining positions in successful law firms.

There has been some deviation from this pattern since 1937, in part because of the increasing availability of legal education. In addition, the increase in size of the legal profession, the judiciary, and the federal government has made high positions in these sectors more accessible to individuals with lower-status backgrounds who previously might have been excluded. If these explanations have some validity, then we should expect that the proportion of justices with lower-status backgrounds will remain relatively large and may increase in the future.

With the exception of Thurgood Marshall, Clarence Thomas, Sandra Day O'Connor, and Ruth Bader Ginsburg, all the justices have been white men. This pattern is not difficult to understand. Until recently, women and members of racial minority groups had extreme difficulty pursuing a legal education because of legal and other restrictions. As a result, the number of potential justices from these groups who passed the first barrier to selection was quite small. Moreover, prejudice against women and members of racial minorities has limited their ability to advance in the legal profession and in politics. For example, O'Connor and Ginsburg graduated very high in their classes at elite law schools, but they could not win positions in prestigious law firms; of course, Marshall would have fared no better if he had sought such a position. Because of such barriers, very few individuals who were not white men could achieve the high positions that people generally must obtain to be considered for nomination to the Court.

The growing representation of women and members of racial minority groups on the Court reflects their increased ability to achieve those positions. And presidents are more willing to consider them in selecting justices. Still, because of the various advantages they enjoy, white men are likely to remain numerically dominant on the Court for some time.

If the Court has been composed primarily of white men with higher-status backgrounds, what has been the effect on its policies? With regard to race and gender, the legal claims of racial minority groups and of women might have been taken seriously at an earlier time, had these groups enjoyed even limited representation on the Court,[51] but it is impossible to be certain.

With regard to the influence of social class, the picture is even more complicated. Certainly people of high socioeconomic status tend to develop social and political attitudes that differ from the predominant political attitudes in groups having lower socioeconomic status. But this is only a tendency. Moreover, some of those born relatively poor have become fairly wealthy in adulthood; Warren Burger is one example. The sympathies of people who have "climbed" upward from a low socioeconomic level may differ little from those of people who started out with social and economic advantages. Notably, the justices with humble backgrounds have included solid conservatives such as Burger and Clarence Thomas as well as liberals such as Earl Warren and Thurgood Marshall. If the Supreme Court's decisions have reflected "essentially the conscience of the American upper middle class," it is only in part because most justices originated in that class.[52]

Prior Judicial Service. The current Supreme Court is unusual in having eight justices who served on lower courts (all but William Rehnquist), but historically a majority of the justices had judicial experience before reaching the Court. Many commentators think that such service is desirable, even a prerequisite to superior work on the Supreme Court. On a different level, some conservatives have argued that a lack of lower court service encourages judicial activism.

Yet a comparison of justices with and without lower court experience indicates that the two groups do not behave very differently. To take one example, the leaders of the activist Warren Court were Earl Warren, with no lower court experience, and former state judge William Brennan. Their strongest opponents were John Marshall Harlan, who came to the Court from a federal court of appeals, and Felix Frankfurter, who came from Harvard Law School. And all four of these justices—those with and without lower court experience—have been viewed as outstanding.

This apparent lack of difference is easy to explain. Of the

twenty justices appointed since 1937 who had lower court experience, the justice with the most experience had served for thirteen years; ten justices had been lower court judges for five years or less. Undoubtedly even a short period on a lower court shapes a justice's perspective, but a stint of three or five years—or even of thirteen years—is not likely to have as much impact on a person's thinking and approach to judicial policy issues as the much longer period of education and professional development that preceded it.

Why, then, have most recent appointees come from lower federal courts? It may be that presidents and senators increasingly see such experience as desirable. Probably more important is the concern of recent presidents with the positions that potential nominees would take as justices. As noted earlier, forecasting of those positions is easier for people who have already served as judges, particularly on the federal courts.

Partisan Political Activity. One characteristic shared by most current justices, like their predecessors, is a degree of involvement in partisan politics. Antonin Scalia, for instance, held several positions in the Nixon and Ford administrations. Anthony Kennedy drafted a state ballot proposition for California governor Ronald Reagan. William Rehnquist was active in the Arizona Republican party. Clarence Thomas worked with John Danforth when Danforth was the Missouri attorney general and a U.S. senator, and Thomas later served in the Reagan and Bush administrations.

This pattern reflects the ways that justices are chosen. Even if nominations to the Court are not used as political rewards, presidents look more favorably on those who have contributed to their party's success. Partisan activity is also a way to come to the attention of presidents, their staff members, and others who influence nomination decisions. Perhaps more important, it enables people to win the high offices and appointive positions that make them credible candidates for the Court. To take the most important current example, lawyers who avoid any involvement in politics are unlikely to win federal judgeships.

Historically, many justices were career politicians who achieved high elective office. Of the current justices, only O'Connor comes close to fitting that pattern. She became majority leader of the Arizona Senate, though she left the legislature after only six years to run for (and win) a trial court judgeship. In filling two Court vacancies in his first term, Bill Clinton seriously considered three people who had won high elective office. But Clinton ultimately followed the example of Ford, Reagan, and Bush in choosing lower court judges who had never run for office.

The Role of Chance. A person does not become a Supreme Court justice through an inevitable process. Rather, advancement from membership in the bar to a seat on the Court is a result of luck as much as anything else. This luck comes in two stages. First, good fortune is often necessary to achieve the high positions in government or law that make individuals possible candidates for the Court; it is not necessarily the "fittest" who become cabinet members or federal appellate judges. Second, once they achieve such positions, whether candidates are seriously considered for the Court and actually win an appointment depends largely on the existence of several favorable circumstances.

For one thing, a potential justice gains enormously by belonging to a particular political party at the appropriate time. Every appointment to the Court between 1969 and 1992 was made by a Republican president. As a result, potential justices who were liberal Democrats had to watch their chances slip away. Further, someone whose friend or associate achieves a powerful position becomes a far stronger candidate for a seat on the Court. David Souter was fortunate that someone who described Souter as "my closest friend" (Warren Rudman) became a U.S. senator and that a person who knew and admired him (John Sununu) became the president's chief of staff.[53]

More generally, everyone appointed to the Court has benefited from a favorable series of circumstances. Eisenhower's attorney general became aware of William Brennan because Brennan gave a conference address in place of a colleague on the New Jersey Supreme Court who was ill. John Paul Stevens has reported that his *pro bono* volunteer services for a client led to favorable publicity that later helped him win a judicial appointment.[54]

This does not mean that the Court's direction, as shaped by presidential appointments, is random. No matter which individuals they choose, Democratic presidents generally nominate people with liberal views and Republicans tend to select conservatives. But it does mean that specific individuals do not obtain appointments through an inevitable process; membership on the Court is achieved in large part through good fortune. "You have to be lucky," said Sandra Day O'Connor about her appointment,[55] a statement that reflects realism as well as modesty.

Changes in Career Paths. Even in the period since 1937, there have been changes in paths to the Supreme Court and in the characteristics of people who become justices. The numerical dominance of people from privileged backgrounds and of white men has declined, a decline reflecting social and political changes in the United States. That trend is unlikely to be reversed.

As noted already, justices' career patterns have also changed. Among the twelve justices appointed since 1969, only one (O'Connor) ever held elective office, only one (Rehnquist) came to the Court directly from the executive branch, and all but two (Rehnquist and Powell) were appellate judges when they received their Court appointments. In a sense, there is less politics and more law in the backgrounds of justices than there used to be. This change may be a transitory phenomenon, the result of a series of specific appointment decisions. But it might represent a long-term shift. If the backgrounds of justices *are* becoming more legal and less political, this represents a noteworthy change in the ways that people reach the Supreme Court.

Leaving the Court

Congress has not changed the size of the Supreme Court for more than a century, and it is not likely to do so in the near future. Thus new members can come to the Court only when a sitting justice leaves that institution.

Voluntary Resignation and Retirement

When Harry Blackmun retired from the Court in 1994, he explained that "it's not easy to step aside, but I know what the numbers are, and it's time."[56] The "numbers" referred to his age. Later, Blackmun said, "Eighty-five is pretty old. I don't want to reach a point where my senility level reaches unacceptable proportions, and I don't want to be asked to retire like Oliver Wendell Holmes Jr." (a distinguished justice whose performance began to decline before he left the Court at the age of 90).[57] What Blackmun did not say, but many observers surmised, was that the moderately liberal justice had wanted his successor to be chosen by a Democratic president. Indeed, two years earlier he had said that he would stay on the Court "until the third day of November 1992"—the day on which the voters would choose between President George Bush and Bill Clinton.[58] And Blackmun talked with a White House assistant about when it would be best to announce his retirement.[59]

Blackmun's retirement illustrates several generalizations about the reasons that justices have left the Court in recent years, reasons shown in Table 2-4. To begin with, Blackmun remained a justice until he was at an advanced age; he did not resign to take up another pursuit. In the Court's first decade, several justices resigned to seek more attractive opportunities, but only a handful of justices have done so in the twentieth century. The most recent was Arthur Goldberg, who resigned in 1965 to become U.S. ambassador to the United Nations. The main reason for this change is simple: the Court's prestige and influence on American life make justices reluctant to relinquish their positions.

Yet Blackmun did retire before he was overcome by infirmities that would have limited his effectiveness. This, too, reflects a change. In the nineteenth century most justices died in office, but that is no longer true. Indeed, the last death of a sitting justice was that of Chief Justice Fred Vinson in 1953.

Not only have recent justices left the Court before their deaths, but few have remained on the Court when they were seriously disabled. William Brennan and Thurgood Marshall had both said they would remain on the Court for life. Marshall went one step further, telling his clerks, "If I die, prop me up and keep on voting."[60] Yet both gave up their positions when they thought it necessary to do so. After Marshall announced his retirement in 1991, he explained to a reporter that "I'm getting old and falling apart."[61] Brennan retired on the advice of his doctors in 1990, as he explained five years later. "They told me I had the one stroke and if I had another one, it might be

TABLE 2-4
Reasons for Leaving the Court, 1965–1994

Year	Justice	Age	Primary reasons for leaving	Length of time from leaving until death
1965	Goldberg	56	Appointment as ambassador to U.N.	24 years
1967	Clark	67	Son's appointment as attorney general	10 years
1969	Fortas	58	Pressures based on possible ethical violations	13 years
1969[a]	Warren	78[a]	Age	5 years[a]
1971	Black	85	Age and ill health	1 month
1971	Harlan	72	Age and ill health	3 months
1975	Douglas	77	Age and ill health	4 years
1981	Stewart	66	Age	4 years
1986	Burger	78	Responsibilities for Commission on the Bicentennial of the Constitution, possibly age	9 years
1987	Powell	79	Age and health concerns	—
1990	Brennan	84	Age and ill health	7 years
1991	Marshall	83[b]	Age and ill health	2 years
1993	White	76[b]	Desire to allow another person to serve, possibly age	—
1994	Blackmun	85	Age	—

Sources: Joan Biskupic and Elder Witt, *Guide to the U.S. Supreme Court,* 3d ed. (Washington, D.C.: Congressional Quarterly, 1997), 931–954; other biographical sources, newspaper stories.

[a] Warren originally announced intent to leave the Court in 1968 at age 77.
[b] Marshall announced intent to leave the Court at 82, White at 75.

my last. So I quit." Brennan added that he had regretted quitting "every minute since I did. God, when I see some of the decisions . . . I think, 'Jeez, if only I were there.'"[62]

In part, the willingness of justices to retire reflects congressional policy. Since 1869 older justices have been encouraged to leave the bench by congressional legislation providing that their salaries will continue if they do so. Today justices who are at least 70 years old and who have served on the federal courts for at least ten years, or who are at least 65 and have served for fifteen years, can retire and continue to receive the salaries they earned at the time of their retirement. Justices who meet these criteria can retire and receive any salary increases granted sitting justices, so long as they perform a certain amount of service for the federal courts—generally equal to one-quarter of full-time work. (A disabled justice is exempt from this requirement.) Thus justices no longer have a strong financial incentive to remain on the Court.

If Justice Blackmun's retirement decision was influenced by the election of a Democratic president, he was not unique in considering who would choose his successor. When Democrat Byron White retired in 1993, one reporter referred to "recurrent rumors for several years that Justice White had grown bored at the Court and would like to retire if a Democrat was elected president."[63] And the continued service of William Rehnquist on the Court in the mid-1990s, despite his age and health problems, may reflect the reluctance of a conservative Republican to allow a Democratic president to choose his successor.

One current justice has already indicated when he will retire. In 1993, two years after he joined the Court, Clarence Thomas told two of his clerks that he would remain on the Court until 2034. He explained, "The liberals made my life miserable for 43 years, and I'm going to make their lives miserable for 43 years."[64]

External Pressure

Financial incentives aside, Congress and the president can try to induce specific justices to leave the Court. Presidents have good reason to do so, in order to create vacancies they can fill. Occasionally they try to induce retirements. John Kennedy reportedly persuaded Felix Frankfurter to retire after ill health had decreased his effectiveness,[65] but Thurgood Marshall responded to a call in which Jimmy Carter's aides suggested retirement by slamming down the phone.[66]

Presidents can also try to lure justices away from the Court by offering them other positions. Lyndon Johnson offered Arthur Goldberg the position of ambassador to the United Nations and then exerted intense personal pressure to induce him to accept that position. But Byron White rejected the idea of becoming

FBI director when the Reagan administration sounded him out about it. James Byrnes's resignation in 1942 was somewhat different; Byrnes was quite unhappy on the Court and wanted to return to the executive branch, but Franklin Roosevelt still had to offer him a central position in the war effort to secure his resignation and his services.[67]

Very different is the use, or threat, of impeachment. Under the Constitution, justices, like other federal officials, can be removed through impeachment proceedings for "treason, bribery, or other high crimes and misdemeanors."[68] President Thomas Jefferson actually sought to gain control of the largely Federalist (and thus anti-Jefferson) judiciary through the use of impeachment, and Congress did impeach and convict a federal district judge in 1803. Justice Samuel Chase made himself vulnerable to impeachment by participating in President John Adams's campaign for reelection in 1800 and by making some injudicious and partisan remarks to a Maryland grand jury in 1803. Chase was impeached, an action justified chiefly by his handling of political trials, but the Senate acquitted him in 1805. His acquittal effectively ended Jefferson's plans to seek the impeachment of other justices.

No justice has been impeached since then. But more recently there was serious discussion about the possible impeachment of two justices. Several efforts were made to remove William Douglas (most seriously in 1969 and 1970), motivated by opposition to his strong liberalism. The reasons stated publicly by opponents were his financial connections with a foundation and his outside writings; the impeachment effort was encouraged privately by President Nixon.[69] A special House committee failed to approve a resolution to impeach Douglas, however, and the resolution died.

Had Abe Fortas not resigned from the Court in 1969, he actually might have been removed through impeachment proceedings.[70] Fortas had been criticized for his financial dealings at the time he was nominated unsuccessfully to be chief justice in 1968. A year later, it was disclosed that he had a lifetime contract as a consultant to the Wolfson Foundation and had received money from that foundation at a time when the person who directed it was being prosecuted by the federal government. The Nixon administration orchestrated a campaign of pressure on Fortas through the mass media and through the

Court itself. Fortas's explanation of his conduct proved unconvincing, and he soon resigned. The resignation came too early to determine how successful an impeachment effort would have been, but it almost certainly would have been serious.

The Fortas incident seems unlikely to be repeated, in part because it reminds justices of the need to avoid questionable financial conduct. The removals of three federal judges through impeachment proceedings between 1987 and 1989 make it clear that impeachment is a real option. But it is used only in cases with strong evidence of serious misdeeds, often involving allegations of corrupt behavior.

Thus the timing of a justice's leaving the Court reflects primarily the justice's own inclinations, health, and longevity. Those who want to affect the Court's membership may have their say when a vacancy occurs, but they have little control over the creation of vacancies.

Conclusion

One theme of this chapter is that the widespread recognition of the Court's importance has a strong impact on the selection of its members. Presidents have an interest in controlling appointments, and they stress competence and policy preferences in selecting justices. The Senate gives nominations to the Court a degree of scrutiny that is unique for presidential appointments. Interest groups regularly attempt to influence the selection process. Because of the prestige attached to membership on the Court, only individuals who have achieved high positions in the field of law or in politics are seriously considered as nominees. The Court's importance also makes justices reluctant to leave it.

The recruitment of justices is a complex process. The Supreme Court is not a body to which people "rise" in an orderly manner. Rather, they reach the point at which they are considered for the Court—and some of them actually obtain appointments—in a series of stages in which there are many participants, many considerations are weighed, and luck plays an important role.

The recruitment process is also subject to change. The criteria for selection of nominees and the balance of power between president and Senate have shifted over time. The backgrounds of today's justices, taken together, differ from those of the justices selected in earlier periods. Undoubtedly there will be more changes in the future; indeed, there are signs that the Senate may soon take a role in the selection of justices that is even more active than its current role.

The recruitment process is consequential because of the strong link between the Court's membership and its decisions. That link is examined more fully in subsequent chapters.

NOTES

1. The four who were nominated and confirmed twice include three individuals elevated from associate justice to chief justice (Edward White, Harlan Stone, and William Rehnquist) and one (Charles Evans Hughes) who resigned from the Court and was later appointed chief justice. Douglas Ginsburg is counted as a nominee even though he withdrew from consideration in 1987, before he was officially nominated.
2. "Excerpts From Clinton's Remarks Announcing His Selection for Top Court," *New York Times*, May 14, 1994, 10.
3. Joan Biskupic, "Promises, Pressure in Court Search," *Washington Post*, March 21, 1993, A13.
4. This discussion is based in part on John Anthony Maltese, *The Selling of Supreme Court Nominees* (Baltimore: Johns Hopkins University Press, 1995); and Gregory A. Caldeira and John R. Wright, "Lobbying for Justice: The Rise of Organized Conflict in the Politics of Federal Judgeships," in *Contemplating Courts*, ed. Lee Epstein (Washington, D.C.: CQ Press, 1995), 44–71.
5. Michael Pertschuk and Wendy Schaetzel, *The People Rising: The Campaign against the Bork Nomination* (New York: Thunder's Mouth Press, 1989); Patrick B. McGuigan and Dawn M. Weyrich, *Ninth Justice: The Fight for Bork* (Washington, D.C.: Free Congress Research and Education Foundation, 1990); Mark Gitenstein, *Matters of Principle: An Insider's Account of America's Rejection of Robert Bork's Nomination to the Supreme Court* (New York: Simon & Schuster, 1992).
6. Richard Hodder-Williams, "The Strange Story of Judge Robert Bork and a Vacancy on the United States Supreme Court," *Political Studies* 36 (December 1988): 628.
7. Gregory A. Caldeira and John R. Wright, "Lobbying for Justice: Organized Interests and the Bork Nomination in the United States Senate" (Paper presented at the annual meeting of the American Political Science Association, Chicago, September 1992).
8. Maltese, *Selling of Supreme Court Nominees*, 90–91.
9. Caldeira and Wright, "Lobbying for Justice: The Rise of Organized Conflict," 59–69.
10. William O. Douglas, *The Court Years, 1939–1975: The Autobiography of William O. Douglas* (New York: Random House, 1980), 247.
11. Henry J. Abraham, *Justices and Presidents: A Political History of Appointments to the Supreme Court*, 3d ed. (New York: Oxford University Press, 1992), 186.

12. Eleanor Randolph, "Husband Triggered Letters Supporting Ginsburg for Court," *Washington Post,* June 17, 1993, A25.
13. "No Litmus Test Needed Here," *New York Times,* September 25, 1992, A12. The case was *Sojourner T. v. Edwards* (5th Cir. 1992).
14. David A. Kaplan, "Campaigning for the High Court," *Newsweek,* July 2, 1990, 61.
15. "No Wonder They're So Stiff," *California Lawyer,* December 1987, 12.
16. Naftali Bendavid, "Just Saying No to Chance for Supreme Court," *Legal Times,* April 18, 1994, 1, 22, 23.
17. David Garrow, "Justice Souter Emerges," *New York Times Magazine,* September 25, 1994, 52.
18. John C. Jeffries, Jr., *Justice Lewis F. Powell, Jr.* (New York: Charles Scribner's Sons, 1994), 1–9.
19. Abraham, *Justices and Presidents,* 266.
20. U.S. Congress, *Nomination of Judge Clarence Thomas To Be Associate Justice of the Supreme Court of the United States,* Committee on the Judiciary, U.S. Senate, 102d Congress, 1st session (Washington, D.C.: Government Printing Office, 1993), 222–223.
21. Ann Devroy and Ruth Marcus, "High Court Playoffs Rival Hoops for Tension, Personal Drama," *Washington Post,* June 15, 1993, A12.
22. David G. Savage, *Turning Right: The Making of the Rehnquist Supreme Court* (New York: John Wiley & Sons, 1992), 180–181.
23. Henry F. Pringle, *The Life and Times of William Howard Taft* (New York: Farrar & Rinehart, 1939), 854.
24. This formulation is adapted from one presented in Sheldon Goldman, "Judicial Appointments and the Presidential Agenda," in *The Presidency in American Politics,* ed. Paul Brace, Christine B. Harrington, and Gary King (New York: New York University Press, 1989), 19–47.
25. "Ginsburg, Economy, Budget Encourage Upbeat Clinton," *Congressional Quarterly Weekly Report,* June 19, 1993, 1602.
26. Fred Barnes, "Reagan's Full Court Press," *New Republic,* June 10, 1985, 18.
27. Savage, *Turning Right,* 169.
28. Data supporting this conclusion are presented in David W. Rohde and Harold J. Spaeth, *Supreme Court Decision Making* (San Francisco: W. H. Freeman, 1976), 107–109.
29. Alyssa Sepinwall, "The Making of a Presidential Myth" (letter), *Wall Street Journal,* September 4, 1990, A11; Tony Mauro, "Leak of Souter Keeps McGuigan In Plan," *Legal Times,* September 10, 1990, 11.
30. Savage, *Turning Right,* 177.
31. *Webster v. Reproductive Health Services* (1989); *Planned Parenthood v. Casey* (1992).
32. "Justice Anthony Kennedy: Surely Reagan's Biggest Disappointment," *Human Events,* May 31–June 7, 1996, 3.
33. J. Anthony Lukas, *Nightmare: The Underside of the Nixon Years* (New York: Viking Press, 1976), 569. (William Rehnquist, also a Nixon appointee, did not participate in the decision because of his prior position in the Justice Department during the Nixon administration.)
34. Robert Scigliano, *The Supreme Court and the Presidency* (New York: Free Press, 1971), 95, updated by the author.
35. Abraham, *Justices and Presidents,* 319.
36. Tony Mauro, "The Court's Religious Conversion," *Legal Times,* July 1, 1996, 8.

37. Barbara A. Perry, *A "Representative" Supreme Court? The Impact of Race, Religion, and Gender on Appointments* (New York: Greenwood Press, 1991), 122.

38. See George L. Watson and John A. Stookey, *Shaping America: The Politics of Supreme Court Appointments* (New York: HarperCollins, 1995), chs. 2–3; and Jeffrey A. Segal, Charles M. Cameron, and Albert D. Cover, "A Spatial Model of Roll Call Voting: Senators, Constituents, Presidents, and Interest Groups in Supreme Court Confirmations," *American Journal of Political Science* 36 (February 1992): 96–121.

39. These percentages are based on figures in Jeffrey Segal, "Senate Confirmation of Supreme Court Justices: Partisan and Institutional Politics," *Journal of Politics* 49 (November 1987): 1008, updated by the author. Percentages differ among sources, chiefly because of differences in assignment of partisan affiliation to some presidents.

40. Based on ibid., updated by the author. Nominations made during a president's fourth year but after the president's reelection are not included.

41. See Maltese, *Selling of Supreme Court Nominees.*

42. Calvin Trillin, "How to Become a Supreme Court Justice," *San Francisco Chronicle,* October 7, 1990, This World section, 5.

43. L. Marvin Overby, Beth M. Henschen, Michael H. Walsh, and Julie Strauss, "Courting Constituents? An Analysis of the Senate Confirmation Vote on Justice Clarence Thomas," *American Political Science Review* 86 (December 1992): 997–1003.

44. "Here Comes the Judge," *Newsweek,* February 2, 1970, 19. Quoted in John Massaro, *Supremely Political: The Role of Ideology and Presidential Management in Unsuccessful Supreme Court Nominations* (Albany: State University of New York Press, 1990), 105.

45. Warren B. Rudman, *Combat: Twelve Years in the U.S. Senate* (New York: Random House, 1996), 181.

46. Bendavid, "Just Saying No to Chance for Supreme Court," 23.

47. Kim Isaac Eisler, "Black Bio Lacks Shades of Gray," *Legal Times,* November 25, 1996, 78. See Roger K. Newman, *Hugo Black: A Biography* (New York: Pantheon, 1994), 233–268.

48. On Thomas's reaction to the confirmation battle, see John C. Danforth, *Resurrection: The Confirmation of Clarence Thomas* (New York: Viking Press, 1994); and Jeffrey Toobin, "The Burden of Clarence Thomas," *The New Yorker,* September 27, 1993, 38–51.

49. For this observation and for much of the information on which the analysis in this section is based, I am indebted to John R. Schmidhauser, *Judges and Justices: The Federal Appellate Judiciary* (Boston: Little, Brown, 1979), 41–100.

50. Lee Epstein, Jeffrey A. Segal, Harold J. Spaeth, and Thomas G. Walker, *The Supreme Court Compendium,* 2d ed. (Washington, D.C.: CQ Press, 1996), 227–238. This source was also used to classify the justices sitting in 1997.

51. See William J. Daniels, "Justice Thurgood Marshall: The Race for Equal Justice," in *The Burger Court: Political and Judicial Profiles,* ed. Charles M. Lamb and Stephen C. Halpern (Urbana: University of Illinois Press, 1991), 235.

52. Schmidhauser, *Judges and Justices,* 99.

53. See Rudman, *Combat,* 152–194. The quotation is on p. 153.

54. Richard C. Reuben, "Justice Stevens: I Benefited from Pro Bono Work," *Los Angeles Daily Journal,* August 11, 1992, 11.

55. Laurence Bodine, "Sandra Day O'Connor," *American Bar Association Journal* 69 (October 1983): 1394.
56. "Departing Justice Blackmun Garners Clinton's Praise," *Congressional Quarterly Weekly Report,* April 9, 1994, 859.
57. Douglas Jehl, "Mitchell Viewed as Top Candidate for High Court," *New York Times,* April 7, 1994, A1.
58. Tony Mauro, "Court 'Name Game' Enters New Inning," *Legal Times,* November 9, 1992, 10.
59. Ruth Marcus, "Good Counsel: More Judge Than Witness," *Washington Post,* July 27, 1994, A18.
60. Stephen Chapman, "Octogenarian Justices Are No Asset to the Court," *Chicago Tribune,* July 4, 1991, sec. 1, 11.
61. Neil A. Lewis, "Marshall Urges Bush to Pick 'the Best'," *New York Times,* June 29, 1991, 7.
62. From an interview with NBC News, quoted in Tony Mauro, "High Court Highs and Lows," *Legal Times,* December 18–25, 1995, 20.
63. Linda Greenhouse, "White Announces He'll Step Down from High Court," *New York Times,* March 20, 1993, 1.
64. Neil A. Lewis, "2 Years After His Bruising Hearing, Justice Thomas Still Shows the Hurt," *New York Times,* November 27, 1993, 6.
65. Juan Williams, "Marshall's Law," *Washington Post Magazine,* January 7, 1990, 29.
66. From an interview with Marshall conducted by Carl Rowan, quoted in "The Justice and the President," *Washington Post,* September 11, 1987, A23.
67. David Robertson, *Sly and Able: A Political Biography of James F. Byrnes* (New York: W. W. Norton, 1994), 301–319.
68. U.S. Constitution, art. 2, sec. 4.
69. John Ehrlichman, *Witness to Power: The Nixon Years* (New York: Simon & Schuster, 1982), 122.
70. Laura Kalman, *Abe Fortas: A Biography* (New Haven, Conn.: Yale University Press, 1990), 359–376; and Bruce Allen Murphy, *Fortas: The Rise and Ruin of a Supreme Court Justice* (New York: William Morrow, 1988).

Chapter 3

The Cases

In 1987 Lora Lohr had a heart pacemaker implanted. Three years later the pacemaker failed, requiring emergency surgery. Lohr's doctor concluded that a defect in a part of the pacemaker probably had caused the failure. In 1993 Lohr and her husband sued Medtronic, Inc., the manufacturer of the pacemaker, in Florida state court. Medtronic removed the case to federal court, where it argued that the Lohrs' claims were preempted by a federal statute regulating medical devices and thus that her lawsuit should be dismissed. A federal district judge agreed with Medtronic; the Lohrs appealed, and the court of appeals reached a mixed decision. Both sides asked the Supreme Court to hear the case. The Court accepted the case by granting a writ of certiorari, and in 1996 it ruled in favor of the Lohrs and reinstated their lawsuit.

This sequence of events fits a common pattern for Supreme Court cases, but from one perspective it is extraordinary. Of those people who have potential lawsuits, most never bring them. Of the cases that do get filed in court, whether civil or criminal, the overwhelming majority are settled by the parties and thus do not go to court for a decision. Of the cases in which trial courts do rule, only a small proportion reach the point at which the losing party could petition the Supreme Court for a hearing, and by no means does everyone whose case reaches that point actually file a petition. And when someone asks the Court to hear a case, the odds against the Court's granting a writ of certiorari, and thereby accepting the case for decision, are very high. *Medtronic, Inc. v. Lohr* was literally a one-in-a-million event.

This chapter examines agenda setting in the Supreme Court, the process by which an enormous number of potential Supreme Court cases is narrowed to the several dozen that the Court fully considers and decides each year. The *Lohr* case illustrates the roles of several participants in that process. The Court could hear the case only because it fell within the Court's jurisdiction and because the federal regulatory statute led to a preemption issue; Congress created the Court's jurisdiction and enacted the regulatory statute. The Court could not reach out and decide the preemption issue but had to await an appropriate case; thus the Lohrs and their lawyers gave the Court an opportunity to address that issue. The Lohrs were assisted by an interest group, the Public Citizen Litigation Group, and one of its lawyers argued their case in the Supreme Court. Finally, the Court was free to hear or reject the *Lohr* case; in this instance, as in others, it had the ultimate power to determine whether it would consider the matter. As I will discuss, this power helps to give the Court a degree of control over its agenda that is far greater than that of most other courts.

In the chapter's first section I examine how and why cases are brought to the Court. The next section considers the Court's selection of cases from those that come to it. The chapter's final section discusses growth in the Court's caseload and its impact on the Court. In that section, and again in Chapter 5, I consider the impact of Congress on the Court's agenda.

Reaching the Court: Litigants, Attorneys, and Interest Groups

In the 1995 term, approximately 6,600 cases were filed in the Supreme Court.[1] In this section I consider how and why these cases came to the Court, examining the activities of litigants, their attorneys, and interest groups. I consider separately the litigation activities of the federal government, the most frequent and most distinctive participant in Supreme Court cases.

Litigants

Every case that comes to the Supreme Court has at least two formal parties, or litigants—at least one on each side. For a case to reach the Court, of course, one or more of the parties must have taken action to initiate the litigation and to move it up-ward through the court system.

As we would expect, litigants in the Supreme Court are a di-verse lot.[2] Of those who petition the Court to hear cases, the great majority are individuals; most of these individuals are criminal defendants. Of the litigants (generally called respon-dents) that are brought to the Court by petitioners, gov-ernments and government agencies from the federal level to the local level constitute the largest category. Individuals are also respondents in many cases. Corporations frequently ap-pear as petitioners or respondents. Other kinds of litigants, such as nonprofit groups and labor unions, also participate in many Court cases. (In cases involving forfeiture of property to the government, the official parties can have names such as "$405,089.23 in United States Currency."[3] But those assets are surrogates for the people who held them.) As this range of liti-gants suggests, it is difficult to generalize about the participants in Supreme Court cases.

The Motivations of Litigants. Perhaps the most important questions concerning litigants are why they become involved in court cases and why they carry them to the Supreme Court. The motives of litigants can be thought of as taking two general forms, resulting in two "ideal types" of Supreme Court litiga-tion; there are also some cases in which litigants have mixed motives.

The first type of case may be called "ordinary" litigation be-cause of its relative frequency. Ordinarily, parties bring cases to court or appeal adverse judgments because of a direct per-sonal or organizational interest that they seek to advance. Plain-tiffs file personal injury suits in court because they think they will probably obtain a monetary advantage from litigation. Sim-ilarly, litigants appeal court decisions because they believe that their potential gain from a successful appeal and the likeli-hood of success are sufficient to justify additional trouble and expense.

One example of ordinary litigation is *O'Gilvie v. United States* (1996). Betty O'Gilvie died in 1983 of toxic shock syndrome, and her husband and children were awarded $1.5 million in compensatory damages and $10 million in punitive damages from the manufacturer of the product that allegedly caused her death. They paid income tax on the punitive damages but then sought a refund of the tax, which was given to the children but not to the husband. He brought a case in the federal district court for Kansas to obtain a refund, and the Internal Revenue Service then brought a case in that court to recover the refund it had given to the children. The district court ruled in favor of the husband and children, but the Tenth Circuit court of appeals reversed that decision. The O'Gilvies took their case to the Supreme Court, which accepted the case but ruled against them on the ground that punitive damages are taxable. For the Court, the case was a chance to rule on an important issue in tax law; for the O'Gilvies, however, the primary concern surely was the millions in dollars that were at stake.

The second ideal type of case may be called "political" litigation. Here the motive of litigants is advancement not of their self-interest but of policies they favor. Most often, political litigation involves an effort to obtain a judicial decision that supports the litigant's policy goals. For instance, a group concerned with environmental protection might bring a suit to obtain a stringent interpretation of a statute that regulates air pollution. Someone who seeks to promote equality for disabled people may challenge a company practice on the ground that it violates protections of disabled workers stated in federal law.

Timmons v. Twin Cities Area New Party (1997) exemplifies political litigation.[4] Wisconsin litigator Sarah Siskind and law professor Joel Rogers, wife and husband, became interested in the tactic by which minor political parties list Republican or Democratic candidates on the ballot as their own candidates as well. Learning that most states prohibit this "cross-endorsement," Siskind and Rogers developed a legal challenge to those prohibitions; in the process, they helped to create a party called the New Party. With the help of the Public Citizen Litigation Group, the same group that assisted the Lohrs, they litigated several cases and won a favorable ruling from the Eighth Circuit court of appeals in a case involving the New Party in Minnesota. With a conflict among lower courts on the issue of cross-endorsement, the Supreme Court accepted that case—one that arose solely from the political goals of the people who initiated it.

When the Court ruled that Minnesota could prohibit cross-endorsements, the defeat was to those political goals, not personal self-interest.

Many cases have a large measure of both ordinary and political elements. For instance, individuals or companies may bring lawsuits to gain something directly, but along the way they may become concerned with the larger policy issues that arise from their cases. In cases brought by government agencies, ordinary and political elements may be difficult to separate: prosecutors file criminal cases to advance the specific mission of their agencies, but that mission is linked to the broader political goal of attacking crime.

The proportion of cases that can be classified as fully or partly political increases with each step upward in the judicial system; political litigation is most common in the Supreme Court. This pattern is not accidental. Ordinary litigation tends to be terminated at a relatively early stage, because the parties find it more advantageous to settle their dispute or even to accept a defeat than to fight on. In contrast, political litigants can often obtain significant victories only by getting a case to the highest levels of the judicial system because a favorable verdict in a trial court may do little to advance their policy goals. And political litigation often attracts the support of interest groups that help to shoulder the costs and other burdens of carrying a case through the judicial system.

Even so, the great majority of cases brought to the Supreme Court are best classified as ordinary litigation. A large proportion are criminal cases in which a convicted defendant who wants to get out of prison, or to stay out, seeks a hearing. Other cases come from business corporations that have a sufficient economic stake in the outcome to justify a petition to the Court. Still other cases concern a variety of individual grievances, big or small; in these cases the aggrieved party cannot resist going to the Supreme Court in one final effort to obtain redress.

Political litigation is more common in the cases that the Court agrees to hear, because those cases are more likely to concern the broad legal issues that interest the justices. Yet, as the *O'Gilvie* case illustrates, ordinary litigation is by no means absent from the cases that the Court hears. Even in the biggest cases, the ones that attract the attention of large numbers of interest groups, the litigants are often motivated chiefly by self-interest.

Attorneys

Few Supreme Court decisions have had the impact of *Roe v. Wade,* the Court's 1973 decision requiring the legalization of abortion. Yet the lawyers who argued this significant case before the Court were not veterans of Supreme Court litigation. The Texas law prohibiting abortion was defended by Jay Floyd, an assistant state attorney general who had never argued a case before the Court. Sarah Weddington, the lawyer who challenged that law, was making her second argument in a contested case in *any* court; her first had been made in federal district court in the same case.[5]

United States v. Chesapeake and Potomac Telephone Co. (1996) resulted in no decision at all; the Supreme Court sent the case back to a court of appeals to consider whether it was moot. But the case involved the right of local telephone companies to provide cable television services, and it had enormous stakes for the telephone and cable industries. Accordingly, both sides were well represented. The lawyer who presented the oral argument for the federal government was Deputy Solicitor General Lawrence Wallace, who had argued well over one hundred cases before the Court—more than any other living lawyer.[6] Opposing Wallace was Laurence Tribe, a Harvard law professor who had participated in more than twenty arguments in the Court and who is one of the most highly regarded Supreme Court advocates.

These two cases illustrate the distinction between two kinds of lawyers who participate in Supreme Court litigation.[7] The first group consists of attorneys who come before the Court only on rare occasions; many of them come only once. Like Sarah Weddington, most become involved in a case at its inception and simply continue to represent their client when the case moves to the Supreme Court. Although they may consider yielding to an experienced Supreme Court practitioner at that point, they choose to keep their case—sometimes, primarily because they do not want to forgo the opportunity to argue a case before the Court.

Most of these lawyers are members of the official Supreme

Court Bar, whose membership requirements are not stiff. The most important one is that lawyers have been admitted to practice in a state for at least three years; experience in arguing cases before the Court is not necessary. Many lawyers who never expect to handle a case in the Court obtain membership in its Bar, mostly for the prestige; about five thousand pay the $100 fee and join each year.[8] Former justice Lewis Powell described the Supreme Court Bar as "primarily a means of providing certificates that applicants can frame and hang in their chambers—if they do practice—to impress (if not deceive) prospective clients."[9]

The second group includes the lawyers who are frequent participants in cases at the Court. Most prominent are members of the solicitor general's staff; Supreme Court practice is their specialty. Some attorneys work for interest groups that frequently become involved in Supreme Court cases. Others have private practices in which Supreme Court advocacy is a major specialty; many of these lawyers have experience in the solicitor general's office or as law clerks in the Court. The box on pages 90–91 presents profiles of three lawyers who are part of this "inner circle." Unlike other attorneys, those in this second group usually become involved in a case at the appellate level, often when it reaches the Supreme Court.

Of the two groups of lawyers who participate in Supreme Court cases, the first is by far the larger. As Table 3-1 shows, most attorneys who argued cases before the Court in its 1995 term were doing so for the first time. Of course, the lawyers who participate frequently are involved in a higher percentage of cases than their numbers suggest. Indeed, the federal government with its experienced advocates participates in a majority of the cases decided on the merits.

Observers of the Court typically perceive that experienced Supreme Court advocates do a better job of arguing their cases. *Romer v. Evans* (1996) was a major case in which Colorado voters' prohibition of gay-rights laws was challenged under the Constitution. The lawyer for Colorado had argued a single case at the Court a few months earlier. The lawyer challenging the law had no experience before the Court and had resisted pressure to step aside in favor of a lawyer who did have such experience. One reporter criticized the performance of both lawyers:

TABLE 3-1

*Prior Oral Arguments (1988–1994 terms) by Lawyers
Arguing One or More Cases in the 1995 Term*

Prior oral arguments	Total	Lawyers Solicitor general's office	Other
0	58	2	56
1	11	1	10
2	7	3	4
3	1	0	1
4	1	1	0
5	2	0	2
6	2	0	2
7	0	0	0
8	3	1	2
9 or more	9	9	0
	94	17	77

Note: Each lawyer who argued one or more case in the 1995 term is counted only once. Since oral arguments prior to the 1988 term are not counted, the table underestimates slightly the overall level of experience.

"*Romer v. Evans* might have been a case where both sides would have benefited from imported representation"—imported from the ranks of highly experienced Supreme Court advocates.[10] Indeed, Kevin McGuire found from his analysis of cases that the side whose lawyer had more experience before the Court enjoyed an advantage in winning a favorable decision.[11]

This advantage, though significant, is not overwhelming. Inexperienced Supreme Court advocates sometimes do very good jobs. More important, the quality of lawyers' work is only one factor that helps to shape the Court's decisions, in part because the justices and their law clerks do their own close analysis of cases. It is hardly rare for a lawyer to secure a victory after arguing a case badly. One experienced advocate before the Court argued that "good lawyering can be a real plus" but "bad lawyering is not necessarily the death knell it is in other courts."[12]

In the legal system as a whole, a relationship exists between the wealth of an individual or institution and the quality of the

Profiles of Three Lawyers Who Participate

H. Bartow Farr III. After serving as law clerk to Supreme Court Justice William Rehnquist and working in the solicitor general's office, Farr went into private practice with a specialization in appellate courts. He is now part of a two-member firm with Richard Taranto, who also served in the Court and the solicitor general's office. Farr is a regular participant in Supreme Court litigation. He presents oral argument about once a term, on average. He has argued in major cases such as *Masson v. New Yorker Magazine* (1991), involving the application of libel laws to misquotations, and *Cipollone v. Liggett Group* (1992), involving liability of tobacco companies for health damage caused by smoking. Farr represents primarily businesses and business associations (including the National Cable Television Association in several cases) and state and local governments.

Carter G. Phillips. Like Farr, Phillips was a Supreme Court law clerk (for Chief Justice Warren Burger) and a member of the solicitor general's staff. He then joined the Washington office of Sidley & Austin, one of the largest law firms in the country. Phillips has represented a wide range of clients who are parties or amici in Supreme Court cases—primarily businesses, local governments, and professional groups (including, quite frequently, the American Medical Association). Having presented several oral arguments before the Court on behalf of the federal government, Phillips has continued to participate regularly in oral argument on behalf of private clients. In two cases decided in 1996, he argued for a railroad in

legal services available to that party. The picture is mixed in the Supreme Court. On the one hand, the experienced Supreme Court advocates in private practice are most readily available to large corporations and other prosperous organizations that can afford their regular fees. Some "inner circle" lawyers charge clients between $300 and $400 an hour, and the total fee for handling a case in the Supreme Court can reach $500,000.[13]

On the other hand, parties without substantial resources often obtain excellent legal services. Many of the attorneys who argue cases before the Court with some frequency and who are most skilled in doing so represent segments of society that are relatively poor or powerless. And Supreme Court specialists in private practice sometimes take cases for clients who have limited resources.

Frequently in Cases before the Supreme Court

a dispute over rules of liability for employee injuries (*Norfolk and Western Railway Co. v. Hiles*) and for chemical companies in a dispute with the federal government over the costs of litigation and settlement with military veterans that resulted from use of the defoliant Agent Orange in Vietnam (*Hercules Incorporated v. United States*).

Laurence Gold. Gold has been a lawyer with the AFL-CIO since 1974, and he has served as its general counsel since 1984. The AFL-CIO and its member unions become involved in Supreme Court cases as parties or amici with some frequency, so Gold is also a regular participant in litigation before the Court. He has participated in about three dozen oral arguments before the Court. *North Star Steel Company v. Thomas* (1995) and *United Food and Commercial Workers Union v. Brown Group, Inc.* (1996) dealt with a federal statute that requires some employers to provide employees with notice before a mass layoff or plant closing; in both cases, Gold argued successfully for interpretations that favored employees and unions. He has helped to write recent amicus briefs in cases whose subject matter ranges from gun control to agricultural marketing agreements along with issues relating more directly to the interests of organized labor.

Sources: Kevin T. McGuire, *The Supreme Court Bar: Legal Elites in the Washington Community* (Charlottesville: University Press of Virginia, 1993); Supreme Court decisions; biographical sources.

A poor person who lacks the support of an interest group may have to petition the Court for a hearing without a lawyer's help, and this certainly constitutes a disadvantage. If the Court accepts such a case, however, it will appoint an excellent attorney to represent the indigent litigant. Despite the very low compensation they receive from the Court, lawyers seldom decline such an appointment. According to one Supreme Court specialist, arguing a case before the Court "is the ultimate professional experience for an appellate lawyer."[14]

Interest Groups

Leaders of interest groups are opportunists: they focus their efforts where they can make the most difference. For that reason, many groups give substantial attention to the Supreme

Court. The Court's decisions establish important policies on issues as diverse as antitrust and obscenity. Groups that care about those issues understand that influencing the Court can be a way to advance their goals or to fight back against other groups with opposing goals. And because so many interest groups are affected by the Court's decisions, a great deal of group activity is focused on the Court. In the Supreme Court, as in the other branches of government, interest groups are major participants in the policy-making process.

The Forms of Group Activity. Groups that seek to influence congressional decisions try to make their case directly to members of Congress. In contrast, it is considered highly improper to lobby judges directly. Because of this norm, Supreme Court justices generally attempt to avoid contact with litigants and the groups that support them.

But interest groups can attempt to influence the Court in other ways. As described in Chapter 2, some groups participate informally in the nomination and confirmation of justices. A group that helps to determine the Court's membership can affect its policies fundamentally.

Groups also can participate in litigation before the Court in two related ways. First, a group can help to get cases to the Court. Interest groups are allowed to bring suits in their own names only if they have legal standing because a case affects them directly. Organizations that exist primarily as interest groups generally lack standing. But other organizations that may be considered interest groups, especially businesses and governments, are often parties in Supreme Court cases.

A group that is not a party can "sponsor" a case on an issue that concerns it, providing attorneys' services and bearing the costs from the start. A very small proportion of all cases brought to the Court involve group sponsorship,[15] chiefly because of the considerable expense and practical difficulties of sponsorship. But cases that the Court actually hears, particularly cases of great significance, are far more likely to be sponsored. One study found that half of the most important decisions in the 1986–1991 terms were in cases sponsored by groups.[16] Alternatively, a group can become involved in cases that others have already initiated, helping to bear financial costs and supplying legal services and advice.

One example of group sponsorship was *Babbitt v. Sweet Home Chapter of Communities for a Great Oregon* (1995). Acting under the Endangered Species Act of 1973, the federal Interior Department restricted logging in the Pacific Northwest to protect the northern spotted owl. The American Forest and Paper Association, representing the timber industry, then organized landowners and small timber companies to bring a lawsuit challenging the government's interpretation of the law. The Association financed the lawsuit, which resulted in a defeat in federal district court, a victory in a court of appeals, and ultimately defeat in the Supreme Court.[17]

Second, by participating in oral argument or submitting briefs, a group can attempt to influence the Court's decisions whether to accept cases and how to decide those that are accepted. If a group is effectively in control of a case, its attorneys will submit a brief in support of (or in opposition to) the Supreme Court's acceptance of the case. If the case is accepted for decision on the merits, the group's attorneys will submit further briefs and participate in oral argument.

When a group does not control the case, it still may submit arguments to the Court in what are called *amicus curiae* (friend of the court) briefs. With the consent of the parties to a case or by permission of the Court, any person or organization may submit an amicus brief to supplement the arguments of the parties. (Legal representatives of government do not need to obtain permission.) Most of the time, the parties give their consent for the submission of amicus briefs. When the Court's consent is needed, it seldom is denied—only about a dozen times from 1990 through 1996. Amicus briefs can be submitted on the issue of whether a case should be heard or, after a case is accepted for hearing, directly on the merits of the case. An amicus can also participate in oral argument if allowed by the Court. It is rare for an amicus other than the federal government to argue a case—though the state of Ohio did so in a 1997 case, *City of Boerne v. Flores.*

Amicus briefs are by far the most common means by which groups other than parties participate in litigation before the Court. As might be expected, amicus briefs are especially common in cases that the Court has accepted for consideration on the merits. In the 1989 through 1993 terms, such briefs were submitted in 85 percent of the cases decided on the merits.[18] In those cases that had amicus briefs during the 1986–1991 terms, an average of more than four per case were submitted. And, because groups or individuals can join in submitting briefs, the number of participants was considerably larger: on average, there were more than four "friends" per brief.[19]

Some major cases attract large numbers of amicus briefs. In *Webster v. Reproductive Health Services,* a 1989 case about state regulation of abortion, the Court received a record 80 briefs representing the views of more than 400 private interest groups, about 250 members of Congress, and more than 1,000 state legislators, as well as state attorney generals, private individuals, and the federal government.[20] The box on page 95 shows the array of groups that participated in amicus briefs in a 1996 punitive damages case and in the two assisted suicide cases that the Court decided in 1997. More than 70 amicus briefs were submitted in the assisted suicide cases (some groups submitted separate briefs in the two cases).

The popularity of amicus briefs reflects the relative ease of this route to the Court. An amicus brief is not inexpensive, typically costing several thousand dollars and often tens of thousands to prepare. But the costs and difficulties of participating as an amicus can be surmounted by a great many groups, at least occasionally. And, because of the widespread perception that amicus briefs influence the Court, groups consider the effort of filing or joining in a brief to be worthwhile. Amicus participation is useful in another way as well, as one group leader explained: "A group has to be able to show its members that their efforts are paying off, and filing amicus briefs is the easiest way to do that."[21]

Groups also lobby the Court outside the litigation process. In 1997 the attorney generals of twenty-four states issued a statement asking the Court to reverse its ruling in *Buckley v. Valeo* (1976), which had greatly restricted government power to regulate the financing of political campaigns. Groups on both sides of the abortion controversy conduct marches and demonstrations while the Court considers abortion cases, in part to put indirect pressure on the justices.

Finally, interest groups seek to influence media coverage of the Court's decisions.[22] After decisions are handed down, group

Selected Groups Participating in Amicus Curiae Briefs Submitted to the Supreme Court in Some Recent Cases

BMW of North America, Inc. v. Gore (1996)

Issue: Was a punitive damages award of $2 million excessive in a case involving a manufacturer's repainting of a new car without disclosure to the customer?

Participating Groups

Chamber of Commerce of the United States
American Automobile Manufacturers Association
Business Council of Alabama
American Tort Reform Association
Washington Post
NBC
American General Life and Accident Insurance Company
National Association of Securities and Commercial Law Attorneys
Association of Trial Lawyers of America
Product Liability Advisory Council
Washington Legal Foundation

Washington v. Glucksberg (1997)

Vacco v. Quill (1997)

Issue: Do state laws that prohibit assisting in suicides violate the due process or equal protection clauses of the Fourteenth Amendment?

Participating Groups

United States
State of Oregon
Michigan Catholic Conference
Lutheran Church—Missouri Synod
American College of Legal Medicine
Christian Medical and Dental Society
Coalition of Hospice Professionals
Hemlock Society USA
Northwest Women's Law Center
National Gray Panthers Project Fund
Family Research Council
American Civil Liberties Union

representatives give interviews in which they try to put those decisions in the most favorable light. When the Supreme Court reporter for the *New York Times* returned to her office after the
Court's major abortion decision in 1992, "there were two huge
stacks of faxes on the floor by my desk, one pile generated by
the right-to-life side and the other by the pro-choice side."[23]
Group leaders understand that the impact of the Court's decisions depends in part on how those decisions are reported.

The Array of Groups in the Court. Every year, hundreds of in-
terest groups participate in Supreme Court cases in some way.
Among them are nearly all the groups that are most active in
Congress and the executive branch.

It is hardly surprising that so many groups focus their attention on the Court. In their efforts to influence government,
interest groups go to the institutions that can affect them in
significant ways. The Supreme Court decides issues that range
from labor-management relations to freedom of expression to
the powers of state governments. Thus it makes good sense for
a wide range of interest groups to involve themselves in the
work of the Court.

Interest group participation in Supreme Court litigation has
increased dramatically in the past few decades. This change is
also unsurprising. Throughout government, the number of active interest groups and the level of their activity have increased
considerably. The apparent success of some groups in shaping
the Supreme Court's policies has encouraged attempts by other
groups to exert a similar impact. And the Court's increased
prominence as a policy maker reminds groups of its potential
importance to their goals.

The diverse groups that come to the Court can be placed in
four broad categories. The largest category includes economic
groups: individual businesses, trade associations, professional
associations, labor unions, and farm groups. Economic groups
predominate in the Court, as they do in the other branches, because they are numerous and relatively well funded. And the
Court does a great deal that they care about. In particular, the
business community is affected by most of the Court's decisions.
Nearly all the subjects that the justices address—even those that
might seem unrelated to the business community—are of concern to it in some way. Cases on state-federal relations often

arise as a result of state taxation or regulation of businesses. Civil rights cases frequently concern the enforcement of anti-discrimination laws against employers.

The second category includes groups that represent segments of the population defined by something other than economics. The most prominent of these groups is the NAACP Legal Defense and Educational Fund (sometimes called the NAACP Legal Defense Fund or simply the Fund), which typifies groups representing segments of the population defined by race, ethnicity, or gender.[24] The Fund was created by the NAACP as a separate litigating group in 1939, and it is now fully independent of the parent organization. It initiates litigation through its staff of about thirty lawyers, most of whom are in New York City, and a large network of cooperating attorneys throughout the United States. The Fund initially focused its efforts on securing voting rights for black citizens and desegregating schools in the South, two issues that are still important today. It has also worked to challenge capital punishment and to obtain effective enforcement of federal laws against employment discrimination.

The Fund's successes in the Court have encouraged the development of similar organizations, such as the Mexican-American Legal Defense and Education Fund and several litigation groups representing women. Religious groups have participated in Supreme Court litigation for a long time, but their involvement has grown considerably in recent years.[25]

The groups in the third category represent broad ideological positions rather than the interests of a specific segment of society; an example is the American Civil Liberties Union.[26] Established in 1920 as an organization for the protection of civil liberties, the ACLU has always relied heavily on litigation as a means to that end. Although it has traditionally emphasized freedom of expression, the ACLU involves itself in virtually every area of civil liberties law. It acts primarily on complaints of civil liberties violations that people bring to local ACLU affiliates, which provide volunteer attorneys for cases they perceive as meritorious. If cases reach the Supreme Court, they are often handled by the national ACLU office. In the past few decades, the ACLU created special projects that have initiated concerted litigation campaigns in specific areas of concern, such as women's rights, capital punishment, prisons, and national security. In the mid-1990s it participated in Supreme Court cases involving such issues as federal regulation of material on the Internet, fee requirements for appeals by indigent litigants, and racial considerations in drawing legislative districts.

The ACLU is one of many groups that work to achieve liberal policy goals. Two other such groups are the Sierra Club, which has a litigation arm devoted to environmental protection, and the Planned Parenthood Federation of America, for which abortion rights are a primary concern. In the 1960s Ralph Nader pioneered public interest law firms, which were established to handle cases that they perceived as serving the public interest from a liberal perspective. These firms have instituted litigation on such issues as consumer rights, civil liberties, and the environment. One of the firms, the Public Citizen Research Group, now gives some emphasis to litigation enforcing the separation of powers between Congress and the executive branch. Its cases have produced several major decisions, including the Court's ruling against congressional vetoes of administrative rules.[27]

Groups that favor conservative positions on legal issues were slower to involve themselves in litigation, but a number of such groups are now active.[28] Americans for Effective Law Enforcement supports narrow interpretations of the procedural rights of criminal defendants. Americans United for Life litigates on abortion and other issues. There are several conservative public interest law firms, modeled in part after their liberal counterparts. One of these firms, the Mountain States Legal Foundation, sponsored the 1995 case in which the Supreme Court made it more difficult for the federal government to justify programs that favor businesses owned by members of racial minority groups.[29]

One major group with conservative aims is the American Center for Law and Justice (ACLJ), established by religious leader Pat Robertson in 1991.[30] The similarity between "ACLJ" and "ACLU" is no accident; the ACLJ was intended as a counterpart to the ACLU in supporting conservative Christian values. The organization gives some emphasis to assisting students who want to participate in religious activities and participants in antiabortion activities. Chief counsel Jay Alan Sekulow has argued cases on both issues in the Supreme Court.

Fourth, governments regularly appear as interest groups in the Court. The federal government is a special case and is examined later in this chapter. State and local governments often come to the Court as litigants, and they file many amicus briefs. It has become standard practice for several states to join in a brief in order to emphasize their strong shared interest in a case. All fifty states joined in an amicus brief asking the Court to hear *Ivy v. Diamond Shamrock Chemicals Co.* (1994), which concerned the jurisdiction of federal and state courts. Groups that represent many governments, such as the National League of Cities, frequently submit amicus briefs as well.

Group Strategies and Tactics. In *Brown v. Board of Education* (1954), the Supreme Court ruled that public school students cannot be segregated by race. *Brown* and the four cases that accompanied it were sponsored by the NAACP Legal Defense Fund, and the Fund's victory was the culmination of a long campaign to achieve desegregation. Under the leadership of Thurgood Marshall, the Fund had begun with challenges to blatant discrimination against black students in graduate and professional schools; its successes in those cases helped move the Court toward the far more sweeping decision in *Brown*.

That litigation campaign was a landmark in American legal history. It has been the subject of a number of books and television movies. (In one movie Sidney Poitier played Marshall, who said that "Sidney was better than I was in the court, but he got paid more than I did."[31]) But the path to *Brown* was not as smooth as it appears in retrospect. The Fund's leaders struggled to garner the funds required to carry out their litigation campaign, and they had to worry about coordinating cases that they had not initiated. More important, the Fund's success in achieving school desegregation resulted not only from the skills and dedication of its lawyers but from favorable circumstances as well. When conditions are less favorable, interest groups—including the Fund itself—are likely to be less successful.

Only a minority of groups map out long-term litigation campaigns, but they all face strategic and tactical decisions.[32] At the strategic level, they must decide how much of their energy and resources to devote to litigation rather than other forms of political action—though groups that are set up specifically to litigate do not face this choice. They must also decide what kinds of issues to emphasize in their litigation work and how to coordinate their efforts with other groups that have similar interests. Groups concerned with racial discrimination have worked together a good deal. At the tactical level, a group's lawyers consider whether bringing a specific case or supporting a litigant in a case that has already been initiated would serve their goals. They sometimes have a choice among different regions in which to initiate cases or between federal and state courts. And, like other lawyers, they have to choose which arguments to make in the cases in which they participate.

Many considerations affect these decisions, including the views of group members and the availability of resources. The high expense of litigation means that even relatively wealthy groups have to set priorities. Perhaps the most fundamental consideration is groups' perceptions of the courts in general and the Supreme Court in particular. It is not surprising that conservative groups have become more active in Supreme Court litigation since the 1970s as the Court has become more receptive to conservative arguments. Similarly, choices of specific cases and arguments reflect judgments about potential responses from the justices.

The Significance of Interest Groups. Interest groups can affect what the Supreme Court does in several ways; here, I focus on their effect in determining whether cases get to the Court. In this respect, cases may be placed in three categories.

The largest category includes the cases that come to the Court without any participation by interest groups. For the most part, these cases constitute what I have called ordinary litigation. The issues in these cases are too narrow to interest any group. They reach the Court because the parties and attorneys have sufficient motivation of their own to seek a Supreme Court hearing and sufficient resources to finance the litigation. These conditions exist in much of the litigation involving businesses, which often have substantial resources and a large financial stake in a case. They also exist in a great many criminal cases, in which defendants face significant prison terms and do not have to pay lawyers' fees or most of the other expenses.

The second category consists of cases that would have reached the Court without any interest group involvement, but in which one or more groups are involved in some way. An interest group may assist one of the parties by providing attorneys' services or financing to ensure that the case does reach the Supreme Court and to gain some control over the position that the party takes. Far more often, a group will submit an amicus brief supporting the petition for a hearing by the Court.

The third category includes cases that would not reach the Court without sponsorship by interest groups. There are many important legal questions in civil liberties that no individual litigant has the capability or sufficient incentive to take to the Supreme Court. Ordinarily, it would be impossible for one parent or even several parents to arrange and finance a school desegregation suit on their own. To take another example, during most of its history the Supreme Court decided few cases concerning the legal rights of the poor; one reason was that the poor seldom could afford the costs of getting a case to the Court. In 1965 the federal government set up the Legal Services Program as a kind of interest group that would represent the poor. Between 1966 and 1975, more than 150 cases sponsored by the program came to the Court. Some of these cases resulted in a series of significant Court decisions on the rights of the poor.[33]

It should be emphasized that only a small proportion of cases brought to the Court fall in this third category, because group sponsorship of cases in the Court is relatively rare. But groups are most likely to sponsor cases that have the potential to be heard by the Court and to produce major legal rulings. Of course, groups can do more than get cases to the Court; they can help to determine whether those cases are heard and how the Court rules. That influence is discussed later in this chapter and in Chapter 4.

The Federal Government as Litigant

Of all the litigants in the Supreme Court, the federal government appears most frequently. In the 1995 term it was a party in more than one-third of the cases brought to the Court for consideration and in nearly half of the cases actually decided by the

Court after oral argument.[34] The federal government is also the most important interest group in the Court. In its own cases, the government takes a position on such major issues as the rights of criminal defendants and the scope of environmental protection. It frequently participates as an amicus in other cases, as it did in 27 of the 90 cases argued before the Court in the 1995 term.

Thus the group of lawyers who have the greatest impact on the Court are the ones who work for the Office of the Solicitor General in the Justice Department. Fewer than two dozen lawyers work in that office, but they are primarily responsible for representing the federal government in the Supreme Court. They decide whether to bring federal government cases to the Court; only a few federal agencies can take cases to the Court without the solicitor general's approval.

Lawyers in the solicitor general's office also do the bulk of the legal work in Supreme Court cases in which the federal government participates, including petitions for hearings, the writing of briefs, and oral arguments. One exception is that the attorney general traditionally makes at least one oral argument before the Court. Janet Reno, attorney general in the Clinton administration, chose a 1997 case involving the power of law enforcement officers to order passengers out of cars.[35]

The solicitor general's office enjoys a unique relationship with the Court, one that has elements of partnership. That relationship is symbolized by the Court's provision of an office for members of the solicitor general's staff to use at the Court. More consequential are the Court's frequent invitations to the solicitor general to participate in a case as amicus with a brief or oral argument, invitations that it seldom extends to anyone else. For its part, the solicitor general's office frequently asks to participate in oral argument as amicus curiae; in recent years, the Court seldom has denied those requests.

One aspect of this partnership is the solicitor general's self-restraint in requesting hearings by the Court. In the cases acted on by the Court in the 1995 term, the federal government filed 27 petitions for certiorari while its opponents filed 2,680. The federal government has fewer potential Court cases than its opponents, because it wins most of the time in the courts of appeals, but the limited number of government petitions reflects primarily the solicitor general's willingness to forgo possible petitions for certiorari. This willingness stems in part from a desire to ease the Court's workload and to maintain the solicitor general's credibility with the justices. An interest in maintaining credibility also helps to explain the solicitor general's unique practice of "confessing error" to the Supreme Court—stating in a brief that a lower court decision in favor of the federal government involved some kind of error. On average, the solicitor general confesses error in two or three cases a year.[36]

The solicitor general's office enjoys considerable independence from the president and attorney general, an independence fostered by its special relationship with the Supreme Court. The solicitor general can argue that positions urged on the office by its formal superiors would weaken its credibility with the Court and thus its effectiveness in representing the executive branch. But the office operates in a general climate created by the president and the attorney general, and officials in the Justice Department and the White House intervene in the making of specific decisions.[37]

This general climate has an impact on the overall pattern of positions that the office takes in litigation. Analyzing individual rights cases in which the solicitor general had a choice about whether to participate, Rebecca Salokar found that the government was far more likely to take a liberal position under a Democratic president than a Republican president.[38] In part, this difference reflects the president's power to choose the solicitor general. Democratic presidents usually choose liberals, while Republicans favor conservatives. Personal views aside, a solicitor general makes some effort to represent the administration's viewpoint. Erwin Griswold served as solicitor general during both the Johnson and Nixon administrations, and his legal positions became more conservative under Nixon.[39]

Intervention by the administration in a specific case is hardly rare. The solicitor general sometimes invites intervention, seeking guidance from higher-level officials. In other instances, presidents or their staff members become aware of a case and try to influence the solicitor general's position.

One instance of intervention came in a case involving a federal statute prohibiting receipt and possession of child pornography. In *Knox v. United States* (1993, 1995), Stephen Knox

asked the Supreme Court to overturn his conviction under the
statute. President Clinton's solicitor general Drew Days argued
for a narrow interpretation of the child pornography statute
and suggested that the Court send the case back to the court of
appeals to reconsider its decision affirming the conviction. The
Court did so. The Clinton administration received heavy criticism for Days's argument in the case, and the Senate unanimously passed a resolution attacking it. Seeking to undo the political damage, Clinton asked the Justice Department to draft a
revision of the statute so that it would have broader coverage.
Meanwhile, the court of appeals reaffirmed the conviction, and
Knox brought the case back to the Supreme Court. At that
point attorney general Janet Reno intervened to overrule Days's
position, personally signing a brief that argued for a broad interpretation of the statute. The Court then denied the defendant a hearing, making his conviction final.[40]

During his tenure as solicitor general from 1993 to 1996,
Days received a good deal of criticism, primarily from conservatives who argued that his positions in cases were unduly liberal. Indeed, the Republican-controlled Senate Judiciary Committee called Days to testify in 1995 and questioned him sharply
about several cases.[41] That hearing was quite unusual, but such
criticism is not. The lawyers who served as solicitor general in
the Reagan and Bush administration were criticized by liberals
who charged them with pressing a conservative agenda on the
Supreme Court and by conservatives for insufficient zeal in ad-
vocating that agenda. (Bush solicitor general Kenneth Starr
came under much closer scrutiny a few years later, after he became independent counsel for the Whitewater investigation.)

Although the Department of Justice is the primary legal representative of the federal government, Congress has its own
legal arms: the House Office of the General Counsel and the
Office of Senate Legal Counsel.[42] Congress sometimes participates as a body in Supreme Court litigation to defend statutes that the solicitor general refused to defend. For instance,
Congress intervened in *Immigration and Naturalization Service v.
Chadha* (1983) to argue for its power to veto administrative
rules, because the solicitor general was supporting the administration's position that legislative vetoes were unconstitutional.
More often, members of Congress submit amicus briefs to the

Court as individuals or sets of individuals, seeking to influence the Court and—in some instances—to appeal to constituents by taking popular positions. Such submissions have become common only in recent years. During the six decades from 1912 through 1971, members of Congress submitted amicus briefs in only fourteen cases. In the decade from 1986 to 1995, they did so in sixty cases.[43]

Deciding What to Hear: The Court's Role

In March 1996 the federal Fifth Circuit court of appeals in New Orleans ruled that the affirmative action program used by the University of Texas law school for student admissions violated the Equal Protection Clause of the Fourteenth Amendment. The court's opinion took a strong position against the consideration of race in school admissions—a position that contrasted with most people's reading of a complex 1978 Supreme Court decision on the subject. If it went into effect, the Fifth Circuit's decision would require substantial changes in many schools' admissions policies. The decision attracted considerable attention, and people in education and law waited to see whether the Supreme Court would agree with the Fifth Circuit and prohibit affirmative action programs in school admissions or whether it would allow such programs to continue.

The Court did neither. Instead, it simply refused to hear *Texas v. Hopwood* (1996).

The Court treats most cases in the same way: it refuses to hear them. In its 1995 term, the Court granted certiorari and reached a decision on the merits in fewer than one in sixty cases brought to it.[44] This ratio is a reminder that the Court has enormous power to set its own agenda.

When the Court decides not to hear a case, its decision allows the lower court decision to become final, but it has no broader legal effect. In *Hopwood*, the Court's denial of certiorari meant that the Fifth Circuit's prohibition of affirmative action in school admissions was the law for the three states in that circuit, but schools in the other eleven circuits were unaffected by that prohibition. Newspapers and television often depict a denial of certiorari as approval of the lower court decision in a case.[45] The Court *is* more likely to deny certiorari when most members agree with the lower court decision in a case, so a denial may provide a clue to the justices' views. But the refusal to hear a case has no legal meaning in itself.

Options

In its screening of petitions for hearings, the Court does not simply either accept or reject individual cases; its choices are broader and more complicated. To begin with, the Court does not consider petitions in isolation from one another; often, cases are linked. The justices may accept a case to clarify or expand on an earlier decision in the same policy area. They may accept several cases that raise the same issue in order to address that issue more fully than a single case would allow them to do. They may even reject a case because they are looking for a more suitable case on the same issue.

When the Court does accept a case, the justices can choose which issues they will consider. The Court often limits its grant of certiorari to one issue raised by the petitioner, and it sometimes asks the parties to address an issue that neither had raised. No matter what issues the parties address, the Court retains the freedom to determine the issues it actually resolves in its opinion. In a 1995 case, Justice O'Connor charged that the Court majority was deciding an issue that the petition for certiorari had not raised, contrary to one of the Court's rules.[46] Whether or not her charge was justified, in practice the Court can decide the issues it wants to decide. One striking example is *Mapp v. Ohio* (1961), in which the Court turned an obscenity case into a landmark decision on police searches and seizures.

When the Court accepts a case, it also determines the kind of consideration it will give that case. It may give the case full consideration, which means that the Court receives a new set of briefs on the merits from the parties and holds oral argument, then issues a decision on the merits with a full opinion explaining the decision. Alternatively, it may give the case summary consideration. This usually means that the case is decided without new briefs or oral argument; the Court relies on the materials that the parties already submitted. A large minority of the cases that the Court accepts receive summary consideration.

In most summary decisions, the Supreme Court issues a "GVR" order—Granting certiorari, Vacating the lower court decision, and Remanding the case to that court for reconsideration. Most of these orders are issued because some event since the lower court decision is relevant to the case. In turn, that event is usually a Supreme Court decision in another case. In *Bailey v. United States* (1995), the Court interpreted the word "uses" in a federal statute that imposed a five-year minimum prison sentence on someone who uses a gun while committing a drug offense. Five days later the Court issued GVR orders in twenty cases that it wanted courts of appeals to reconsider "in light of *Bailey v. United States.*"[47] The justices sometimes disagree about the appropriateness of a specific GVR order, and in two 1996 cases they debated the circumstances under which such orders should be issued.[48] Still, these orders are usually unanimous and routine.

In other summary decisions, the Court actually reaches a decision on the merits and issues an opinion of several paragraphs or even several pages. This opinion typically is labeled *per curiam* (by the Court) rather than being signed by a justice, but it has the same legal force as a signed opinion.[49] When the Court takes this kind of action, as it did several times in the 1995 term, justices sometimes complain that it should not have decided the case without getting full information from the parties through briefs that directly address the merits of the case and through oral argument. In 1997 the Court resolved an issue involving federal sentencing rules with a summary decision, even though the existence of two concurring opinions and two dissenting opinions suggested that the issue was not a simple one. In their dissenting opinions, Justice Stevens and Justice Kennedy argued that the case should have been given full consideration.[50]

Even after accepting a case, the Court can avoid a decision by issuing what is called a "DIG" (for "Dismissed as Improvidently Granted"). A DIG occurs a few times each term, when the parties' briefs on the merits or the oral arguments suggest to the justices that the case is inappropriate for a decision. In *Grimmett v. Brown* (1997) the Court issued a DIG a week after oral argument, in which one of the lawyers argued that the Court's ruling on the issue before it would have no effect on the outcome of the case for the parties.[51] On the same day, however, the Court accepted another case raising the same issue. That action underlines the impact of the Court's having so many cases to choose from; if it misses one opportunity to address an important question, another is likely to be available soon.

Screening Procedures

The Court uses a series of complex procedures to screen petitions for hearing, and these procedures are made more complex by two distinctions between types of cases. The first is between the certiorari cases, over which the Court's jurisdiction is discretionary, and the very small number of cases that the Court is required to decide, labeled appeals. Before 1988, the number of appeals was greater, and the Court used dismissals or summary affirmances to avoid granting full hearings in most of these cases. In 1988 Congress limited appeals to those cases decided by three-judge federal district courts. Few appeals now reach the Court—on average, about a dozen a term.[52] But the Court retains, and uses, the option of deciding them without holding oral argument or issuing full opinions. The second distinction, between paid cases and paupers' cases, requires more extensive discussion.

Paid Cases and Paupers' Cases. Only about one-third of the requests for hearings that arrive at the Supreme Court are "paid" cases, for which the Court's filing fee of $300 has been paid and all required copies of materials have been provided. The remaining cases, a growing majority, are brought *in forma pauperis* by indigent people for whom the fee and the requirement of multiple copies are waived. The great majority of the "paupers' cases" are brought by prisoners in federal and state institutions. (A person responding to a petition may also be given pauper status.)

Criminal defendants who have had counsel provided to them in the lower federal courts because of their low incomes are automatically entitled to bring paupers' cases in the Supreme Court. Other litigants must submit an affidavit supporting their motion for leave to file as paupers. The Court has never developed precise rules specifying when a litigant can claim pauper status. But in recent years, it has denied a number of litigants the right to proceed as paupers in particular cases on the grounds that they were not truly paupers or that their petitions were frivolous or malicious. The Court has also gone further, issuing a general denial of pauper status to several litigants who had filed large numbers of paupers' petitions. In 1996, for instance, it ordered its Clerk of the Court not to accept any further paupers' petitions from a litigant who had filed at least eighteen petitions with the Court. According to the Court, the litigant "has a history of frivolous, repetitive filings," and her latest petition was "nearly incomprehensible, and alludes to, among other things, fraud by the staff of this Court and impending impeachment proceedings" against the Court's Clerk.[53]

A very small proportion of paupers' petitions are accepted for full decisions on the merits—less than one-third of 1 percent in the 1995 term, compared with 3 percent of the paid cases in the same term.[54] The lack of inherent merit in many of these cases and the fact that many litigants have to draft petitions without a lawyer's assistance help to account for the low acceptance rate. But because there are so many paupers' petitions, even the small proportion that are accepted add up to a significant number of cases—thirteen in the 1995 term—and they constitute an important part of the Court's work on issues of criminal procedure.

Prescreening: The Discuss List. The ultimate decision to hear a case is made at the Court's conference, but requests for hearings are considered and voted on at conference only if they are put on the Court's "discuss list."[55] The chief justice creates the discuss list, but other justices can and do add cases to it. Cases left off the discuss list are denied hearings automatically. This is the fate of most cases; Justice Ginsburg has estimated that, typically, only 10 to 13 percent of the petitions for hearing get on the discuss list.[56]

The discuss-list procedure serves to limit the Court's workload. But this procedure also reflects a belief that most petitions do not require collective consideration, because they are such poor candidates for acceptance. A great many petitions raise only very narrow issues, and many others make very weak legal claims, so it is easy to reject them.

Action in Conference. In conference, the chief justice or the justice who added a case to the discuss list opens discussion of the case. In order of seniority, from senior to junior, the justices then speak and usually announce their votes. If the discussion does not make the justices' positions clear, a formal vote is taken, also in order of seniority. Despite the prescreening of weak cases, a substantial majority of the petitions considered in conference are denied.

Most cases receive very brief discussion in conference, and ordinarily the justices simply state the positions they reached individually before the conference. In this sense, the conference usually serves only as a place for individual votes to be added together.

But some cases are given more extensive consideration, which sometimes extends beyond the initial discussion. In conference, any justice can ask that a case be "relisted" for a later conference. This might be done to obtain additional information, such as the full record of the case in the lower courts. A justice also might ask for relisting to circulate an opinion dissenting from the Court's tentative denial of a hearing and thereby try to change the Court's decision. As Justice Stevens once noted, such an opinion "sometimes persuades other Justices to change their votes and a petition is granted that would otherwise have been denied."[57]

When it accepts a case, the Court also decides whether to allow oral argument or to decide the case summarily on the basis of the available written materials. Four votes are required for oral argument. A case that is not given oral argument may be granted a hearing and decided on the merits at the same conference, so that the two stages of decision in effect become one.

The Court does not issue an opinion to explain its acceptance or rejection of a case, and individual votes are not announced systematically. But justices occasionally record their dissents from denials of petitions for hearings, and these votes may be accompanied by opinions. During the 1995 term there were two cases in which three justices dissented and a third in which Justice Thomas dissented alone. Justices who voted not to grant a hearing sometimes write an opinion to comment on the Court's decision. In *Texas v. Hopwood* (1996), the affirmative action case involving the University of Texas, Justice Ginsburg wrote a short opinion "respecting the denial of the petition for a writ of certiorari" that Justice Souter joined. Ginsburg's opinion said that the university had discontinued the program in question, so there was no longer a live controversy. Ginsburg probably wrote the opinion to deter observers from inferring that the Court approved of the Fifth Circuit's decision in the case.

The Clerks' Role. A key function of the justices' law clerks is to help in scrutinizing requests for hearings.[58] In 1997 eight of the nine justices—all but John Paul Stevens—were part of the "certiorari pool." Petitions and other materials on each case are divided among the clerks for these eight justices. The clerk who has responsibility for a case writes a memorandum of two to twenty-five pages. The memo typically includes a summary of the relevant facts and the parties' contentions and a recommendation for the Court's action on the petition. Some justices then have their own clerks examine and react to the memo for each case, thus providing a second point of view on the case.

Because of the press of time, the justices rely heavily on law clerks' analyses of cases. William Brennan, who retired in 1990, was the last of the justices who regularly read the petitions themselves. Some justices and other observers have expressed particular concern about the justices' collective reliance on the pool memo.[59] One recent law clerk has argued that this reliance is less problematic than it might appear: clerks typically write their pool memos with care, and justices frequently vote contrary to the memo's recommendation. "Still," he concluded, "any system that depends to a considerable degree on the views of a single novice lawyer is fairly subject to criticism."[60] Justice Stevens lessens this problem by staying out of the pool. But he delegates a good deal of responsibility to his own clerks, who write memoranda or refer petitions directly to him in only a minority of cases.

Substantial though it is, the impact of the law clerks on certiorari decisions should not be exaggerated. For one thing, the large majority of petitions would elicit the same reaction from any justice or clerk: an obvious denial. And justices involve themselves most fully in the screening process at the point where individual judgments make the most difference—in selecting cases to hear from those on the discuss list.

The Criteria for Decision

Supreme Court justices are free to choose cases to hear on any basis they wish, and they need not justify or explain their choices. When the Court decides a case, its opinion often includes a rationale for accepting the case, but the rationale is usually brief and not very illuminating. The Court seldom explains denials of petitions for hearing.

The Court's Rule 10 does provide general guidance by specifying some of the conditions under which the Court will hear a case. The rule emphasizes the Court's role in ensuring the certainty and consistency of the law. The criteria for accepting a case cited in Rule 10 include the existence of important legal issues that the Court has not yet decided, conflict among courts of appeals on a legal question, conflict between a lower court's decision and the Supreme Court's prior decisions, and departure "from the accepted and usual course of judicial proceedings" in the courts below.

These criteria make sense, but they suggest a conception of the Court's function and of its members' interests that is unrealistically narrow. Thus, it is necessary to take a broader view of the criteria for decision. The Court's pattern of screening decisions and evidence from other sources suggest the significance of several considerations.

The Technical Criteria. The Supreme Court will reject a petition for hearing if it fails to meet certain technical requirements. Some of these requirements are specific to the Court. For instance, paid petitions must comply with the Court's Rule 33, which establishes requirements on such matters as the size of print and margins used, type of paper, format and color of cover, and maximum length. These requirements are relaxed for the paupers' petitions, but even paupers' petitions may be rejected if their deviation from the rules is extreme.

The Court also imposes the same kinds of technical requirements for the hearing of cases that other courts apply. One specific requirement is that petitions for hearing be filed within ninety days of the entry of judgment in the lower court, unless the time has been extended in advance. In 1996 the Court refused to accept two certiorari petitions because they were one day late, apparently because the lawyers involved failed to take into account the extra day in February during a leap year.[61]

More fundamental are the requirements of jurisdiction and standing. If the Court receives a case that clearly falls outside its jurisdiction, it cannot accept that case for hearing. For instance, the Court could not hear a state case in which the petitioner raised no issues of federal law in state court.

The rule of standing holds that a court may not hear a case unless the party bringing the case is properly before it. The most important element of standing is the requirement that a party in a case have a real and direct legal stake in its outcome. This requirement precludes hypothetical cases, cases brought on behalf of another person, "friendly suits" between parties that are not really adversaries, and cases that have become "moot" (in effect, hypothetical) because the parties can no longer be affected by the outcome. In 1997 the Court chose not to address the merits of a challenge to an Arizona law requiring that state employees speak only English on the job, holding that the case had become moot when the employee who originally brought the challenge resigned from her position.[62]

The technical requirements sometimes are easy to apply. But their application can be more ambiguous, arousing disagreement among the justices. Those disagreements often reflect views about the underlying merits of cases. For example, the justices who are most likely to grant standing to environmental groups are generally the ones most favorable to the policy positions of those groups. As this example indicates, the rules of jurisdiction and standing are not only requirements imposed on the Court but means by which the Court itself can regulate access to its judgments in accordance with its members' goals.

The technical criteria serve as preliminary screening devices by which some cases are eliminated. But most cases meet these criteria, and the Court must use others to choose among them.

Conflict between Courts. Because the Supreme Court accepts so few cases, we might expect that every case it *does* accept involves an issue that has been the subject of considerable controversy in government and society. But this is hardly the case. A substantial proportion of the cases heard by the Court involve obscure questions in fields such as tax law and bankruptcy. In one 1996 case, the Court framed the question before it as follows: "whether Federal Rule 4, which authorizes an extendable 120-day period for service of process, supersedes the Suits in Admiralty Act provision that service on the United States be made 'forthwith'."[63]

Why does the Court hear such cases? One reason is that seemingly narrow and technical issues can have considerable impact on many people. But the primary reason is that those issues often evoke disagreements between lower courts. On the relationship between Federal Rule 4 and the Suits in Admiralty Act, for instance, the courts of appeals that addressed the issue in various cases had reached conflicting conclusions. All justices believe that resolving such conflicts over the interpretation of federal law is a major part of the Court's responsibilities. That belief is reflected in the Court's Rule 10, which gives primary emphasis to the existence of such conflicts as a criterion for accepting cases. (It should be kept in mind that conflict between courts over interpretation of a legal provision is different from disagreement between two lower courts about the outcome of the same case.)

Conflict in interpretation does strongly incline the Court to hear a case. Most of the law clerks interviewed by H. W. Perry said that the first thing they looked for in a petition was a genuine conflict.[64] Gregory Caldeira and John Wright found that intercourt conflict was one of the strongest considerations inclining the Court to accept a case.[65] Indeed, a high proportion of cases that the Court hears on the merits involve conflicts, and the Rehnquist Court seems especially inclined to hear conflict cases.[66]

This does not mean that the Court accepts all conflict cases. One scholar estimated that in its 1989 term, the Court refused to hear more than two hundred cases in which there were real conflicts in the interpretation of the law between courts of appeals.[67] That number makes clear the primary reason that the Court does not hear every case involving such conflicts: there are simply too many.

Whether the Court accepts a conflict case depends in part on the extent of the conflict, and in part on the seriousness of its effects. The Court emphasized the latter criterion in 1995 when it revised its Rule 10 by inserting the word "important" in three places, indicating that it was inclined to hear cases involving conflicts only if they involved important matters or legal questions. But the Court occasionally accepts a case to resolve a conflict even though only two courts are in conflict on a seemingly minor issue. That was true of a 1993 case involving the issue of whether Antarctica is a "foreign country" under the Federal Tort Claims Act, an issue that one commentator said was "of singular unimportance to the nation and its ever-growing body of federal law."[68] In contrast, the Court sometimes turns down cases involving fairly serious conflicts among several courts. Eventually, however, the Court may have little choice but to resolve a serious issue on which several courts have lined up on the two sides.

Importance of the Issues. Whether or not a case involves conflict between lower courts, the importance of the issues has considerable influence on the Court's willingness to accept the case. Rule 10 also emphasizes this consideration, for good reason: the best way for the Court to maximize its impact is to decide those cases that affect the most people and that raise the most significant policy issues.

This consideration in itself eliminates most cases that come to the Court. The Court's rules require that a petition for hearing list the "questions presented" by the case on the first page, and a scanning of petitions makes the reason for this requirement clear: in a great many cases, the questions presented are almost certainly too narrow to merit the Court's attention. Cases that seem to be of minor importance are heard from time to time, especially when several justices strongly disagree with a lower court decision, but such cases are clearly exceptions to the rule.

A case may seem important to members of the Court for various reasons. Cases typically are important not in themselves but because they raise broader legal or policy issues. It is not surprising when the Court hears cases on issues such as the power of state governments to set term limits for members of Congress or the right of physicians to assist in suicides by terminally ill patients. More broadly, justices may feel that certain policy areas merit continuing attention because of their importance. This feeling helps to explain the Court's long-standing interest in federalism cases and the prominence of civil liberties cases on its agenda in the current era.

Although a case raising an important issue has a relatively good chance to be accepted, the Court often rejects such cases. Justices may vote against hearing them for a variety of reasons, such as agreement with the lower court decision or a desire to delay before tackling a difficult issue. The press of conflict cases has also caused the Court to reject some relatively important cases that involve no conflicts.

Policy Preferences. Rule 10 does not mention justices' personal conceptions of good policy as a criterion for accepting or rejecting cases, but those conceptions are quite weighty in guiding the Court's choices. Because case selection is such an important part of the Court's policy making, members of the Court could scarcely resist use of the agenda-setting process as a way to advance their policy goals.

Justices could act on their policy goals primarily in two ways. First, they might vote to hear cases because they disagree with the lower court decision that they are reviewing; seeing what they think was an error by the lower court, they want to correct that error. Second, they might act strategically by voting to hear cases when they think that the policy they favor would gain a majority if the Court decided those cases on the merits. There is considerable evidence that both approaches are common in the Court's decisions whether to grant certiorari.

Chief Justice Rehnquist has attested to the justices' use of the first approach: "The most common reason members of our Court vote to grant certiorari is that they doubt the correctness of the decision of the lower court."[69] Justices and clerks attest that cases are sometimes accepted simply because the decision under review was "egregious."[70] These statements suggest that the Court overturns most of the lower court decisions it reviews, and this is indeed true. In the 1995 term, the Court affirmed lower courts in only 32 percent of the certiorari cases that it accepted and decided with full opinions,[71] a proportion far lower than the rate in appellate courts that must hear all the cases they receive. Of course, the justices' evaluations of lower court decisions reflect their ideological positions. If a lower court has reached a conservative decision, a liberal justice is more likely to view it as wrongly decided and vote to hear the case than is a conservative colleague.

The second, strategic, approach requires justices to predict how the Court would decide a case if it were accepted. It is clear that they frequently do make such predictions. Justices often vote against hearing a case because they fear that the Court would reach a result they dislike if the case were accepted. H. W.

Perry found that justices and clerks routinely referred to this practice as "defensive denials." As one justice told Perry, "I might think the Nebraska Supreme Court made a horrible decision, but I wouldn't want to take the case, for if we take the case and affirm it, then it would become a precedent."[72] Defensive denials are especially appealing to the members of the Court's ideological minority at any given time (such as the liberals on the Rehnquist Court), since they have the most reason to fear the Court's prospective decisions. But justices may engage in this practice whenever they anticipate an unfavorable decision.

Conversely, justices who think the Court would decide a case in accord with their preferences may vote to hear it for that reason. One apparent example in 1996 also illustrates the Court's ability to set its agenda.[73] On April 25th, President Clinton signed the Anti-Terrorism and Effective Death Penalty Act of 1996, which placed substantial limits on the ability of state prisoners to bring more than one habeas corpus action in federal court. Nine days later the Court accepted a case in which a state prisoner had filed a second habeas application, and it asked the parties to address only the meaning and constitutionality of the habeas limitations in the new act—issues that the parties themselves had not raised, because the act had not existed when they wrote their briefs. The Court also set oral argument for one month later and asked the parties to file briefs within two weeks, both unusually short intervals, in order to decide the case by the end of the 1995 term.

Justice Stevens took the unusual step of dissenting from the Court's order, protesting that the Court's consideration of the issues in the case "should be undertaken with the utmost deliberation, rather than unseemly haste."[74] Stevens, the Court's most liberal justice, was joined in his dissent by the three colleagues who ranked next in liberalism. The Court's ideological split suggests that the conservatives wanted to uphold the new statute as soon as possible. On June 28th, about two months after the act became law, the Court reached a decision holding that its habeas corpus provisions were acceptable under the Constitution but interpreting it to maintain the Court's own power to accept habeas petitions. (The decision was unanimous, but three of the Court's liberals joined in concurring opinions that diverged from the majority opinion in important respects.) The conservative justices got what they apparently wanted—a quick and clear message to federal judges that the act's limits on habeas corpus should be carried out.

It is uncertain how these two ways of acting on policy preferences fit together. But research on this question indicates that both are important. Justices respond to both their evaluations of lower court decisions and their expectations about the Court's decision if a case is accepted.[75] And it is clear that justices' preferences, expressed in these ways, have considerable effect on their choices of cases.

Identity of the Petitioner. During its 1995 term, the Supreme Court considered 27 petitions for certiorari filed by the federal government. It granted 21. The government also filed five amicus briefs supporting petitions for certiorari; the Court granted hearings in three of the five cases. Thus, the solicitor general's office secured hearings in 24 cases—a success rate of 75 percent. The Court considered 6,451 other petitions for hearings, granting certiorari in 75—about 1 percent.[76]

What accounts for this extraordinary rate of success? It can be ascribed chiefly to the advantages of what Marc Galanter calls a "repeat player"—a litigant engaged in many related cases over time.[77] This status provides the government with at least three advantages.

First, the solicitor general's staff chooses cases to bring to the Court from a large pool of cases that are eligible for Court consideration. Thus the staff can select those that are the most likely to be accepted. Almost any litigant who could be so selective would enjoy a fairly high rate of success in the Supreme Court.

Second, the solicitor general's selectivity earns some gratitude from the Court and builds credibility as well. If the federal government brought petitions at the high rates that other litigants bring them, the Court's caseload would be much heavier than it is. Thus the solicitor general plays an important role in easing pressures on the Court. In the last decade, the office of the solicitor general has brought even fewer cases to the Court than it did in the past; whether intentionally or not, the government has reduced its demands on the Court at a time when the justices have sought to reduce the number of cases they hear. The justices reciprocate for this restraint by viewing the government's petitions in a favorable light. Further, the justices know that the government takes to the Court only the cases that its lawyers deem most worthy, so they, too, are inclined to view those cases as worthy.

Third, the attorneys in the solicitor general's office handle a great many Supreme Court cases, so they develop an unusual degree of expertise in dealing with the Court. Few other lawyers learn as much about how to appeal to the Court's interests. As a result, the government can do more than most other litigants to make cases appear worthy of acceptance.

Of course, it helps that the solicitor general represents the federal government, a litigant with unique status. This status is reflected in the Court's treatment of the solicitor general's office as something of a partner. But it is primarily the advantage of the repeat player that accounts for the remarkable record of the solicitor general as a petitioner for certiorari.

Some other litigants and interest groups also enjoy advantages in securing hearings from the Court. As noted earlier, large corporations can hire experts in Supreme Court litigation, and lawyers who handle litigation for interest groups such as the AFL-CIO often develop that expertise. These expert lawyers—and certain interest groups themselves—may develop a degree of credibility with the Court. But no other litigant or group has anything like the full set of advantages that account for the solicitor general's success.

Avoiding Problematic Cases. Whatever their value in other respects, some cases are rejected by the Court because of characteristics that make their acceptance inconvenient, characteristics of two types.

First, the facts of some cases may be inappropriate. The facts may be too muddled to allow a clear decision, or they may require justices to reach a decision on grounds different from the ones they would like to use. In other cases, the circumstances of a dispute or the identity of the litigants may put the Court's likely decision in an unfavorable light.

Sometimes the justices select the "best" case on an issue after rejecting a large number of related cases because of their facts. In 1961 members of the Court had resolved that they would establish the right of indigents to a free attorney in felony cases.

Then, with the assistance of their clerks, the justices searched for a case whose facts were appropriate for establishment of that principle. A large number of cases were rejected before Clarence Gideon's petition was accepted. His case was ideal for the Court's purposes, in part because it concerned the relatively minor felony of breaking and entering a poolroom with intent to commit a misdemeanor. A reversal of Gideon's conviction would provoke less public wrath than the reversal of a conviction for a violent offense.[78]

Second, justices may seek to avoid certain issues altogether because of their controversial nature, which can make them difficult to decide and—more important—can lead to attacks on the Court for the decisions it does reach. A good example is the Court's refusal to rule on the constitutionality of participation by the United States in the war in Vietnam. Few issues brought to the Court have been so important, but the Court refused to hear the cases that raised this question between 1967 and 1972. Undoubtedly, some justices wanted to avoid injecting the Court into the most important and most disputed issue of national policy.

The desire to avoid controversy may help to explain other denials of hearings in recent years. In *Thomasson v. Perry* (1996) the Court refused to hear the first legal challenge to the "don't ask, don't tell" policy under which gay and lesbian members of the armed services can be discharged for disclosing their sexual orientation, a highly emotional issue in an area—military policy—in which the justices usually hesitate to intervene. Having been criticized for its 1995 decision striking down state term limits for members of Congress, the Court in 1997 refused to decide whether states could punish officials who failed to support term limits by labeling them on the ballot as having "disregarded voter instruction on term limits."[79]

Often the Court refuses to address a difficult issue only temporarily, accepting a case later, after the issue has been allowed to "percolate" in the lower courts. In 1995 the Court refused to hear two related cases involving state prohibitions on assisted suicide, one of them brought to the Court by Dr. Jack Kevorkian, but two years later it decided two other assisted-suicide cases.[80] And certainly the Court does accept a good many cases that are likely to embroil it in controversy. In a way, the Court's frequent willingness to take such cases is more noteworthy than is its avoidance of other difficult cases.

Summary. The Supreme Court's decisions about whether or not to hear cases are based on a complex set of considerations, reflecting the wide range of goals that the justices seek to advance through the selection of cases. Votes on the question of whether to hear cases are subjective decisions that depend on the values and perspectives of the justices. Justices differ in the priority they give to resolving conflicts between lower courts. They assess the importance of cases in various ways. And they work from quite different sets of policy preferences.

It follows that the Court's selection of cases to decide fully, like everything else it does, is affected by its membership at any given time. Most cases are unlikely to be accepted no matter who is on the Court. But the composition of the few dozen cases that the Supreme Court actually does accept in a term strongly reflects the identities of the justices who serve during that term.

Caseload Growth and the Court's Response

The Growth in Caseloads

Litigants brought 6,633 cases to the Supreme Court during the 1996 term. That figure reflects a massive increase in the number of filings in the past several decades. The Court never received even two thousand cases in a term until 1961, and 1979 was the first term in which it received as many as four thousand. The growth in the Court's caseload from 1956 to 1995 is shown in Figure 3-1.

Explaining the Growth. The growth in the Court's caseload over the past forty years has several sources. First, the increase reflects changes in American society. The population of the United States increased by more than 50 percent between 1956 and 1996, and a larger population produces more potential cases. There has probably been an increase in "rights consciousness," as Americans have shown an increased willingness to take action—including litigation—to protect what they consider to be their rights. Interest groups have played a part in that process, increasingly helping people to carry forward such litigation.

Actions by other government institutions are a second source

FIGURE 3-1
Cases Filed in the Supreme Court per Term, by
Five-Year Averages, 1956–1995

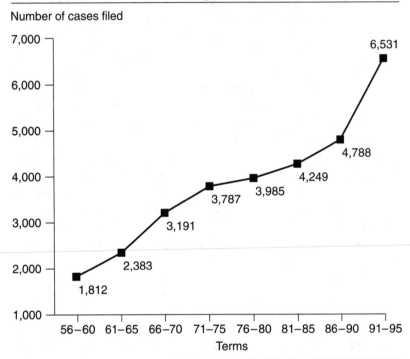

Number of cases filed

Sources: Lee Epstein, Jeffrey A. Segal, Harold J. Spaeth, and Thomas G. Walker, *The Supreme Court Compendium: Data, Decisions, and Developments* (Washington, D.C.: Congressional Quarterly, 1994), 60–61; "Statistical Recap of Supreme Court's Workload During Last Three Terms," *United States Law Week* 65 (August 6, 1996): 3100.

of caseload growth. New federal legislation, such as the civil rights laws of the 1960s and 1970s, has created new sources of litigation. Statutes that raise the penalties for criminal offenses and changes in policy by prosecutors and judges have increased enormously the number and length of prison sentences; there were five times as many people serving sentences of more than one year in 1994 as there were in 1970.[81] This development has brought substantial growth in the numbers of criminal appeals, many of which ultimately reach the Supreme Court.

Third, the Court itself has played a major role. Its willingness to waive its ordinary requirements for the filing of cases has made it possible for thousands of indigent litigants to bring paupers' petitions to the Court each year. Its establishment of the right to free counsel for indigent criminal defendants and its elimination of the cost of the first appeal for them have increased the opportunity to challenge convictions.

For a long time, the Court's general policy direction also contributed to the growth in its caseload. Particularly in the 1960s, the Court showed considerable sympathy for challenges to government action that were based on alleged violations of civil liberties. This sympathy encouraged those who felt their rights had been violated to bring cases to the Court. The Court's support for civil liberties probably had its greatest impact in two issue areas: criminal procedure, in which the Court encouraged appeals by defendants through its tightening of due process requirements; and equality, in which its support for the rights of disadvantaged groups spurred challenges to government action based on the constitutional guarantee of equal protection of the laws.

The pattern of growth in the caseload helps to make clear the impact of these forces. The number of petitions increased rapidly during the 1960s, more slowly during the 1970s and early 1980s, then rapidly once again in the late 1980s and early 1990s. The growth in the 1960s reflected the establishment and broadening of new rights by the Court during that decade. The slower growth in the years that followed came at a time when the Court was establishing fewer new rights and the decisions of the 1960s had already achieved most of their impact. The recent spurt of growth has come entirely in the paupers' petitions, whose numbers doubled from about 2,000 a year in the early 1980s to more than 4,000 a year in the early and mid-1990s; the numbers of paid petitions have remained stable since the late 1970s. Paupers' petitions result primarily from criminal prosecutions, so they reflect the burgeoning numbers of convictions and prison sentences.

Responding to Caseload Growth

Growth as a Problem. Observers of the Court and the justices themselves have seen growth in the Court's caseload as a problem for the Court and for federal law. For the Court, the perceived problem is that its ability to do its job well is compromised. The growing caseload makes the justices busier. As a result, they may give less careful consideration to their work, particularly the cases they decide on the merits. Some observers think the justices write opinions with less care, fail to take the time needed to reach truly collective decisions, and delegate too much responsibility to law clerks.[82]

For the federal law, the perceived problem is that the Court does not resolve as many legal issues as it should. If the number of cases heard by the Court increased at the same rate as the number of petitions for hearing, the Court's workload would become impossible to handle. To avoid this outcome, over the years the justices have raised the standards for their acceptance of cases. As a result, seemingly meritorious cases are denied hearings. As Chief Justice Rehnquist said in 1987, "Today we decline to review cases involving important questions of federal law not previously decided by our Court, cases which the Court would have unquestionably heard and decided as little as thirty years ago."[83]

Jurisdictional Change as a Solution. The current period is not the first time that the Court's caseload has grown. During most eras it has faced substantial increases in the numbers of cases brought to it. At least since the late nineteenth century, such increases have prompted complaints by the justices that they were overburdened and unable to handle their work effectively.

The primary solution that the justices sought and that Congress provided was to give the Court greater discretion in deciding whether to hear cases, primarily in two major steps. The first was the Court of Appeals Act of 1891, which created a new set of intermediate appellate courts and gave the Court discretionary jurisdiction over a large minority of cases for the first time. The second was the Judiciary Act of 1925, which expanded the discretionary jurisdiction by requiring that most cases come to the Court as requests for writs of certiorari, which the Court could reject without reaching any decision on the merits, rather than as appeals, which the Court could not.

The 1925 statute had an enormous impact. Its most obvious effect was to limit justices' workloads by allowing them to concentrate on only a portion of the cases brought to them. More subtly, it gave the Court more freedom to determine the scope of its activity, the kinds of issues it would address, and its role as a policy maker.

As the Court's caseload grew further, the justices sought to have the remaining categories of appeals eliminated. In 1988 Congress did eliminate most of those categories, but the number of appeals already was so low that they added little to the Court's workload—especially because the Court often gave them less than full consideration. For that reason, more radical changes in the Court's jurisdiction were proposed during the 1970s and 1980s.

The proposed changes would have involved creation of a new court between the courts of appeals and the Supreme Court. In some proposals, the new court would help the Supreme Court to screen petitions for hearings. Like increases in the Court's discretionary jurisdiction, these proposals were aimed at reducing the Court's burdens. In others, which received more serious consideration, the new court would actually decide some cases in place of the Supreme Court. These proposals were aimed at resolving more issues in federal law. While some justices supported these proposals, there was nothing approaching a consensus on the Court or elsewhere in government that a new court of a particular type was desirable. In the absence of such a consensus Congress is unlikely to make a major change in the structure of government, and it did not.

Accepting Fewer Cases as a Solution. Acting on their own, justices could reduce their workloads simply by hearing fewer cases. In fact, over the past decade the Court has taken that step. As Table 3-2 shows, the number of cases that the Court accepts each term and the number that it decides with full, signed opinions have declined substantially—by nearly half.

A variety of explanations for this reduction have been put forward,[84] and the justices themselves have offered several explanations.[85] Some justices have said that there is no single overriding reason for the reduction, and one scholar's close analysis of the reduction supports this judgment.[86] But the central factor is that the justices collectively have raised their standards for granting of certiorari.

Of the justices who commented on the case reduction, none said that the justices simply wanted to work less, and Justice Ginsburg said that "the cutback in opinions doesn't mean that the court is becoming a lazy lot."[87] The *effect* of the cutback, however, is a reduced workload. Thus, if the quality of the

TABLE 3-2

*Size of the Court's Agenda for Decisions
on the Merits, 1984–1995 Terms*

Term	Petitions granted	Signed opinions
1984	185	139
1985	186	146
1986	167	145
1987	180	139
1988	147	133
1989	122	129
1990	141	112
1991	120	107
1992	97	107
1993	99	84
1994	93	82
1995	105	75

Source: "Statistical Recap of Supreme Court's Workload During Last Three Terms," *United States Law Week,* various years.

Court's decisions suffered from its heavy workload, the justices have solved that problem themselves.

Of course, accepting fewer cases might aggravate problems in the federal law. If the Court left too many important issues unresolved in 1987, as Chief Justice Rehnquist thought at the time, there would seem to be even more such issues now. This is not necessarily true. Some justices and commentators have suggested that new issues are arising at a slower rate than in the past, and the Court today seems to concentrate more on establishing general legal rules than on correcting misapplications of those rules by lower courts. Still, the Court almost surely leaves more important questions unanswered today than it did a decade ago.

In any event, the difficulty of gaining a hearing in the Supreme Court has become even greater. One lawyer who handles cases in the Court complained that "they're engaging in their own mini-shutdown of the government."[88] Recently an amicus curiae brief tried to use the Court's reduced workload as an argument for accepting the case in question. "Our point is that the clear absence of a crushing workload for the next term eliminates any need to pass over a petition . . . that raises important and recurring issues of constitutional law."[89] The Court did not accept the case.

Conclusion

A central theme of this chapter is the Supreme Court's ability to set its own agenda. Congress and litigants both play an important part in shaping that agenda, but what the Court hears is largely under its own control. From the wide variety of legal and policy questions brought to the Court, the justices can choose those few that they will address fully. They can also choose which issues in a case they will decide. And the Court affects the choices of lawyers and interest groups through its opinions by suggesting the kinds of legal claims that it will view favorably in future cases.

The Court has been criticized for the ways it uses its agenda-setting powers, but the justices employ these powers rather well to serve their purposes. They accept and reject cases on the basis of individual and collective goals such as avoiding troublesome issues, resolving legal conflicts, and establishing policies that the justices favor. Thus justices employ the process of selecting cases for full decisions to shape the Court's role as a policy maker. They also use that process to limit their workloads.

After the Court selects the cases to be decided, of course, it actually decided those cases. In the next chapter I examine the process by which the Court makes its decisions.

NOTES

1. "Statistical Recap of Supreme Court's Workload During Last Three Terms," *United States Law Week,* August 6, 1996, 3100.
2. This summary of the distribution of litigants across categories is based in part on Gregory A. Caldeira and John R. Wright, "Parties, Direct Representatives, and Agenda-Setting in the Supreme Court" (Paper presented at the annual conference of the Midwest Political Science Association, Chicago, April 1989).
3. *United States v. $405,089.23 in United States Currency* (1996).
4. See Marcia Coyle, "This Team Hopes to Revolutionize Politics," *National Law Journal,* December 2, 1996, A1, A12.

5. Sarah Weddington, *A Question of Choice* (New York: G. P. Putnam's Sons, 1992), 64.

6. See Joan Biskupic, "Deputy Solicitor Heads for New Bench Mark," *Washington Post,* October 31, 1994, A21.

7. This discussion is based in part on Kevin T. McGuire, *The Supreme Court Bar: Legal Elites in the Washington Community* (Charlottesville: University Press of Virginia, 1993).

8. Tony Mauro, "This Argument Shed Little Light," *Legal Times,* October 23, 1995, 10.

9. Tony Mauro, "Marshall Nugget," *Legal Times,* December 6, 1993, 11.

10. Mauro, "This Argument Shed Little Light," 8. See Joan Biskupic, "Legal Elite Vie for Court Time in Pursuit of Supreme Challenge," *Washington Post,* December 2, 1996, A19.

11. Kevin T. McGuire, "Repeat Players in the Supreme Court: The Role of Experienced Lawyers in Litigation Success," *Journal of Politics* 57 (February 1995): 187–196.

12. Marcia Coyle, "High Court Bar's 'Inner Circle'," *National Law Journal,* March 3, 1997, A16.

13. Ibid.

14. Biskupic, "Legal Elite Vie for Court Time."

15. Caldeira and Wright, "Parties, Direct Representatives, and Agenda-Setting," tables 1 and 2.

16. Lee Epstein, "Interest Group Litigation during the Rehnquist Court Era," *Journal of Law & Politics* 9 (Summer 1993): 715–717.

17. Keith Schneider, "Power to Protect Species May Hang on a Word," *New York Times,* January 6, 1995, A23.

18. Calculated from data in Lee Epstein, Jeffrey A. Segal, Harold J. Spaeth, and Thomas G. Walker, *The Supreme Court Compendium: Data, Decisions, and Developments,* 2d ed. (Washington, D.C.: CQ Press, 1996), 647.

19. Epstein, "Interest Group Litigation," 645.

20. Based in part on Susan Behuniak-Long, "Friendly Fire: Amici Curiae and *Webster v. Reproductive Health Services,*" *Judicature* 74 (February–March 1991): 262. This source gives a total of 78 briefs, not counting a brief by the federal government on whether to hear the case and a private group's brief that the Court did not allow to be filed.

21. Karen O'Connor and Bryant Scott McFall, "Conservative Interest Group Litigation in the Reagan Era and Beyond," in *The Politics of Interests: Interest Groups Transformed,* ed. Mark P. Petracca (Boulder, Colo.: Westview Press, 1992), 271.

22. This paragraph is based primarily on Richard Davis, *Decisions and Images: The Supreme Court and the Press* (Englewood Cliffs, N.J.: Prentice-Hall, 1994).

23. Linda Greenhouse, "Telling the Court's Story: Justice and Journalism at the Supreme Court," *Yale Law Journal* 105 (April 1996): 1554.

24. This paragraph is based in part on Stephen L. Wasby, *Race Relations Litigation in an Age of Complexity* (Charlottesville: University Press of Virginia, 1995), esp. 61–64.

25. Gregg Ivers, "Religious Organizations as Constitutional Litigants," *Polity* 25 (Winter 1992): 243–266.

26. See Samuel Walker, *In Defense of American Liberties: A History of the ACLU* (New York: Oxford University Press, 1990).

27. *Immigration and Naturalization Service v. Chadha* (1983).

28. See Lee Epstein, *Conservatives in Court* (Knoxville: University of Tennessee Press, 1985).

29. *Adarand Constructors, Inc. v. Pena* (1995). See Marcia Coyle, "Supreme Court Ponders Racial Set-Aside Case," *National Law Journal,* January 23, 1995, A1, A17.

30. James H. Andrews, "Religious Right Fights for Rights," *Christian Science Monitor,* February 7, 1994, 14; Tim Stafford, "Move Over ACLU," *Christianity Today* 37 (October 25, 1993): 20–24.

31. George Stevens, Jr., "His Life's Work: When Thurgood Marshall Saw the Movie," *Washington Post,* January 29, 1993, A23.

32. See Wasby, *Race Relations Litigation in an Age of Complexity.*

33. Susan E. Lawrence, *The Poor in Court: The Legal Services Program and Supreme Court Decision Making* (Princeton, N.J.: Princeton University Press, 1990).

34. Data on the 1995 term discussed here and later in this section were provided by the Office of the Solicitor General.

35. *Maryland v. Wilson* (1997). See Joan Biskupic, "Neither Miscues Nor Pizazz Mark Reno's High Court Appearance," *Washington Post,* December 12, 1996, A30; and Tony Mauro, "At Last, Reno Answers Questions," *Legal Times,* December 16, 1996, 8–9.

36. David M. Rosenzweig, "Confession of Error in the Supreme Court by the Solicitor General," *Georgetown Law Journal* 82 (July 1994): 2079–2117.

37. See Rebecca Mae Salokar, *The Solicitor General: The Politics of Law* (Philadelphia: Temple University Press, 1992); Cornell W. Clayton, *The Politics of Justice: The Attorney General and the Making of Legal Policy* (Armonk, N.Y.: M. E. Sharpe, 1992), 52–61; and Louis Fisher, "Is the Solicitor General an Executive or a Judicial Agent? Caplan's *Tenth Justice,*" *Law & Social Inquiry* 15 (Spring 1990): 305–320.

38. Salokar, *The Solicitor General,* 159.

39. Ibid., 170–171.

40. See Pierre Thomas, "Reno Reverses Child Pornography Stance," *Washington Post,* November 11, 1994, A4; and Linda Greenhouse, "Court Rejects Child-Smut Case With Political Overtones," *New York Times,* January 18, 1995, C18.

41. Eva M. Rodriguez, "Senators Train Sights on Solicitor General," *Legal Times,* November 20, 1995, 1, 20, 21.

42. This discussion is based primarily on Rebecca Mae Salokar, "Legal Counsel for Congress: Protecting Institutional Interests," *Congress and the Presidency* 20 (Autumn 1993): 131–155.

43. Epstein, Segal, Spaeth, and Walker, *Supreme Court Compendium,* 612–614.

44. "Statistical Recap of Supreme Court's Workload during Last Three Terms."

45. Elliot E. Slotnick and Jennifer A. Segal, "'The Supreme Court Decided Today . . . ,' Or Did It?" *Judicature* 78 (September–October 1994): 89–95.

46. *Lebron v. National Railroad Passenger Corp.,* 130 L. Ed. 2d 902, 923–928 (1995).

47. The orders are found at 133 L. Ed. 2d 514–518.

48. *Lawrence v. Chater* (1996); *Thomas v. American Home Products* (1996).

49. On per curiam opinions in general, see Stephen L. Wasby, Steven Peterson, James Schubert, and Glendon Schubert, "The Per Curiam Opinion: Its Nature and Functions," *Judicature* 76 (June–July 1992): 29–38.

50. *United States v. Watts* (1997).

51. Harvey Berkman, "High Court Dismisses RICO Case," *National Law Journal,* January 27, 1997, A16.
52. This figure is taken from data provided by the Office of the Solicitor General.
53. *In re Gaydos,* 136 L. Ed 2d 369, 371–372 (1996).
54. "Statistical Recap."
55. This examination of the discuss list and of the conference are based in part on H. W. Perry, Jr., *Deciding to Decide: Agenda Setting in the United States Supreme Court* (Cambridge, Mass.: Harvard University Press, 1991), 43–51, 85–91.
56. Ruth Bader Ginsburg, "Remarks for American Law Institute Annual Dinner May 19, 1994," *Saint Louis University Law Journal* 38 (Summer 1994): 884.
57. *Singleton v. Commissioner of Internal Revenue,* 439 U.S. 940, 945–946 (1978).
58. This discussion of the clerks' roles is drawn in part from Perry, *Deciding to Decide,* 51–84; Dan T. Coenen, review of Perry, *Deciding to Decide,* in *Constitutional Commentary* 10 (Winter 1993): 180–193; and Sean Donahue, "Behind the Pillars of Justice: Remarks on Law Clerks," *The Long Term View* 3 (Spring 1995): 79–80.
59. Tony Mauro, "Ginsburg Plunges into the Cert Pool," *Legal Times,* September 6, 1993, 8.
60. Donahue, "Behind the Pillars of Justice," 80.
61. Martha M. Hamilton, "A Leap Year Lapse Abruptly Ends an Appeal to the Supreme Court," *Washington Post,* March 12, 1996, C1, C4.
62. *Arizonans for Official English v. Arizona* (1997).
63. *Henderson v. United States,* 134 L. Ed. 2d 880, 888 (1996).
64. Perry, *Deciding to Decide,* 246.
65. Gregory A. Caldeira and John R. Wright, "Organized Interests and Agenda Setting in the U.S. Supreme Court," *American Political Science Review* 82 (December 1988): 1109–1127; Caldeira and Wright, "Nine Little Law Firms? Justices, Organized Interests, and Agenda-Setting in the Supreme Court" (Paper presented at the annual conference of the Midwest Political Science Association, Chicago, April 1994).
66. Jeffrey A. Segal and Harold J. Spaeth, *The Supreme Court and the Attitudinal Model* (New York: Cambridge University Press, 1993), 201.
67. Arthur D. Hellman, "By Precedent Unbound: The Nature and Extent of Unresolved Intercircuit Conflicts," *University of Pittsburgh Law Review* 56 (Summer 1995): 720–724.
68. Kenneth W. Starr, "Trivial Pursuits at the Supreme Court," *Wall Street Journal,* October 6, 1993, A19. The case was *Smith v. United States* (1993).
69. William H. Rehnquist, "Oral Advocacy: A Disappearing Art," *Mercer Law Review* 35 (1984): 1027.
70. Perry, *Deciding to Decide,* 265–268.
71. "The Supreme Court, 1995 Term," *Harvard Law Review* 110 (November 1996): 372.
72. Perry, *Deciding to Decide,* 198–207. The quotation is on p. 200.
73. *Felker v. Turpin* (1996).
74. *Felker v. Turpin,* 134 L. Ed. 2d 685 (1996).
75. Saul Brenner and John F. Krol, "Strategies in Certiorari Voting on the United States Supreme Court," *Journal of Politics* 51 (November 1989): 828–840; Robert L. Boucher, Jr., and Jeffrey A. Segal, "Supreme Court Justices as Strategic Decision Makers: Aggressive Grants and Defensive

Denials on the Vinson Court," *Journal of Politics* 57 (August 1995): 824–837; Gregory A. Caldeira, John R. Wright, and Christopher J. W. Zorn, "Strategic Voting and Gatekeeping in the Supreme Court" (Paper presented at the annual conference of the American Political Science Association, San Francisco, August–September 1996).

76. These data were provided by the Office of the Solicitor General.
77. Marc Galanter, "Why the 'Haves' Come Out Ahead: Speculations on the Limits of Legal Change," *Law & Society Review* 9 (Fall 1974): 97–125.
78. Nathan Lewin, "Helping the Court with Its Work," *New Republic,* March 3, 1973, 18. The case was *Gideon v. Wainwright* (1963).
79. *Arkansas Term Limits v. Donovan* (1997).
80. *Kevorkian v. Michigan* (1995); *Hobbins v. Kelley* (1995); *Washington v. Glucksberg* (1997); *Vacco v. Quill* (1997).
81. Kathleen Maguire and Ann L. Pastore, eds., *Sourcebook of Criminal Justice Statistics 1995* (Washington, D.C.: Government Printing Office, 1996), 556.
82. See, for example, Paul M. Bator, "What Is Wrong with the Supreme Court?" *University of Pittsburgh Law Review* 51 (Spring 1990): 685–687.
83. "Chief Justice Urges National Appeals Court, Repeal of Court's Mandatory Jurisdiction," *The Third Branch,* July 1987, 1, 5.
84. Arthur D. Hellman, "The Shrunken Docket of the Rehnquist Court," in *The Supreme Court Review* 1996, 403–438.
85. Joan Biskupic, "The Shrinking Docket," *Washington Post,* March 18, 1996, A15; Biskupic, "Female Justices Attest to Fraternity on Bench," *Washington Post,* August 21, 1994, A24; Richard Carelli, "Supreme Court's Decisions Dwindle," *Montgomery Advertiser,* January 24, 1996, 17A; David J. Garrow, "The Rehnquist Reins," *New York Times Magazine,* October 6, 1996, 71, 82.
86. Hellman, "Shrunken Docket."
87. Biskupic, "Female Justices Attest to Fraternity on Bench."
88. Biskupic, "The Shrinking Docket."
89. Biskupic, "The Shrinking Docket." The case was *Dalkon Shield Claimants Trust v. Shadburne-Vinton* (1996).

Chapter 4

Decision Making

At the heart of the Supreme Court's work is its decision making. The Court's importance as an institution stems chiefly from its decisions on the merits of cases—decisions with impact extending beyond the litigants to the nation as a whole. This chapter examines how and why the Court makes its decisions on the merits.

Decisions and the Decisional Process

Elements of the Court's Decision

Supreme Court decisions usually have two components. One component is the Court's treatment of the parties to the case. The Court can affirm the lower court decision, leaving undisturbed that court's treatment of the parties. Alternatively, it can modify or reverse the lower court decision, overturning that court's judgment altogether or in part. The terms *modify* and *reverse* are imprecise. In general, a reversal overturns the lower court decision altogether or nearly so, while modification is a more limited, partial overturning. The Court may also vacate (make void) the lower court decision, an action whose effect is similar to that of reversal.

In most cases the Court's treatment of the parties has little impact beyond those parties themselves. But the Court's decisions in such cases may be important because of their second component, the statement of general legal rules on which the Court bases its treatment of the parties. This statement of rules is included in the Court's written opinion. In most cases that the Court decides on the merits, the decision is accompanied by an opinion that explains the decision. Generally at least five justices subscribe to this opinion, so that it constitutes an authoritative statement by the Court.

One function of the Court's opinion is to justify the decision. When the Court overturns a criminal conviction, it can explain the principles that led it to make that decision and thus seek to convince readers of the opinion that its decision was correct. This function is most important when a decision is likely to arouse disapproval in other government institutions or in the public at large.

If the Court modifies or reverses a lower court decision, the case is usually sent back, or remanded, to the lower court for reconsideration. A second function of the Court's opinion is to provide directions for that reconsideration. If the Court reverses a court of appeals decision in a freedom of speech case, its opinion can specify the rules for interpretation of the First Amendment that the court of appeals should follow in the case. The language at the end of the Court's opinion in a 1997 case was in the standard form: "The judgment is reversed, and the case is remanded to the Ninth Circuit for further proceedings consistent with this opinion."[1]

The third and most important function of the opinion is to lay down general principles of law that are applicable to other cases, principles that theoretically are binding on lower court judges whenever they are relevant. Together, the principles that the Court's opinions establish in a field of law constitute its policies in that area.

The importance of this function is illustrated by *Maryland v. Wilson* (1997), the case argued by Attorney General Janet Reno. Jerry Lee Wilson was a passenger in a car that was stopped for a traffic violation by a state trooper. Believing that Wilson was acting suspiciously, the trooper ordered him to step out of the car. When Wilson did so, some crack cocaine fell to the ground, and he was arrested and charged with drug offenses. Two Maryland courts ruled that the drugs could not be used as evidence, because the trooper's ordering Wilson out of the car was an unreasonable seizure under the Fourth and Fourteenth Amendments. The Supreme Court reversed the decision, holding that the order was reasonable and that the resulting evidence could be used in court.

Had the Court written no opinion, the decision would have affected only Wilson. But the Court's opinion held that a police officer can always order a passenger to step outside a vehicle that has been stopped for a lawful reason. Because of that opinion, the Court's decision affected the enormous number of encounters involving law enforcement officers and auto passengers every year. More broadly, the *Wilson* decision was an addition to the Court's line of decisions in recent years that has expanded the freedom of police officers to engage in searches and seizures.

Just as the Court chooses which party to favor in its decision, so it chooses the basis for its decision. A ruling for one of the parties often could be justified on several grounds, and the ground chosen by the Court helps to determine the long-term impact of its decision. If the Court overturns the death penalty for a particular defendant, it might base that decision on a whole range of grounds—from the existence of a specific error in that defendant's trial to the unconstitutionality of the death penalty under all circumstances. Obviously, a decision based on the second ground would have a much greater impact than one based on the first ground.

The Decision-Making Process

Presentation of Cases to the Court. The written briefs that the Court receives when it considers whether to hear a case often touch on the merits of the case. Once a case has been accepted for oral argument and decision, attorneys for the parties submit new briefs that focus on the merits. In most cases that reach this stage, interest groups submit amicus curiae briefs stating their own arguments on the merits.

Most of the material in these briefs concerns legal issues. The parties muster evidence to support their interpretations of relevant constitutional provisions and statutes. In their briefs they frequently offer arguments about policy as well, seeking to convince the justices that support for their position constitutes not only good law but good public policy.

Material in the briefs is supplemented by attorneys' presentations in oral argument before the Court. Oral argument is strictly limited in time; in most cases each side is provided half an hour for argument to the Court. Attorneys for the parties to a case sometimes share their time with the lawyer for an amicus, almost always the federal government.

Oral argument allows attorneys to supplement and highlight material in their briefs. More important, it allows the justices to probe issues that concern them by questioning the lawyers. Presentations by lawyers are interrupted frequently by questions and comments from members of the Court, and it is the justices who control the flow of argument.

Justices differ in how often they ask questions. The current Court includes several justices who ask questions frequently, including Antonin Scalia, David Souter, Ruth Bader Ginsburg, and Stephen Breyer. As a result, argument sessions are more lively than they were in the 1980s.[2] At the conclusion of a 1993 argument, Chief Justice Rehnquist told a lawyer, "I think you did very well in the four minutes that the Court allowed you."[3]

The justices differ in their styles of questioning.[4] Rehnquist sometimes takes a stern approach, rebuking lawyers who have misstepped. In contrast, John Paul Stevens has a polite and self-effacing style, sometimes beginning a question, "Excuse me, there's one thing that puzzles me."[5] Scalia is the most likely to try to control the direction of the argument in a case. "Often," one observer noted, "if an attorney fails to make the argument Scalia favors, the Justice simply intervenes and takes over the argument."[6] Sometimes, Scalia cannot wait to see whether a lawyer says the right thing. After a Breyer question in a 1996 argument, Scalia immediately offered his own answer to the lawyer; he began, "I think your response is that . . .".[7] Occasionally, Scalia adds his own question to that of a colleague before the latter can be answered. After he did so in one 1997 argument, Rehnquist "turned to Scalia and snapped: 'Let him answer Justice O'Connor's question.'"[8]

Justices often ask questions to clarify issues for themselves, but they also use questions to shape their colleagues' perceptions of a case. As Rehnquist points out, this is the only time before the conference discussion of a case "when all of the judges are expected to sit on the bench and concentrate on one particular case."[9]

Tentative Decisions. After oral argument the Court discusses each case in one of its conferences later the same week. The conference is a closed session attended only by the justices. The discussion is fairly structured.[10] The chief justice presides and begins by summarizing the case, then states personal views on the case and usually a vote on the decision. The associate justices, starting with the most senior member (in terms of service on the Court, not age) and ending with the most junior, then present their own views and votes. Because their colleagues have already voiced similar positions, the more junior justices generally speak quite briefly. Typically, little or no additional discussion follows this presentation of positions. According to Justice Scalia, "To call our discussion of a case a conference is really something of a misnomer, it's much more a statement of the views of each of the nine Justices, after which the totals are added and the case is assigned."[11]

We might expect a more freewheeling discussion of cases, with justices speaking at length and arguing back and forth. But the Court's workload creates time pressures that preclude extended discussions. Just as important, the justices usually bring to the conference fixed views on the cases. They have already read the written materials and listened to oral argument, and often they have discussed the case with their law clerks. Furthermore, their views on cases are influenced by their own, frequently strong, attitudes about policy. As a result, Chief Justice Rehnquist reported, "it is very much the exception" for justices' minds to be changed in conference. He added that extended discussion ordinarily would have little impact on the justices' positions.[12]

After each two-week sitting, the writing of the Court's opinion in each case is assigned to a justice. If the chief justice voted with the majority, the chief assigns the opinion. In other cases, the most senior justice in the majority makes the assignment. Primarily because so many conference votes are lopsided, the chief justice is usually among the majority. If there is no majority, because some justices want to reserve judgment or because the Court is split in complex ways, the chief justice assigns the opinion.

Reaching Final Decisions. The justice who is assigned the opinion in a case writes an initial draft. This justice is guided by the views expressed in conference concerning the appropriate rationale for the Court's decision. Other justices may also work on the case, reconsidering their positions or writing alternative opinions. During this process, views on the case may change even before the assigned opinion is produced in draft form.

Once this opinion is completed and circulated, it often becomes a focus of negotiation. Ordinarily the justice assigned to write the opinion wants to obtain the support of as many colleagues as possible for it. The writer seeks to convince justices who were originally in the minority to change their positions, and it also may be necessary to discourage allies in conference from leaving the fold. At the least, the assigned justice wants to maintain the original majority for the outcome supported by the opinion and a majority in support of the rationale expressed in the opinion, so that the opinion becomes the official statement of the Court. The justice may fail in this task, so that another justice's opinion supporting the same outcome or a different one becomes the opinion of the Court.

The negotiation that occurs during this period focuses on the wording of the opinion. The assigned justice and rival opinion writers may be willing to change arguments or the ways in which arguments are expressed in order to satisfy other justices and thus enlist their support. As Justice Ginsburg has described, a justice might respond to a draft majority opinion with a note reading, "I will join [the opinion] if you take out, put in, alter or adjust as follows."[13] When the Court is deeply divided, this process may be quite complex and difficult, and the result may be a final opinion that lacks clarity and coherence.

Occasionally no opinion gains the support of a majority. Table 4-1, which lists several characteristics of the Court's decisions in the 1995 term, shows that there were six decisions without majority opinions and two others in which a majority could be mustered for only part of the Court's opinion. Without a majority opinion there is no authoritative statement of the Court's position on the legal issues in the case, though the opinion on the winning side with the greatest support—the "plurality opinion"—may specify the points for which majority support exists. Lower court judges and other observers can attempt to discern what positions are shared by the justices on the majority side, but this is not always an easy task. In *Bush v. Vera* (1996), a case involving racial considerations in legislative districting, there were four opinions for the five-member majority, two written by the same justice (O'Connor). It would be quite difficult to dis-

TABLE 4-1

Selected Characteristics of Supreme Court Decisions, 1995 Term

Characteristic	Number	Percentage
Number of decisions	83	—
Vote for Court's decision[a]		
Unanimous	35	42
Nonunanimous	48	58
Support for Court's opinion		
Unanimous for whole opinion	31	37
Unanimous for part of opinion	1	1
Majority but not unanimous	43	52
Majority for only part of opinion	2	2
No majority for opinion	6	7
Cases with		
Dissenting opinions[b]	47	57
Concurring opinions[c]	29	35
Total number of		
Dissenting opinions	67	—
Concurring opinions	49	—

Note: The decisions included are decisions on the merits that are listed in the front section of *Supreme Court Reports, Lawyer's Edition.*

[a] "Decision" refers to outcome for the parties. Partial dissents are not counted as votes for the decision.

[b] Opinions labeled "concurring and dissenting" are treated as dissenting opinions. Opinions labeled "separate statements" are treated as concurring opinions.

[c] Some concurring opinions are in full agreement with the Court's opinion.

cern from all these opinions a clear set of rules on race and redistricting.

Concurring and Dissenting Opinions. In most cases, an opinion gains a majority but lacks unanimous support. Disagreement with the majority opinion can take two forms. First, a justice may cast a dissenting vote, which expresses disagreement with the result reached by the Court as it affects the parties to a case. If a criminal conviction is reversed, for instance, a justice who believes it should have been affirmed will dissent. Second, a justice may concur with the Court's decision, agreeing with the result in the specific case but differing with the rationale expressed in the Court's opinion. Both kinds of disagreement are common;

in the 1995 term, as Table 4-1 shows, an opinion received full support from every justice in only 37 percent of the Court's decisions.

A justice who disagrees with the majority opinion generally writes or joins in a dissenting or concurring opinion. Dissenting opinions are so routine that when the conference vote on a case is split, the senior justice in the minority assigns the writing of a dissenting opinion.[14] Because they are individual expressions rather than statements for the Court, both types of opinions can vary a great deal in form and tone. For the same reason, they usually reveal more about the author's views, and often express those views in more colorful language, than do majority opinions.

Dissenting opinions typically begin as efforts to win support from colleagues during the decision process, to convert a minority into a majority. Some dissenting opinions, of course, begin as draft opinions for the Court but fail to gain majority support. After a case has been decided, issuing a dissenting opinion can serve several purposes.

For one thing, dissenting opinions give justices who disagree with the result in a case the satisfaction of expressing unhappiness with that result and justifying their disagreement. Justice Scalia has said that the right to dissent "makes the practice of one's profession as a judge more satisfying."[15]

Dissenting opinions can have more concrete purposes. Through their arguments, dissenters may try to set the stage for a later Court to adopt their view. This may be one reason why the majority opinion sometimes responds to the arguments made by a dissenter. In the short term, a dissenting opinion may be intended to subvert the Court's decision by pointing out how lower courts can interpret it narrowly or by urging Congress to overturn the Court's reading of a statute.

When more than one justice dissents, all the dissenters may join in a single opinion. Alternatively, they may write multiple opinions. In *Shaw v. Reno* (1993), another case concerning racial discrimination in the drawing of legislative districts, each of the four dissenters wrote an opinion. In such instances dissenters often express agreement with each other's opinions.

One type of concurring opinion disagrees with the majority opinion, taking the position expressed by Harry Blackmun in one case: "I concur in the result the Court reaches in this case, but I cannot follow the route the Court takes to reach that result."[16] Sometimes this disagreement on doctrine is virtually total. In *Lewis v. United States* (1996), Justice Kennedy's concurring opinion agreed with the majority opinion that Lewis had not been entitled to a jury trial. But he rejected entirely the majority's holding that a defendant who faced more than six months of imprisonment could be denied a jury trial under some circumstances, and he called that holding "one of the most serious incursions on the right to jury trial in the Court's history."[17] Sometimes the disagreement is more limited. In her concurring opinion in *Michael H. v. Gerald D.* (1989), Justice O'Connor agreed with the majority opinion except for one potentially significant footnote.

Another type of concurring opinion is written by justices who join the majority opinion. In most of these opinions, justices interpret the majority opinion in order to influence people's reactions to the Court's decision. Sometimes an opinion includes direct advice to the lower court to which the case will be remanded. In *Shalala v. Whitecotton* (1995), Justice O'Connor offered advice to the losing litigant about arguments to make when the case was reconsidered. More often, the concurring justice seeks to affect application of the Court's ruling to other cases or situations. Concurrences frequently offer a narrow interpretation of the Court's ruling.

Announcing the Decision. The process of decision making in a case ends when all the opinions have been put in final form and all justices have determined which opinions they will join. The decision is then announced in open court.

Typically, the justice who wrote the majority opinion reads a portion of the opinion. Justices occasionally offer further commentary. The authors of dissenting opinions also may read their opinions, though Chief Justice Rehnquist reportedly has an informal rule allowing each justice to do so only once a term.[18] Sometimes a dissenter adopts a forceful tone in disagreeing with the Court's ruling. In summarizing his strongly worded dissent in a 1996 decision, Stevens said that the majority opinion "flies in the face of the Constitution's text."[19]

The length of time required for a case to go through all the stages from filing in the Court to the announcement of a decision can vary a good deal, depending primarily on the backlog of cases scheduled for oral argument and the time the justices take to settle on a decision and set of opinions. In June 1996 the Court decided cases that were filed as early as November 1994 and as late as May 1996, though the speed with which the Court accepted and decided the latter case was quite extraordinary.

After the Court decides a case—or declines to hear it—the losing party may petition for a rehearing. Such petitions are rarely granted.[20]

Influences on Decisions: Introduction

In June 1992 the Supreme Court handed down its decision in *Planned Parenthood v. Casey*, in which the issue was whether Pennsylvania's regulations on abortion were unconstitutional. There was no majority opinion, but an unusual joint opinion by Justices O'Connor, Kennedy, and Souter defined the Court's position. The joint opinion upheld all but one of the challenged Pennsylvania regulations. In doing so, it held that the restrictions on state regulation of abortion established in *Roe v. Wade* (1973) should be modified to allow more regulation, but it reaffirmed "the essential holding" of *Roe*. Justices Stevens and Blackmun wrote concurring and dissenting opinions, arguing that all the Pennsylvania regulations should be struck down and that *Roe* should be fully maintained. Chief Justice Rehnquist and Justices White, Scalia, and Thomas each joined in concurring and dissenting opinions written by Rehnquist and Scalia, arguing that each regulation should be upheld and that *Roe* should be overturned altogether.

The Court's decision in *Casey* was noteworthy because many people had expected the Court to announce that it was abandoning *Roe v. Wade* rather than largely reaffirming it. How can that decision be explained? We can never know with certainty why the Supreme Court reaches the decisions it does. Like other policy makers, the justices are influenced by a broad range of considerations that interact in a complex way. But we do have some understanding of what shapes the Court's decisions, and the opinions in *Casey* tell us far more about the justices' thought processes than we usually learn. Thus this case helps in identifying the factors that affect the Court's decisions.

As in other cases, the justices were engaged in the task of interpreting the law—in this case, the Constitution and the Court's prior decisions. Each opinion argued that its own position was most consistent with the applicable legal rules. The joint opinion emphasized the desirability of adhering to *Roe* because of the value of following precedent. For their part, Rehnquist and Scalia argued that *Roe* was inconsistent with the Constitution and thus ought to be overturned.

Justice Scalia charged that in this and other decisions, the Court was making "value judgments" rather than simply interpreting the law. Blackmun pointed out that he was 83 years old and that when he left the Court, "the confirmation process for my successor well may focus on the issue before us today." What Scalia lamented and what Blackmun accepted was that the positions taken by justices on abortion law reflected their own conceptions of good policy as well as good law. It is noteworthy that Blackmun and Stevens, the justices who supported the broadest legal protections for abortion, were the justices with the most liberal records of votes and opinions on civil liberties issues in general, while three of the four justices who sought to overturn *Roe* had strongly conservative records. That pattern strongly suggests that the way the justices read the legal issues in *Casey* reflected a wider set of policy preferences.

The Court's decisions are ultimately group products. As the writing of a joint opinion suggests, O'Connor, Kennedy, and Souter worked together closely in reaching a position that each could accept. Their interactions may have been important in moving Kennedy from his position in a 1989 case, where he seemed committed to overturning *Roe,* to the quite different moderate position of the joint opinion. That shift was unexpected, and according to one report, Scalia "was so upset that he walked over to Kennedy's nearby house in McLean to upbraid him."[21] Scalia's opinion in *Casey* took a harsh tone in refuting the joint opinion. This tone was not a new one for Scalia, and his opinion in the 1989 case had attacked O'Connor vehemently for taking no position on whether *Roe* should be overturned. It is possible that Scalia's style alienated O'Connor and the other authors of the joint opinion, increasing their resolve to stake out their own position.

The justices knew they were deciding an issue that had

aroused strong public feeling. The joint opinion concluded that overturning *Roe* would lead to "profound and unnecessary damage to the Court's legitimacy" with the American people. Scalia said that he was "distressed" about the "political pressure" directed at the Court on the abortion issue in the form of marches, protests, and mail, and he argued that the Court had brought this pressure on itself with decisions that were not properly rooted in the law. These concerns with public reactions and public pressures on an issue of great salience to many people may well have influenced some justices' choices.

The Court's decisions as a whole are shaped by the same broad forces that operated in *Casey:* the law, the personal values of the justices, interaction among them, and the Court's environment. By looking closely at each of these forces, we can gain a sense of why the Court reaches the decisions it does.

The State of the Law

Every case requires the Supreme Court to choose among alternative interpretations of the law, usually provisions of the Constitution or federal statutes. In doing so, the justices rely on several time-honored techniques: analyzing the "plain meaning" of the words to be interpreted; ascertaining the intent of the lawmakers who wrote that language; and examining the Court's own past decisions, its precedents.

The Law's Significance in Decisions

To what extent does the state of the law explain the Court's decisions? One possible position is that the law is the *only* explanation of what the Court does: its decisions simply reflect the provisions of law that it is called upon to interpret. But that position does not accord with some important realities about the Court.

One reality is that justices care about more than just the law. In particular, they often hold strong preferences about the policy issues involved in cases, and they want to see their preferences reflected in the Court's decisions. For that reason they could be expected not just to accept the freedom that results from the legal ambiguity of cases but to seize upon that freedom to make what they view as good policy. As Stephen Breyer said,

"If you see the result is going to make people's lives worse, you'd better go back and rethink it. The law is supposed to fit together in a way that makes the human life of people a little bit better."[22]

A second reality is the legal ambiguity of the cases that the Supreme Court decides. The Court ordinarily chooses to hear only cases that involve ambiguous applications of the Constitution or federal statutes—cases that have more than one "right answer" under the law. Inasmuch as justices care about things other than the law, the law's ambiguity leaves them considerable room to take those other things into account. Thus it is not surprising that in most cases the justices disagree about the outcome for the litigants, the appropriate legal rules, or both; in those cases, the law's ambiguity causes justices with different policy preferences to reach different conclusions.

But the state of the law still can affect the justices. Even if decisions on either side could be justified under the law, the law may weigh more heavily on one side than the other. If the justices care about making good law, they would be drawn toward the side that seems to have a stronger legal argument.

And there is excellent reason to think that justices do care about making good law. They are trained in a tradition that emphasizes the law as a basis for judicial decisions. They are judged by a legal audience that cares about their ability to reach well-founded interpretations of the law. Perhaps most important, they work in the language of the law. The arguments they receive in written briefs and oral arguments are primarily about the law. And the same is true of arguments they make to each other in draft opinions and memoranda.[23]

As a result, justices are affected by the state of the law they interpret. That effect is clearest when they reach judgments that seem to conflict with their conceptions of good policy. Concurring with a 1996 decision that upheld a state's taking of an automobile under its forfeiture power, Justice Thomas expressed his concern about such uses of power. But, he concluded, "this case is ultimately a reminder that the Federal Constitution does not prohibit everything that is intensely undesirable."[24] When Justice O'Connor's majority opinion in a 1994 case took a similar position, one reporter summarized her opinion by saying that "sometimes the Supreme Court just holds its nose."[25]

Sometimes, in fact, the justices are sufficiently unhappy with their interpretation of a statute that they ask Congress to consider rewriting the statute to override their decision—to establish a policy that they feel powerless to adopt themselves because of their reading of the law.[26]

Means of Interpretation

Judges can employ a complex array of techniques with which to interpret provisions of law, but most of these techniques fit into a few broad approaches. We can get a fuller sense of the role of law in the Court's decisions by looking at those approaches.

"Plain Meaning." The most basic approach is analysis of the literal meaning of the words in question. Nearly everyone agrees that interpretation should begin with a search for plain meaning, and many possible interpretations of the law are ruled out because they are inconsistent with the plain meaning of a provision. For instance, the Twenty-second Amendment to the Constitution states, "No person shall be elected to the office of the President more than twice." It is difficult to imagine how the Supreme Court could justify a ruling that a twice-elected person can be elected to a third term.

The Court, of course, seldom faces such easy issues. Most of the Court's decisions involve ambiguous provisions such as the Fourteenth Amendment's protection of "due process of law," which has no plain meaning. And even a provision that may seem to have a plain meaning can be susceptible to multiple interpretations. The First Amendment states that "Congress shall make no law . . . abridging the freedom of speech," but justices and commentators have disagreed about the meaning of "freedom of speech" and even of "speech." Legal scholar Cass Sunstein has written that "on so many of the central constitutional questions . . . the Constitution's words tell us much less than we need to know."[27]

The same is often true of federal statutes. One statute requires at least five years' imprisonment for someone who "during and in relation to any crime of violence or drug trafficking crime . . . uses or carries a firearm."[28] In *Smith v. United States* (1993), the defendant offered to trade a machine gun to an undercover officer for cocaine. In *Bailey v. United States* (1995), one defendant had a loaded gun in a locked car trunk; the other had an unloaded gun in a trunk in a closet. Did any or all of these defendants "use" the gun in question? As Justice Breyer said in oral argument on *Bailey*, "the dictionary, at least to me, doesn't answer the question" as to what "use" meant in the statute.[29] The Court ruled that Smith had "used" a gun while the two defendants in *Bailey* had not, but in neither case was there an obvious plain meaning for the justices to adopt.

Intent of Framers or Legislators. Where the plain meaning of a legal provision is unclear, justices can seek to ascertain the intentions of those who wrote the provision. Evidence concerning legislative intent can be found in congressional committee reports and floor debates, which constitute what is called the "legislative history" of a statute. For provisions of the original Constitution, similar evidence is found in records of the Constitutional Convention of 1787.

Sometimes the intent of the Framers of the Constitution or of Congress is fairly clear. Frequently, however, it is not. The body that adopted a provision may not have spoken on an issue; the members of Congress who wrote the broad language of the Fourteenth Amendment could hardly indicate their intent concerning all the issues that have arisen under that amendment. And evidence about intent may be contradictory. When Congress adopts a statute, its members sometimes offer differing interpretations of language in the statute, trying in this way to influence the courts. This was the case with the Civil Rights Act of 1991, which changed the law's language on a number of civil rights issues. In speeches and statements, congressional liberals and conservatives put forward their own versions of what the new language meant. And some evidence of legislative intent comes from sources such as committee reports that may represent the views of congressional staff more than those of the members.

The use of intent has been the subject of considerable controversy in constitutional interpretation. Some people argue that the Court should adhere to the intent of the framers of each provision as closely as possible; others believe it is appropriate to interpret the Constitution in terms of the current meaning of its language and its underlying values. To a considerable extent this is an ideological debate, with liberals wanting the freedom to adopt broad interpretations of constitutional rights. For instance, conservative justices point to evidence that the writers of the Eighth Amendment did not view capital punishment as "cruel and unusual," while some liberals argue that the Court should interpret the Eighth Amendment in light of changing standards about punishments.

In the past decade justices have debated the use of legislative intent in interpreting statutes. Justice Scalia consistently refuses to refer to legislative history. Most fundamentally, he views it as illegitimate; it is the laws, not the intentions of legislators, that govern. Further, he views it as an uncertain guide to congressional intent, highly susceptible to being used as justification "for decisions arrived at on other grounds."[30]

Scalia has gained some support from other conservatives on the Court. But more liberal justices—most vocally, Justice Stevens—continue to favor the use of legislative history. In *Bank One Chicago v. Midwest Bank & Trust Company* (1996), for instance, Stevens strongly contested Scalia's arguments against legislative history. Justice Souter has also expressed his support for the use of legislative history: "Believers in plain meaning might be excused for thinking that the text answers the question [in a 1995 case]. But history may have something to say about what is plain, and here history is not silent."[31]

Precedent. The Supreme Court's own past decisions, its precedents, provide another guide to decision making. A basic doctrine of the law is stare decisis (let the decision stand). Under this doctrine a court is expected to adhere to its past interpretations of law as well as those of higher courts. Aside from legal doctrine, precedents have a practical value. By following precedent, a judge relies on past practice rather than taking new and perhaps risky directions in legal interpretation. Following precedent also simplifies the task of decision making.

Technically, a court is bound to follow not everything stated in a relevant precedent but only the rule of law that is necessary for decision in that case—what is called the holding. Other statements, called obiter dicta or simply dicta (the singular is dictum), have no legal force. The Court might strike down a special tax on newspapers on the ground that the First Amendment prohibits any tax on publications that does not apply equally to other products. That would be the holding of the

case. If the Court's opinion provided examples of other regulations of newspapers that would also violate the First Amendment, those examples—unnecessary for the decision in this
case—would be dicta. But the line between holding and dicta is
not always easy to draw.

Even if strictly followed, the rule of adhering to precedent
would not eliminate all ambiguity in legal interpretation. Most
cases before the Supreme Court concern issues that are at least
marginally different from those decided in past cases, so precedent seldom determines a decision in a strict way. Justices often
"distinguish" precedents, holding that they do not apply in particular situations. They also cut back on precedents, narrow-
ing them without overturning them altogether. Through both
methods, the Burger and Rehnquist Courts have limited substantially the reach of major Warren Court decisions on the
rights of criminal defendants such as *Mapp v. Ohio* (1961) and
Miranda v. Arizona (1966).

Sometimes the Court simply abandons precedents, and it has
done so at an unusually high rate since 1960. By the best count,
the Court overturned 156 precedents between 1960 and 1996,
an average of more than four per term.[32] The fragility of precedent is suggested by the issue of whether the federal minimum
wage law can be applied to employees of state and local governments. In 1968 the Court said that the law can be applied; in
1976 it overturned that decision and held that the law cannot
be applied; and in 1985 it overturned *that* decision and returned to its 1968 position—which Justice Rehnquist in dissent
predicted the Court would abandon again.[33] Sometimes the
Court eliminates a precedent in even less time: in *United States
v. Dixon* (1993), it overturned a three-year-old interpretation of
double jeopardy for criminal defendants.

The Court's overturning of its precedent on double jeopardy
reflected change in its membership: two members of the 5–4
majority that established the precedent left the Court, and the
justices who dissented in the precedent-setting case were joined
by one new justice who agreed with them to create a 5–4 majority on the other side. As this example suggests, justices who
opposed the creation of a precedent tend to adhere to their positions even after the precedent has been established.[34]

Yet precedents do have some weight; there is a degree of reluctance—perhaps stronger for some justices than for others—

to overturn them directly. To take one example, Chief Justice Rehnquist certainly does not regard precedents as sacred, but in a 1996 case he supported a precedent on state taxing powers while expressing his continuing disagreement with that precedent.[35] And Rehnquist's prediction that the Court would abandon its 1985 minimum-wage precedent has not yet been proved right, even though only one of the five justices who voted for that precedent remains on the Court and in all likelihood a majority of the current justices disagree with it. In 1994 the Court chose not to hear a case that would have allowed it to reconsider that precedent.[36] Like the law in general, the rule of adhering to precedent hardly controls the Court's decisions, but it does structure and influence them.

Justices' Values

The Influence of Policy Preferences

In 1971 President Richard Nixon nominated Assistant Attorney General William Rehnquist to the Supreme Court. Rehnquist had a long record of conservative positions on political and legal issues—views that he had expressed as a Supreme Court law clerk, a participant in Arizona politics, and a member of the Nixon administration. Rehnquist's nomination drew opposition from liberals who expected that his conservative views would be reflected in his votes and opinions on the Court. Rehnquist told the Senate Judiciary Committee, however, that "my fundamental commitment, if I am confirmed, will be to totally disregard my own personal belief."[37]

Yet Rehnquist's record on the Court has confirmed the expectations of his opponents in 1971. His positions have been strongly conservative, particularly on civil liberties issues, and he seldom surprises observers of the Court. The consistency between the views he indicated before his appointment to the Court and his record on the Court is symbolized by his position that a criminal conviction need not be overturned just because an involuntary confession was introduced as evidence—a position that he expressed in strong terms as a law clerk in 1952 and as chief justice in 1991.[38]

Clearly, Rehnquist's "personal belief" has had a good deal of impact on his record as a justice. And the same is true of his colleagues on the Court. There has been less consistency between the pre-Court records of some justices and their votes and opinions on the Court, but those who seek to predict the general stance that a nominee will take on the Court have been fairly successful.[39] And when justices express their personal views on policy issues outside the Court, their positions in cases are usually consistent with those views. To take one example, the conservative values that underlie Clarence Thomas's positions on legal issues are apparent in his speeches.[40]

This should not be surprising. As discussed earlier, the state of the law cannot, and does not, fully control the Court's decisions. For that reason the justices' choices must be based in part on other considerations. Among the other considerations that come into play, the justices' policy preferences are the most powerful; like other policy makers, members of the Supreme Court make decisions largely in terms of their personal attitudes about policy. Indeed, because the Court has a degree of freedom from external pressures, policy preferences may play a larger role in its collective choices than they do in legislatures and administrative agencies.

Some scholars argue that the justices' policy preferences are essentially a complete explanation of the Court's decisions.[41] In contrast, I think that the justices' preferences exert their effects in combination with other important forces, such as the political environment—and, for that matter, the law. But policy preferences certainly provide the best explanation for differences in the positions that the nine justices take in the same cases, because no other factor varies so much from one justice to another.

Of course, the views of Supreme Court justices on policy issues derive from the same variety of sources as do political attitudes generally. Chief Justice Rehnquist meant to be sarcastic when he said that his conservatism "may have something to do with my childhood,"[42] but certainly a justice's upbringing can be an important source of the values expressed on the Court. Powerful experiences such as military service in wartime may affect a justice's reactions to issues such as constitutional protection for flag burning.[43] Career experiences can also have an impact: the years that Justice O'Connor spent as a state legislator and state judge undoubtedly help to explain her support for state powers vis-à-vis those of the federal government. Because justices have different backgrounds and learn different things from those backgrounds, each brings a particular set of attitudes to the Court.

The justices' policy preferences could be reflected in their behavior on the Court in different ways. Justices might simply take the positions that best reflect their views of good policy. Or they might act strategically, adjusting their positions to achieve the best results. In Chapter 3, I discussed strategy in decisions whether to accept cases: to a degree, justices vote to hear cases in which they think that the Court would rule the way they want if it accepted these cases. In decisions on the merits, justices might write opinions that do not fully reflect their own views in order to win the support of other justices. Or the Court collectively could modify its position on an issue in order to reduce the chances that Congress will override the Court's decision and substitute a policy that most justices greatly dislike.

It is not entirely clear to what extent the justices behave strategically and what forms their strategies take.[44] But it appears, on the whole, that strategic considerations do not move justices very far from their own favored positions in cases. Thus the impact of justices' policy preferences can be considered initially without taking strategy into account. In the next two sections, strategy aimed at other justices and at the Court's political environment will be considered.

The Ideological Dimension

Liberal and Conservative Positions. The preferences of justices, as reflected in their votes and opinions, may be understood in ideological terms. On most issues that come to the Supreme Court, opposing positions can be labeled as liberal and conservative. The labeling of positions is easiest on civil liberties issues; the position more favorable to legal protection for liberties is considered liberal. Some civil liberties issues involve the right to equal treatment by government and private institutions under the Constitution and federal statutes. The liberal position on these issues is more sympathetic toward challenges to inequality than is the conservative position. Similarly, the liberal position gives greater weight to procedural rights, such as those protecting criminal defendants, and substantive rights, such as freedom of expression and privacy. In contrast, the conservative position gives greater weight to values that compete with these rights, such as the capacity to fight crime effectively.

On economic issues, liberal and conservative positions are more difficult to define. But the liberal position is basically more sympathetic to economic "underdogs" and to government policies intended to benefit those groups. Thus, for example, the conservative position is more favorable to businesses in conflicts with labor unions and more supportive of their efforts to limit government regulation of their operations.

Some cases that come before the Supreme Court do not have obvious liberal and conservative sides. This is true of boundary disputes between two states and most cases involving contracts between businesses. It is also true of cases in which two civil liberties—freedom of expression and equality, for instance— conflict. In some cases people might disagree about how to label the two sides: is a decision favoring the federal government over other creditors in a bankruptcy case liberal, conservative, or neither? On the whole, ideological lines in American society and thus in the Court have become more complicated. Still, most issues that the Court decides do have clearly defined conservative and liberal sides.

Ideology and Decisions. If opposing positions in most cases can be identified as liberal or conservative, we can describe the justices' voting patterns in terms of the frequency with which they support the conservative side and the liberal side. Table 4-2 shows the ideological patterns of votes for the justices in the 1995 term. As the table shows, every justice cast a good many votes on both sides. But the justices also differed considerably in their ideological tendencies: Justice Stevens supported the liberal side nearly three times as often as Justice Scalia.

As I have suggested, the votes that justices cast and the opinions they write reflect the influence of several different forces. For that reason we cannot say that Justice Breyer is a liberal simply because a majority of his votes supported liberal positions. With a different mix of cases and under different circumstances, Breyer might have cast a majority of conservative votes. But because differences in justices' positions reflect primarily differences in their policy preferences, it is appropriate to conclude—at least if the 1995 term is typical—that Breyer is more conservative than Stevens and substantially more liberal than

TABLE 4-2
Proportion of Liberal Votes Cast by Justices, 1995 Term

Justice	Liberal votes
Stevens	67.1
Ginsburg	53.5
Breyer	52.1
Souter	49.2
Kennedy	42.3
O'Connor	35.2
Rehnquist	31.0
Thomas	28.6
Scalia	23.9

Note: Cases are included only if votes could be classified as liberal or conservative by conventional criteria. Cases in which two liberal values or two conservative values conflicted are omitted. Seventy-one cases are included. Votes in unanimous decisions are classified according to which side is primarily favored by the decision. Votes in non-unanimous decisions are classified according to whether the justice voted for the more liberal or the more conservative outcome favored by members of the Court.

Scalia and Thomas. And, indeed, the relative positions of the justices tend to remain fairly stable from term to term. That stability underlines the importance of policy preferences in shaping the positions that justices take.

It is reasonable to describe the justices in terms of their overall liberalism or conservatism, because there is considerable ideological consistency in their positions across issues. A justice who is strongly conservative on the issue of privacy is also likely to be quite conservative on conflicts between business and labor. In this respect, of course, the justices are similar to other policy makers.

But this consistency is far from absolute. A justice who takes liberal positions on economic issues may be conservative on civil liberties issues. Some members of the current Court give considerably more support to freedom of expression than they do to the rights of criminal defendants.

Within specific areas of policy, the degree of consistency is somewhat greater. This consistency can be illustrated by what is called a scalogram. If the nine justices can be ranked from most liberal to most conservative in the same way for all the issues that arise in a category such as criminal cases, we would expect a distinctive pattern of votes on cases in that category. Each time the most conservative justice votes for the liberal position in a case, every other justice should do so as well; each time the second most conservative justice casts a liberal vote, the seven more liberal justices should also do so; and so on. Any deviation from that pattern represents an ideological inconsistency. Scalograms, limited to nonunanimous decisions, lay out the actual pattern of liberal and conservative votes to show how closely they follow this expected pattern.

Figure 4-1 is a scalogram of criminal cases in the Supreme Court's 1995 term. It shows that the justices varied a good deal in their support for criminal defendants, from Stevens at the liberal end of the spectrum (that is, most supportive of defendants) to Scalia at the conservative end. To a considerable extent, the divisions among the justices in individual cases followed the same ideological lines as the overall rankings of justices. For instance, in the three cases in which the Court divided 8–1 in a conservative direction, Stevens was the dissenter in each case. There were only a few exceptions to perfect ideological consistency, and none was extreme. But, as noted in the figure, two cases were excluded because votes for the criminal defendant in those cases had conservative as well as liberal elements, and those cases would not have scaled well with the others. Further, criminal cases involve unusually sharp ideological divisions, and more substantial deviations from ideological consistency would be found in other areas.

Patterns of Agreement. Analysis of patterns of agreement among justices provides another perspective on the Court's ideological divisions. For each pair of justices who served in the 1994 and 1995 terms, Table 4-3 shows the average percentage of the time that they supported the same opinion in the two terms. While Figure 4-1 focuses on votes, Table 4-3 focuses on doctrine; justices who voted for the same outcome but who could not support the same opinion are treated as disagreeing.

The table shows that some pairs of justices agreed with each other much more often than other pairs. Not surprisingly,

FIGURE 4-1

*Scalogram of Justices' Votes in Nonunanimous Decisions Arising
from Criminal Prosecutions, 1995 Term*

Case citation[a]	Justices' votes									Liberal votes
	St	Br	So	Gi	Ke	O'C	Re	Th	Sc	
134–911	+	+	+	+	+	+	+	+	–	8
133–383	+	+	+	+	+	+	–	–	+	7
135–457	+	+	+	+	–	–	–	–	–	4
133–1	+	+	+	+	–	–	–	–	–	4
134–68	+	+	+	–	+	–	–	–	–	4
135–361	+	+	+	–	–	+	–	–	–	4
135–590	+	+	–	–	–	–	–	–	–	2
135–1031	+	–	–	+	–	–	–	–	–	2
134–613	+	–	–	–	+	–	–	–	–	2
135–606	+	–	–	–	–	–	–	–	–	1
133–271	+	–	–	–	–	–	–	–	–	1
134–687	+	–	–	–	–	–	–	–	–	1
135–549	+	–	–	–	–	–	–	–	–	1
Total liberal votes	13	7	6	5	4	3	1	1	1	

Note: Cases are those arising from criminal prosecutions. Two cases (135–392 and 135–427) were excluded because votes for the criminal defendant supported conservative positions on broader issues. Liberal votes (favoring defendants) are designated +, conservative votes (opposing defendants) are designated –. The stepped vertical line divides votes into two groups according to conventional rules of scalogram analysis; – signs to the left of the line and + signs to the right may be interpreted as votes inconsistent with the ideological ordering of the justices.

Key: St = Stevens; Br = Breyer; So = Souter; Gi = Ginsburg; Ke = Kennedy; O'C = O'Connor; Re = Rehnquist; Th = Thomas; Sc = Scalia.

[a] Numbers refer to volumes and pages of citiations in *United States Supreme Court Reports, Lawyers' Edition.*

agreement was most frequent between the justices whose ideological positions in Court decisions were closest. Scalia supported the same opinion as Thomas in seven of every eight cases, and the rates of agreement for pairs of the three most conservative justices averaged 84 percent. Breyer and Souter had the second highest rate of agreement at 86 percent, and the average rate of agreement among the four most liberal justices was 77 percent. The justices in the middle of the Court, O'Connor and Kennedy, were about as likely to agree with the justices to their ideological left (except for Stevens) as they were

TABLE 4-3

Average Percentage of Cases in Which Pairs of Justices
Supported the Same Opinion, 1994 and 1995 Terms

Justice	Gi	Br	So	O'C	Ke	Re	Sc	Th
Stevens	74	72	70	58	63	50	45	44
Ginsburg		79	82	67	76	66	59	55
Breyer			86	75	70	63	57	54
Souter				78	74	68	60	57
O'Connor					77	78	70	70
Kennedy						81	74	71
Rehnquist							81	82
Scalia								88
Thomas								

Sources: "The Supreme Court, 1994 Term," *Harvard Law Review* 109 (November 1995): 341; "The Supreme Court, 1995 Term," *Harvard Law Review* 110 (November 1996): 368.

Note: Numbers are averages, for the two terms, of the percentages of cases in each term in which a pair of justices agreed on an opinion. Both unanimous and nonunanimous cases are included.

with justices to their right. Stevens agreed with Scalia and Thomas only about 45 percent of the time, the lowest rates for these two terms. Even so, the fact that the most disparate members of the Court joined in the same opinion nearly half the time underlines the frequency with which the justices agree on a single interpretation of the law.

We should be careful not to make too much of the overall patterns of agreement. For one thing, the justices do not always line up in expected ways. Unusual alliances appear most often in cases in which the liberal and conservative positions are not clear. During the 1995 term, one case found Scalia joining in a dissenting opinion by Breyer against a majority opinion on which all seven of their colleagues agreed; in another case, it was Stevens and Thomas who joined together against all the other justices.[45]

More important, we should not assume that patterns of agreement reflect self-conscious alliances or blocs of justices. This is not to say that the justices are unaware of general patterns of agreement among themselves. And like-minded justices sometimes do work together closely; this was true, for instance, of Earl Warren and William Brennan during the 1960s. But ideological allies do not always form close working relationships, and those who agree most often in cases do not necessarily have the closest personal relationships. When alliances do develop, they are chiefly the result of agreement about judicial issues rather than the source of that agreement. Shared preferences, not concerted action, best explain the tendency for certain justices to agree on opinions.

Preferences and Policy Change

The process of policy change in the Supreme Court is difficult to analyze systematically, because the issues before the Court are constantly changing. For example, a decline in the proportion of decisions favorable to taxpayers might reflect a change in the Court's policies on tax law or simply a change in the kinds of tax cases that the Court decides, and it is not always easy to distinguish between the two possibilities. Still, at times it is clear that the Court's collective approach to a policy area or a set of policy areas such as civil liberties has changed.

Such changes can occur for many reasons. But shifts in the preferences of the justices as a group are a primary source of policy change in the Court. These shifts could come from change in the views of people already serving on the Court or from change in the Court's membership. In practice, both are significant.

Changes in Views. New justices come to the Supreme Court with fundamental values that are well formed. Yet as members of the Court they are exposed to new influences and confront issues in new forms. The result is a general stability in the preferences that justices express in their votes and opinions but many small changes—and, occasionally, a fundamental change—in their views.

A justice who serves on the Court for several years is likely to shift positions on some specific issues, usually because of experience with cases that concern those issues. In the Court's major decisions on the death penalty in 1972 and 1976, Justice Harry Blackmun took the position that capital punishment was constitutionally acceptable, despite his personal view that it was highly undesirable. But Blackmun gradually came to the position that the death penalty was unconstitutional as well as undesirable, a position that he finally articulated directly in a 1994 opinion.[46]

Individual issues aside, most justices retain the same basic ideological position throughout their career. A justice who begins as a liberal, such as Thurgood Marshall, generally remains a liberal; the same is usually true of a conservative such as William Rehnquist. When a justice's position shifts relative to that of the Court as a whole, it is usually because new appointments have shifted the Court's ideological center, while the justice has retained the same general views. This appears to be the case with John Paul Stevens, who moved to the liberal end of the Court as more liberal justices were replaced by conservatives.

Blackmun is an example of the relatively rare cases in which a justice's basic views seem to undergo a fundamental shift. Blackmun came to the Court in 1970 as a Nixon appointee, and early in his tenure he aligned himself chiefly with the other conservative justices. He and Chief Justice Burger, boyhood friends from Minnesota, were dubbed the "Minnesota Twins." In the 1973 term, Blackmun agreed with Burger on opinions in 84 percent of the decisions, and with liberal William Brennan in only 49 percent.[47] But gradually Blackmun moved toward the center of the Court, and from the 1980 term on he usually had higher agreement rates with Brennan than with Burger—in 1985, Burger's last term, 30 percent higher. By the early 1990s Blackmun had become one of the two most liberal justices on the Court.

This shift to the Court's left resulted in part from the replacement of liberal colleagues with conservatives. But Blackmun's own positions clearly became more liberal; his change of mind on capital punishment is a dramatic example of a broader change. Although the reasons for this change are uncertain, it appears that his experiences in dealing with cases that came to the Court—particularly *Roe v. Wade,* in which he wrote the Court's opinion—were important. And it also seems that Blackmun wanted to help maintain an ideological balance on the Court as it became increasingly conservative.[48]

More recently, some observers have perceived a more limited but significant shift to the left by Reagan appointee Anthony Kennedy—a shift highlighted by his participation in the decisive joint opinion in *Planned Parenthood v. Casey* in 1992. A year later, a dismayed conservative commentator likened Kennedy to Blackmun.[49] Kennedy's positions in major cases and his levels of agreement with liberal and conservative colleagues suggest that he *has* become somewhat more liberal, but not to nearly the degree that Blackmun did.

Perhaps more common than individual ideological shifts are changes in the views of the justices as a group on a particular issue. These shifts typically result from developments in American society that shape the views of the justices along with other groups.

One striking example concerns the legal status of women. The liberal Warren Court gave unprecedented support to the goal of equality under the law, but it did not attack legal rules that treated women and men differently. In contrast, the more conservative Burger and Rehnquist Courts have handed down a series of decisions promoting legal equality for men and women. By the mid-1990s even the most conservative justices were using a rigorous standard to evaluate laws that treat women and men differently, a standard that might have been unthinkable in the 1960s.[50] The most fundamental cause of this change seems to be the direct and indirect impact of the feminist movement on the Court's agenda and, even more, on justices' views about women's social roles. In any event, this example underlines the potential for significant changes in justices' collective views on policy issues.

Membership Change. Although shifts in the positions of sitting justices can produce major policy changes in the Court, membership change is probably the most important source of policy change in the Court. If Supreme Court policies are largely a product of the justices' preferences, and if those preferences tend to be stable, then change will come most easily through the replacement of one justice with a successor who has a different set of policy preferences.

Change in the Court's membership often alters its positions on specific issues. As noted already, the overturning of recent precedents usually results from the replacement of justices who helped create that precedent with others who disagree with it. And even when the Court maintains a precedent, a critical shift in membership may ensure that it is extended no further.

More broadly, changes in the Court's overall ideological position through new appointments typically lead to change in the general content of its policies. The Court's civil liberties policies since the 1950s demonstrate this effect of membership change. Table 4-4 shows the proportions of decisions favorable to parties with civil liberties claims during successive periods in the 1958–1995 terms. Because changes in the content of civil liberties cases can make these proportions misleading, the table also shows civil liberties support with an adjustment for the content of cases based on a statistical technique.

The early Warren Court was closely divided between liberals and conservatives; from 1958 until 1961 there was a relatively stable division between a four-member liberal bloc and a moderate to conservative bloc of five. By the standards of the 1920s and 1930s, the Court's decisions were quite liberal, but the table shows that parties with civil liberties claims won only a little more than half their cases between 1958 and 1961.

President Kennedy's 1962 appointments created a liberal majority; a law clerk during the 1962 term referred to it as "a turning point in the modern history of the Supreme Court."[51] The Johnson appointments later in the decade maintained that majority. The period from 1962 to 1968 was probably the most liberal in the Court's history. The Court established strikingly liberal positions in a variety of policy areas, and the proportion of pro–civil liberties decisions increased substantially.

Between 1969 and 1992, every appointment to the Court was made by a Republican president, and all but Ford sought to use their appointments to make the Court more conservative. Thus the Court gained a distinctly more conservative set of justices. The impact of these membership changes on the Court's civil liberties policies has been somewhat ambiguous. The Court has adhered to some policies of the Warren Court and has even taken new liberal directions on issues such as women's rights. Yet, on the whole, the Burger Court was distinctly less supportive of civil liberties than was the Court of the 1960s, and the Rehnquist Court has been even less supportive.

TABLE 4-4

Proportions of Supreme Court Decisions Favoring Parties
with Civil Liberties Claims and Changes in Court Membership,
1958–1995 Terms

Terms	Proportions of pro–civil liberties decisions		New justices (appointing presidents) and justices leaving the Court
	Actual	*Adjusted*[a]	
1958–1961	57.8	57.8	—
1962–1968	74.1	78.9	*New:* White, Goldberg (Kennedy); Fortas, Marshall (Johnson). *Leaving:* Whittaker, Frankfurter, Goldberg, Clark.
1969–1975[b]	48.8	59.4	*New:* Burger, Blackmun, Powell, Rehnquist (Nixon). *Leaving:* Warren, Fortas, Black, Harlan.
1975–1980[b]	39.1	51.8	*New:* Stevens (Ford). *Leaving:* Douglas.
1981–1985	37.2	50.4	*New:* O'Connor (Reagan). *Leaving:* Stewart.
1986–1989	41.7	49.5	*New:* Scalia, Kennedy (Reagan). *Leaving:* Burger, Powell.
1990–1992	40.1	38.2	*New:* Souter, Thomas (Bush). *Leaving:* Brennan, Marshall.
1993–1995	45.5	37.7	*New:* Ginsberg, Breyer (Clinton). *Leaving:* White, Blackmun.

[a] Adjusted using a statistical technique to control for changes in the content of civil liberties cases decided by the Court. The technique is described in Lawrence Baum, "Measuring Policy Change in the U.S. Supreme Court," *American Political Science Review* 82 (September 1988): 905–912.

[b] 1969–1975 includes the part of the 1975 term with William Douglas on the Court; 1975–1980 includes the part of that term with John Paul Stevens on the Court.

As Table 4-4 shows, the appointments from 1969 through 1975 were followed by substantial reductions in the proportion of decisions favorable to civil liberties. If change in the content of cases is taken into account, another major decline in support for civil liberties occurred after David Souter and Clarence Thomas replaced the Court's two strong liberals in the early 1990s. Because Ruth Bader Ginsburg and Stephen Breyer succeeded a liberal justice and a moderate, their appointments had limited impact on the Court's support for civil liberties— none at all if the content of cases is taken into account.

The lack of a more substantial policy shift between the early 1970s and the early 1990s cautions against exaggerating the impact of membership change. But the change in policies that did occur is noteworthy, and it strongly suggests that appointments are the most important mechanism by which the Court's policies can be altered.

Role Values

Policy preferences are not the only kinds of values that can affect the Court's decisions. The choices that justices make may also be influenced by their role values, their views about what constitutes appropriate behavior for the Supreme Court and its members. In any body, whether it is a court or a legislature, members' conceptions of how they should carry out their jobs structure what they do and affect their policy decisions.

A variety of role values can shape the behavior of justices. Their views about the desirability of unanimous decisions can affect the extent of dissent in the Court's decisions. Their judgments about the legitimacy of "lobbying" colleagues on decisions may determine the outcomes of some cases. But the most important role values concern the considerations that justices take into account in reaching their decisions and the desirability of judicial activism.

It is clear that several different forces shape the justices' votes and opinions in significant ways. The relative weight of these forces depends in part on what justices think they ought to do. In particular, justices have to create a balance between their strong policy preferences on many issues and the expectation that they will decide cases by making accurate interpretations of the law.

There is some evidence that justices differ in the relative weight they give to these legal and policy considerations.[52] These differences are not as sharp as they sometimes appear, however. At any given time, for instance, some justices are considerably more willing than others to uproot some of the Court's precedents. But their attitudes toward precedent as such may be less important than their attitudes toward the policies embodied in particular precedents. In the 1960s, the Court overturned conservative precedents on civil liberties in thirty-two cases, but it overturned liberal precedents only once. In the

1980s, in contrast, the Court overturned ten liberal precedents and only two conservative precedents in civil liberties.[53] Not surprisingly, it was conservatives in the 1960s and liberals in the 1980s who adhered most strongly to the Court's precedents.

The heart of judicial activism is the making of significant policy changes. Because activism has overtones of illegitimacy, justices often emphasize the value of judicial restraint—the avoidance of activism. But this view has not been unanimous; some justices, such as William Brennan, have made strong defenses of activism. And observers of the Court often label some justices as activists and others as proponents of restraint.

Here, too, however, historical patterns are illuminating. During the 1920s and early 1930s, the laws that the Court struck down were primarily government regulations of business practices. Conservative justices were the most willing to strike down such laws, while liberals on the Court and elsewhere argued for judicial restraint. Since the 1940s, however, the Court has struck down primarily laws that conflict with civil liberties. Liberals have been most likely to act against these laws, while conservatives have called for judicial restraint. This history suggests that positions on activism and restraint have served chiefly as justifications of policy choices rather than determining those choices themselves.

This is not to say that the justices' views about activism and other role values have no impact on their behavior. Undoubtedly, such values help to structure the ways in which justices perceive their jobs. But it appears that justices' conceptions of good public policy have a more fundamental impact on their choices.

Group Interaction

In discussing the impact of justices' policy preferences, I presented a simple picture—one in which justices act directly and straightforwardly on their preferences. But justices vote on case outcomes and write and join opinions in a larger context. They are part of a Court that makes decisions as a group, and they are also part of American government and society. As suggested earlier, justices might act strategically by taking into account the possible actions of their colleagues and other institutions. And colleagues and other institutions can shape justices' positions in other ways. Thus both the Court as a group and the Court's environment must be considered.

A Quasi-Collegial Body

In historical accounts of the Supreme Court, some of the most dramatic events concern the interaction among justices in major cases. Newly appointed chief justice Earl Warren, engaging in what Justice Douglas called "a brilliant diplomatic process," moved the Court from sharp division to a unanimous decision in *Brown v. Board of Education* (1954).[54] Members of the Court competed over a period of several months to influence the outcome in *Roe v. Wade* (1973).[55] And, as discussed earlier, the Court's adherence to most of the tenets of *Roe* in *Planned Parenthood v. Casey* (1992) reflected the close collaboration among three justices on a joint opinion.

Yet justices and those close to them often describe a quite different picture of the Court, one in which its members work by themselves and make their own judgments. One legal scholar, a former law clerk, wrote that

it's really nine separate courts. The Justices lead separate, even isolated lives. They deal with each other only in quite formalized settings. They vote the way they want to and then retreat to their own chambers.[56]

Contradictory though they may seem, both of these depictions of the Court are accurate; they simply portray different aspects of the same reality. On the one hand, several conditions limit interaction and influence among the justices. The most basic is the Court's workload. Conference discussion of cases must be abbreviated, and justices often have little time to engage in extended give-and-take during the process of writing and joining opinions. Other conditions also work against direct face-to-face interaction among justices: each has law clerks with whom to discuss cases, and improvements in technology have made it easier for them to communicate with each other in writing. As a result, "the constant personal exchanges in the Warren Court . . . have given way to mostly written contacts through notes and memoranda."[57] David Souter reportedly engages in the practice of "strolling into his colleagues' chambers and gently lobbying for his positions,"[58] but few justices do so routinely.

The justices' ability to influence each other is also limited by the strength of the views that they hold on many issues. When they apply their general positions on an issue to a specific case, the resulting judgment about that case may be too firm for colleagues to sway. As Chief Justice Rehnquist wrote, when justices who have prepared themselves "assemble around the conference table on Friday morning to decide an important case presenting constitutional questions that they have all debated and written about before, the outcome may be a foregone conclusion."[59]

Yet interaction among the justices still can affect the Court's decisions. No matter how great their isolation from each other, justices have powerful incentives to interact and work together on decisions. Even if they did not care very much about the content of the Court's decisions, they would want to achieve opinions that at least five members endorse, so that the Court is laying down authoritative legal rules. And they would seek even greater consensus, to give more weight to the Court's decisions.

Of course, justices often care a great deal about the content of the Court's decisions. Holding strong views about issues that the Court addresses, they would like those views to win as much support as possible from colleagues—particularly the support of a majority. Thus they have good reason to engage in persuasion of other justices.

These incentives are reflected quite clearly in the workings of the Court's decision-making process. The negotiation among justices that was described in the first section of the chapter reflects their interest in winning support from colleagues. It also reflects their willingness to modify their positions as a means to achieve a collective result that reflects their own views at least moderately well. Not all cases feature such negotiation, but it is quite common. One study examined memos with "bargaining statements," in which justices ask for a change in the language of the majority opinion so that they can join the opinion. The study found that such memos were written in 43 percent of the Court's 1983 term decisions. They occurred even more often, 65 percent of the time, in important decisions of the Burger Court.[60]

Moreover, this negotiation and other forms of group interaction account for much of what J. Woodford Howard called "the fluidity of judicial choice,"[61] the shifting of individual votes and collective decisions after tentative decisions are reached in conference. During the seventeen years of the Burger Court, 7.5 percent of the justices' individual votes to reverse or affirm shifted from one side to the other, and at least one such shift occurred in 37 percent of the cases. Most vote shifts increase the size of the majority, as the Court works toward consensus. During the Burger Court, the justices who initially voted with the majority switched their votes 5 percent of the time, but those who initially voted with the minority switched 18 percent of the time.[62] But occasionally—in about 9 percent of the cases between 1956 and 1967—shifts of position turn an initial minority into a majority.[63]

Beyond the outcomes of cases, the legal rules that the Court lays down in its opinions can also change in the decision process. In the Burger Court, slightly more than half of all cases had at least three drafts of the majority opinion circulated by its author.[64] While successive drafts may differ only on minor matters, they sometimes differ substantially—and sometimes with important consequences for constitutional and statutory law.[65]

The effects of interactions among the justices should not be exaggerated. In the great majority of cases, the side that won in the Court's first vote on the merits of the case wins in the final vote as well. Most of the majority opinions that the Court issues look similar to the original drafts of those opinions. But votes and opinions do change; the Court's decisions are often more than simply an adding together of the positions with which each justice begins.

The group life of the Court has effects on its decisions that are broader and more subtle than shifts of position in individual cases. Interactions among the justices create general patterns of influence within the Court, and the Court's ability to reach consensus is affected by the extent of conflict among its members. Both these effects merit consideration.

Patterns of Influence

Felix Frankfurter and William O. Douglas both joined the Supreme Court in 1939. Frankfurter was a Harvard law professor, one of the most renowned legal scholars in the United States. Douglas, who had been a law professor at Columbia and

Yale, was widely regarded as brilliant. Each would serve a long time on the Court—Frankfurter for twenty-two years, Douglas for a record thirty-six years. And each has been included in lists of the greatest justices. Yet neither exerted a great deal of influence over his colleagues on the Supreme Court.

When William Brennan came to the Court in 1956 his work as a lawyer and state judge had given him a reputation for competence, but he was hardly regarded as a great legal thinker. Yet during most of his thirty-four years on the Court, Brennan was probably the most influential justice—even more influential than the chief justices with whom he served. In this sense at least, Brennan was a more successful justice than either Frankfurter or Douglas. How can this result be explained?

In the case of Douglas, the best explanation is a straightforward one: he had only a limited interest in exerting influence over his colleagues. Certainly he devoted some efforts to winning support for his positions, especially in the cases that concerned him most. But in contrast with some other justices, whom he called "evangelists,"[66] he generally preferred to go his own way. One colleague reported, with some overstatement, that "Bill Douglas is positively embarrassed if anyone on the court agrees with him."[67]

Frankfurter is a more complicated case. He came to the Court expecting to play a major leadership role, and he was one of Douglas's "evangelists." But these efforts suffered because of his weak interpersonal skills. Justice Potter Stewart said that Frankfurter "courted" him, but "Felix was so unsubtle and obvious that it was counterproductive."[68] Further, Frankfurter's arrogance caused him to lecture to colleagues, and he reacted sarcastically to opinions with which he disagreed. His behavior alienated several colleagues, with an inevitable impact on his influence within the Court.

Brennan differed from Douglas and Frankfurter in crucial ways. Unlike Douglas, he devoted enormous effort toward influencing his colleagues—not just in individual cases, but in the long term as well. One biographer described his long-term goal as follows: "attract moderate justices to the liberal fold and move the Court's conservative members more to the center by having them write their opinions more narrowly."[69] In his commitment to winning support from his colleagues and his careful consideration of how to do so, Brennan was among the most strategic-minded justices ever to sit on the Court.[70] One striking indication of his commitment to winning support for his positions on legal issues was the apparent continuation of his efforts to gain that support even after retirement. According to one report, Chief Justice Rehnquist was "sometimes said to be near apoplectic at the way [Brennan] still insinuates his eloquent liberal arguments over morning coffee with the likes of Justice Souter."[71]

Frankfurter was also strategic, but Brennan was far better suited to win support from his colleagues. Most important, he had the advantage of a personal style that was much warmer than Frankfurter's. "Everybody got along with him," according to one observer, "even those who bitterly opposed him from a doctrinal view."[72] Brennan was also perceptive about how to win majorities; one commentator said that he could "accurately judge his colleagues and figure out what is doable."[73]

Brennan's commitment and skills were reflected in the results. As a member of the Warren Court, working closely with Warren, he helped to forge a liberal majority for expansion of civil liberties. In the Burger and Rehnquist Courts, he did much to shape the Court's decisions and thereby to limit its conservative shift.

One justice who seems to stand out on the current Court is John Paul Stevens. One observer concluded that Stevens, like Douglas, "makes little effort to win over other members of the Court."[74] Frequently writing opinions for himself rather than joining his colleagues, he has been called the Court's "Lone Ranger."[75]

Antonin Scalia's situation illustrates the difficulty of determining a justice's influence from outside the Court.[76] Scalia does some things that seem likely to bother his colleagues. His very active role in oral argument creates at least temporary frictions.[77] More important, his opinions often attack his colleagues' views in forceful terms—attacks that sometimes could be characterized as ridicule. Dissenting from the Court's 1996 ruling that the Virginia Military Institute must admit women, Scalia denounced not only Justice Ginsburg's majority opinion but the concurring opinion by Chief Justice Rehnquist, a fellow conservative. The concurrence, he wrote, "finds VMI unconstitutional on a basis that is more moderate than the Court's but only at the expense of being even more implausible."[78] Two days later, the Court ruled that a trash hauler could not have his contract with a county government terminated because of his political expression. That decision and a similar one in a second case, said Scalia, "demonstrate why this Court's Constitution-making process can be called 'reasoned adjudication' only in the most formalistic sense."[79] It may be that this kind of language has alienated some colleagues.

Yet Scalia is a gregarious person who has close relationships with some colleagues. More important, his intellectual power clearly gives him influence. For instance, he has attracted support for his position that the Court should give no weight to legislative history in interpreting statutes. And federal judge Alex Kozinski, who is close to Scalia, has argued that Scalia "sets the terms of the debate" on issues before the Court and that he is creating a foundation for long-term influence over development of the law.[80] Thus he may be engaging in a patient but potentially effective long-term strategy within the Court.

As the discussion thus far suggests, justices differ a great deal in their influence over the Court's collective decisions. But these differences should not be exaggerated. For one thing, no justice can dominate the strong-minded people who serve on the Court. Under highly unfavorable conditions, even the most influential justice will lose most of the time. Brennan enjoyed a surprising degree of success as the Court became more conservative in the 1970s and 1980s, but he lost more and more battles as new appointments caused the Court to move further away from his views. Further, every justice has considerable power simply by holding one of only nine votes. No matter how unskilled or unpopular a justice might be, that justice still can vote to affirm or reverse, to support one opinion or another.

The Chief Justice

The chief justice is formal head of the Supreme Court, but there are significant limits on the chief's capacity to influence the Court. One limitation lies in the burden of administrative duties, which reduce the time that the chief can spend on cases. More fundamental is the difficulty of leading colleagues who strongly resist control. As Chief Justice Rehnquist has written, the chief "presides over a conference not of eight subordinates, whom he may direct or instruct, but of eight associates who, like him, have tenure during good behavior, and who are as independent as hogs on ice. He may at most persuade or cajole them."[81] Yet the chief holds significant formal powers, powers that provide considerable potential for leadership.

The Chief Justice's Powers. One important source of power is the role of presiding over the Court in oral argument and in conference. In presiding over the conference, the chief can direct discussion and frame alternatives, thus helping to shape the outcome of the discussion. Most important, the chief ordinarily speaks first on a case in conference. Also significant is the chief's part in creating the discuss list, the set of petitions for hearing that the Court considers fully. The chief, aided by clerks, makes up the initial version of the discuss list. This task gives the chief the largest role in determining which cases are set aside without group judgment.

Opinion Assignment. The power to assign opinions merits more detailed consideration. By custom, the chief justice assigns the Court's opinion whenever the chief is in the majority on the initial vote in conference. (In other cases, the senior justice in the majority makes the assignment.) As a result, the chief justice assigns the great majority of opinions, a little over 80 percent in the period from 1953 to 1990.[82]

In making assignments, chief justices balance different considerations.[83] Administrative considerations relate to spreading workload and opportunities among the justices. Chief justices generally assign about the same number of opinions to each colleague, taking into account assignments from senior associate justices and the workload of opinion writing that a justice already faces at a given time. These considerations have been especially important to Chief Justice Rehnquist, who announced in 1989 that he would be inclined against assigning opinions to colleagues who were behind in their work. One example was justices who had not circulated a draft majority opinion within four weeks of its assignment.[84]

Other considerations relate to the substance of the Court's decisions. The legal rules proclaimed by the Court may depend in part on who writes its opinion. For this reason, chief justices

tend to favor themselves and colleagues who have similar ideological positions when assigning opinions in important cases.

The selection of the opinion writer may help to determine
whether the initial majority remains a majority. When the initial
majority is slim, the chief justice is likely to assign opinions to a
relatively moderate member of that majority, even if the assigned justice is ideologically distant from the chief. This practice stems from the belief that a moderate typically has the best
chance to write an opinion that will maintain the majority and
perhaps win over justices who were initially on the other side.

Because chief justices favor ideological allies in assigning important opinions, in effect they reward the justices who vote
with them most often. They might also use the assignment
power more directly to reward and punish colleagues, as Chief
Justice Burger apparently did. Justice Blackmun said that a justice who was "in the doghouse" with Burger might be assigned
one of the "crud" opinions "that nobody wants to write."[85]

Under any chief justice, the assignment power gives other
justices something to think about. Asked why he joins Rehnquist in singing carols at the Court's Christmas party, David
Souter said, "I have to. Otherwise I get all the tax cases."[86]
Souter was joking, but he touched on an important reality.

Variation in Leadership. What particular chief justices make of
their formal powers and how much leadership they exert vary a
good deal. These differences result from several conditions, including the chief's interest in leading the Court, the chief's skill
as a leader, and the willingness of the associate justices to be led.

The two chief justices who preceded William Rehnquist—
Earl Warren and Warren Burger—are of particular interest.
Earl Warren could not compete with some colleagues as a
scholar. He presided over a Court that had several skillful and
strong-minded members, such as Douglas and Frankfurter, and
that was closely divided between liberals and conservatives during most of his tenure. Under these conditions, Warren hardly
could have dominated the Court.

But Warren did have some major assets. Most important, he
possessed excellent leadership skills, a product of his personal-
ity and his experience as a political leader. He had a good sense
of how to build majorities for his positions, and he was effective

at persuasion: several of his colleagues told one observer "how hard it had been to withstand the Chief Justice when he was able to operate in a one-on-one setting."[87] Thus Warren was able to play an important leadership role on the Court, albeit one that was shared with and contested by some colleagues.

Warren Burger was ambitious for leadership. He achieved some success in securing administrative changes in the federal courts and procedural changes in the Court itself. Simply by being chief justice, he exerted considerable influence over the Court's decisions. But he was far less effective than Earl Warren.

To a considerable extent, Burger's limited impact on the Court's decisions stemmed from his own qualities and predilections. Colleagues chafed at what they considered a poor style of leadership in conference, and they disliked Burger's practice, apparently unique to him, of casting "false" votes in conference for strategic purposes. "All too damned often," said one justice, "the Chief Justice will vote with the majority so as to assign the opinion, and then he ends up in dissent."[88] He was also accused of bullying his colleagues. One scholar concluded that Potter Stewart "loathed" Burger,[89] and other colleagues also disliked his leadership style. Apparently they were not alone; Justice Marshall's messenger said that when Burger retired, "it was just like Christmas morning."[90]

But Burger also faced obstacles that were beyond his control. Perhaps most important, as a strong conservative he had the disadvantage of standing near one end of the Court's ideological spectrum. In any case, his example shows that even a chief justice who wants to be a powerful leader does not always achieve that goal.

When William Rehnquist was promoted to chief justice in 1986, he brought important strengths to that position, and his appointment was welcomed by colleagues and other Court personnel.[91] His well-respected intellectual abilities help to make him an effective leader at conferences, and he conducts the conferences efficiently as well. He is straightforward in taking positions in cases. And he is affable—well-liked even by colleagues who strongly disagree with his views about law and policy.

Rehnquist is even more conservative than Burger, and he began his tenure as chief justice at one end of the Court's ideological spectrum. Appointments to the Court since then have moved its center a bit closer to Rehnquist, enhancing his potential for leadership, but even today only Antonin Scalia and Clarence Thomas are more conservative than he is. Yet Justice Brennan said in 1989 that Rehnquist was "the most all-around successful" of the last three chiefs.[92]

Harmony and Conflict

Disagreement is a regular feature of Supreme Court decision making. In most cases, justices reach different conclusions about the outcome for the parties. In even more cases, they differ over the legal rules they would establish. These differences, of course, are reflected in concurring and dissenting opinions.

Disagreement over specific decisions and broader lines of legal policy does not necessarily reflect personal conflict among the justices, nor does such disagreement necessarily lead to personal conflict. But the potential for such conflict always exists, as it does in other groups of people who work together on matters that involve high stakes.[93]

Yet justices also have incentives to limit frictions. Of course, a harmonious Court is a more pleasant place in which to work. Personal relations can also affect the decisional process. A Court in which conflicts are minimized finds it easier to achieve consensus in decisions. Such a Court also may function more efficiently because good interpersonal relations speed the process of reaching decisions and resolving internal problems. And justices who seek to win the support of their colleagues for the positions they favor certainly want to maintain amity with those colleagues. In part for these reasons, justices make some effort to defuse tensions and achieve good working relationships with each other.

Today, as always, it is difficult for people outside the Court to assess the extent of conflict within it. On the one hand, there are signs of significant conflict. Justices sometimes state their disagreements in opinions that attack other opinions, or even their authors, in strong terms. One federal judge concluded that "the printed abuse of colleagues is more common in the Supreme Court than in any court of appeals."[94] Some of the justices' out-of-court statements also suggest the existence of frictions. Yet it is easy to exaggerate the import of such expressions, and the justices themselves typically minimize their importance. Justice Ginsburg told a judicial conference in 1994 that "you have to appreciate that what appears to be a war of words, in fact, doesn't indicate any lack of friendship or lack of respect."[95] In the same year, Justice Scalia said in a lecture that

I doubt whether any two Justices have dissented from one another's opinions any more regularly, or any more sharply, than did my former colleague Justice William Brennan and I. I always considered him, however, one of my best friends on the Court, and I think that feeling was reciprocated.[96]

Looking at the available evidence, some observers have concluded that the current Court is significantly, and unusually, conflictual. Robert Bork, whose nomination to the Court was defeated in 1987, said in 1991 that the Court was "a snake pit." According to Bork, "they're locked in that building and they're fighting all the time."[97] That judgment may be accurate, but it may exaggerate the breadth and depth of conflict among the justices. And the Court today almost certainly is a happier group than it was in some past eras.

The Court's Environment

As members of Congress do their work, they constantly deal with people who want to influence them: constituents who seek help from the government, reporters who look for good stories, lobbyists who argue for the positions of interest groups, and executive branch officials who want to build support for their legislative proposals. Members could try to ignore all these people. But they do not, because their ability to stay in office and their effectiveness as legislators depend on building favorable relationships with constituents, interest groups, and others in their political environment.

The Supreme Court is a very different kind of institution. The justices make their decisions in relative isolation from people outside the Court. As Justice Harold Burton replied when asked about his move from Congress to the Court, "Have you ever gone direct from a circus to a monastery?"[98] This isolation stems in part from norms associated with courts in general and the Supreme Court in particular, norms that require a certain distance between the Court and those who seek to influence its decisions. Unlike members of Congress, the justices do not interact with lobbyists while they consider cases. Perhaps more important, the life term frees the justices from worries about maintaining their positions. Popular or unpopular, they can continue to do their work on the Court.

But this does not mean that the Court is completely insulated from its political and social environment. Because its decisions are important, people outside the Court care about those decisions, often a great deal. A wide range of individuals and groups try to influence those decisions. For their part, the justices may respond to the views and demands of people outside the Court. In fact, the various elements of the Court's environment do have a substantial impact on its decisions.

Mass Public Opinion

On many issues that come before the Supreme Court there is no public opinion to speak of. It is doubtful that many people knew or cared about the issues in *General Motors Corporation v. Tracy* (1997), which concerned the constitutionality of a tax exemption for natural gas sales by local public utilities that was not extended to independent marketers of natural gas. But many other decisions address salient issues such as crime and civil rights, issues on which a large segment of the public has strong views. And some decisions, such as the Court's major rulings on abortion, are highly visible and controversial in themselves.

Even on issues that do attract strong public views, we might not expect those views to influence justices who hold life terms. But justices might want popularity for its own sake. Justices also care about public regard for the Court, because high regard can help the Court in conflicts with other branches of government and increase people's willingness to carry out its decisions.

The Court itself sometimes indicates that it was influenced by public opinion, referring in its opinion to the views of the public on an issue or the need to preserve the Court's legitimacy with the public. The joint opinion in *Planned Parenthood v. Casey*, for instance, emphasized a concern with Court legitimacy.

TABLE 4-5
Selected Supreme Court Decisions Favoring the Government on Issues Related to Illegal Drugs, 1990–1996

Employment Division v. Smith (1990)
An Oregon statute that prohibits the use of the drug peyote, when applied to its use in a ceremony of the Native American Church, does not violate the constitutional protection of freedom of religion. (Vote 6–3)

Harmelin v. Michigan (1991)
A state law requiring a sentence of life imprisonment without the possibility of parole for possession of more than 650 grams of cocaine does not violate the Eighth Amendment prohibition of cruel and unusual punishment. (Vote 5–4)

United States v. Alvarez-Machain (1992)
The extradition treaty between the United States and Mexico does not prohibit the kidnapping of a suspect in the murder of a Drug Enforcement Administration agent and the forcible transportation of that suspect from Mexico to the United States for trial. (Vote 6–3)

Vernonia School District No. 47J v. Acton (1995)
A requirement that athletes at a public school take random drug tests even if there is no reason to suspect them as individuals does not constitute an unreasonable search under the Constitution. (Vote 6–3)

Whren v. United States (1996)
Police officers who have probable cause to stop a vehicle for traffic violations can search the vehicle for drugs even if the traffic violations were an excuse for the drug search. (Vote 9–0)

In other instances the Court adopts a line of policy that largely mirrors public attitudes. One example is public concern about illegal drugs. In the last decade the Court generally has approved of government actions aimed at controlling illegal drugs that are challenged as violations of civil liberties, on issues that range from drug testing to searches and seizures; Table 4-5 describes some of those decisions.

In part, such decisions reflect the Court's growing conservatism on civil liberties issues. But they also reflect the desire of some justices to support government action against what most people view as a major national problem. Dissenting in one of these cases, Justice Thurgood Marshall charged that the majority had been "swept away by society's obsession with stopping the scourge of illegal drugs."[99]

If Marshall was correct, it is uncertain why the Court was "swept away." Perhaps some of the justices sought to take positions that were popular with the general public and with the other branches of government. But it may be that the justices had simply come to share the concern about drugs that pervaded American society as a whole. If so, this line of policy is similar in its source to the Court's growing support for equality between women and men.

Beyond specific issues, the Court might follow general tides of public opinion. As the public moves to the political left or right, so may the Court. For instance, some commentators perceived that the voters' election of new Republican majorities to both houses of Congress in 1994 influenced the Court. "Once more," one writer said, "the Justices have fallen smartly in step with the voters."[100] Scholars have disagreed about the extent to which the Court does follow ideological trends among the public,[101] but it is at least plausible that they do so.

On the other hand, the Court sometimes exhibits a striking independence from public opinion. Examples of highly unpopular decisions include the Court's rulings limiting religious exercises in public schools, striking down state and federal laws against flag burning, and holding that states could not establish term limits for members of Congress. The justices sometimes try to present such rulings in a way that will limit criticism, indicating that they do care about public reactions. In *Texas v. Johnson* (1989), one of the flag burning decisions, both Justice Brennan's majority opinion and Justice Kennedy's concurring opinion stressed their authors' reverence for the flag. Still, the Court's majority was willing to take action that ran strongly contrary to public views.

Compared with the legislative branch, then, public opinion has a limited impact on the Court. But that impact is real. As Chief Justice Rehnquist concluded:

Judges, so long as they are relatively normal human beings, can no more escape being influenced by public opinion in the long run than can people working at other jobs. And if a judge on coming to the bench were to decide to hermetically seal himself off from all manifestations of public opinion, he would accomplish very little; he would not be influenced by current public opinion, but instead would be influenced by the state of public opinion at the time he came to the bench.[102]

Elite Opinion: The Mass Media and the Legal Community

Along with general public opinion, the opinions of particular groups may also have some effect on the Supreme Court. Two groups whose opinions are potentially relevant to all justices are the mass media and the legal community.

After his confirmation as a justice, Clarence Thomas reportedly canceled all his newspaper subscriptions.[103] But most justices seem to pay attention to coverage of the Court by the mass media.[104] They read and react to stories about the Court, and they sometimes try to influence media coverage. Some justices meet with reporters, though often in off-the-record sessions.

All this attention to the mass media suggests that they may influence what the justices do. The media are important as the Court's primary source of information on public opinion and on the views of other policy makers, and justices' interest in favorable coverage might influence some of the choices they make in deciding cases.

Some conservatives believe that the media have a more pervasive effect. In their view, Supreme Court reporters are primarily liberals who praise justices for taking liberal positions. Thus justices may be tempted to move to the left to win approval in the short term and a favorable image in history. Conservative commentators have labeled this impact the "Greenhouse Effect," after Linda Greenhouse, long-time Court reporter for the *New York Times*. One commentator suggested that Justice Kennedy had become more liberal in his positions because of the Greenhouse Effect.[105]

The legal community is important as a professional reference group. Justices draw many of their acquaintances from this community, and most justices interact a good deal with lawyers and lower court judges. Lawyers are also the primary source of expert evaluation of the Court, particularly through articles in the law reviews published by law schools and edited by their students. The legal community helps to make legal considerations important to the justices in reaching decisions. And if a particular view of legal issues is dominant among lawyers or in a segment of the bar that is important to a justice, this view may affect the one that the justice adopts.

The law reviews can have another kind of impact as well. Because law review articles are often discussed in briefs and read by justices and clerks, they constitute one source of the information that enters into the Court's decisions. Justices frequently cite law review articles in support of their positions, and on occasion articles may help to determine their positions. For their part, members of the Court sometimes write law review articles to influence the legal community. By doing so, they underline the importance of that community to them.

Litigants and Interest Groups

Simply by bringing cases to the Supreme Court, litigants and interest groups can have an impact on the Court's policies. Once the Court has accepted a case, they may influence its decision on the merits. Because of the requirement that communications to the Court go through formal channels, the potential for such influence comes primarily through advocacy in written briefs and oral arguments.

Certainly justices pay attention to the material provided by litigants and interest groups. Opinions for the Court address the arguments raised by the parties to the case, and they often refer to positions taken in amicus briefs as well. When justices question lawyers closely during oral argument, they are often looking for responses to strong arguments by the other side.

One result is that the way lawyers frame arguments in a case can affect the justices' thinking and ultimately their decisions. Lee Epstein and Joseph Kobylka have argued that opponents of the death penalty and of state restrictions on abortion could have been more successful with the Court if they had taken positions that better addressed the concerns of the Court's moderates.[106]

More broadly, as discussed in Chapter 3, the quality of advocacy on the two sides of a case has an impact. Once again, the federal government provides a good example. In the Court's decisions on the merits in its 1995 term, the government had a 63 percent success rate, the same as its overall success rate over the last half century.[107] One source of that success, perhaps the most important source, is the expertise of the experienced advocates in the solicitor general's office.[108]

Undoubtedly, the justices respond primarily to the arguments in cases rather than to the identities of the litigants and interest groups that present those arguments. Yet it is likely that at least some justices react positively or negatively to the participants in cases. Such reactions might not be conscious, but they could affect a justice's perception of the issues sufficiently to make a difference.

Congress and the President

Several sets of policy-making institutions are important to the Court. Lower courts and some administrative agencies implement the Court's decisions. The president plays a part in enforcing decisions, helps to shape public attitudes toward the Court, and sometimes interacts with justices. Congress has significant power over the Court as an institution, as well as the power to change Court-made policies. Thus the justices may take these other policy makers into account—especially Congress and the president—when they cast votes and write opinions.

Congress. Congressional powers over the Court range from its ability to reverse the Court's interpretations of statutes to its control over salary increases for the justices. Because of this array of powers, the justices have good reason to think about congressional reactions to their decisions. Relations with Congress can affect their prestige and their comfort. And justices who think strategically in a broad sense, who care about the ultimate impact of the Court's policies, want to avoid congressional actions that undercut those policies.

The most obvious way that the Court could act to maintain good relations with Congress is to limit serious conflicts between the two institutions. From time to time during its history, the Court's general line of policy has aroused dissatisfaction in Congress that was sufficiently broad and deep to generate a serious threat of concrete action against the Court. In several of these periods, the Court acted to reduce this dissatisfaction and thus the threat to it.[109]

The first such period was the early nineteenth century, when John Marshall's Court faced congressional attacks because of its activist policies. Marshall, as the Court's dominant member, was careful to limit the frequency of decisions that would further anger its opponents. Probably the most dramatic episode of this type, discussed in Chapter 1, was the Court's shift from opposition to support of New Deal legislation in 1937 while Congress was considering President Roosevelt's Court-packing plan. In the late 1950s, members of Congress reacted to the Court's expansions of civil liberties by seeking to override its policies and limit its jurisdiction; the Court reversed some of its own positions and thereby helped to quiet congressional attacks on the Court.

There have been no clear retreats of this sort since the 1950s. Indeed, the Court has exhibited considerable resistance to congressional pressures. It has been attacked in Congress for its positions on a variety of civil liberties issues, including school desegregation, legislative districting, abortion, school prayer, and flag burning. On each of these issues efforts have been made to overturn the Court's decisions, to limit its jurisdiction, or both. Yet in the face of these attacks the Court has adhered to many of its unpopular policies, and it changed others only when its collective policy preferences became more conservative. Recent history is thus a reminder that the justices do not automatically shy away from decisions that create conflict with Congress.

Aside from its responses to open conflicts with Congress, the Court might respond strategically to Congress in a more routine way. The Court's decisions interpreting statutes are the most vulnerable, since Congress and the president can override them simply by enacting a new statute. Thus justices might try to calculate whether their preferred interpretation of a statute would make enough members of Congress sufficiently unhappy to produce such an override. If so, these justices would modify their interpretations to avoid that result. By making that implicit compromise with Congress, they could get the best possible result under the circumstances: not the interpretation of a statute that they favor most, but one that is closer to their preferences than the new statute that Congress would have adopted if the Court's decision had triggered an override.

On the other hand, it may be that most justices do not care that much whether Congress overrides their decisions, except on issues that are particularly important to them. Or the justices might feel that the chances and form of an override are so difficult to predict that there is little to be gained by taking Congress into account when they interpret statutes. In any case, it is not yet clear how often justices take this strategic approach.[110]

The President. Presidents have multifaceted relationships with the Supreme Court, and these relationships provide several sources of potential influence. Two of these sources, discussed in earlier chapters, are quite important. The appointment power gives presidents considerable ability to determine the Court's direction. And the president helps to shape the federal government's litigation policy, and thus affects the Court's decisions, through appointment of the solicitor general and occasional intervention in specific cases.

Personal relationships between justices and presidents are a third source of influence. Some members of the Court were close associates of the presidents who later selected them. And justices may interact with presidents while serving on the bench. Some, such as Abe Fortas, have been frequent visitors to the White House for advisory or social purposes. Such relationships hardly compel justices to support the president's position in litigation, but they may affect a justice's responses to cases with which the president is concerned.

Finally, presidents can help to shape the Court's impact by influencing both the public's view of the Court and responses of other institutions to the Court's decisions. Because presidents may exert such influence, justices have reason to keep the peace with the president just as they do with Congress. As a result, presidents undoubtedly exert a subtle influence on the Court's policy choices.

But this does not mean that presidents can get what they want from the Court simply by pressuring it. During the Reagan administration, both the president and Justice Department officials criticized the Court and some of its justices, but it does not appear that these attacks caused the Court to retreat at all. And Dwight Eisenhower was unsuccessful in a rare presidential attempt to influence a justice directly, when he argued with his appointee Earl Warren against mandating school desegregation. At one point Warren reportedly responded, "You mind your business, and I'll mind mine."[111] This example illustrates a general point: the considerable power of the president and Congress over the Supreme Court ordinarily falls far short of control over the Court's policies.

Conclusion

Of all the considerations that may influence the Supreme Court's decisions, I have given primary emphasis to the justices' policy preferences. Because the application of the law is usually ambiguous and because environmental constraints are generally weak, the justices have considerable freedom to choose positions in accordance with their own conceptions of good policy. Thus the Court's membership and the process of selecting the justices have the greatest impact on the Court's direction.

If justices' preferences explain a great deal, they do not explain everything. The law and the political environment rule out some possible options for the Court at a given time on a particular issue, and they influence the justices' choices among the options that remain. The group life of the Court affects the behavior of individual justices and thus the Court's collective decisions. In particular, the justices regularly adjust their positions to win support from colleagues and help build majorities. These forces are reflected in results that might seem surprising: strikingly liberal decisions from a seemingly conservative Court, and the maintenance of precedents even when most justices no longer favor the policies they embody.

The discussion of influences on decisions began with a look at *Planned Parenthood v. Casey,* the Court's 1992 decision on state regulation of abortion. That decision illustrates the multiple forces that determine what the Court does and the intertwining of these forces. We can discuss specific factors one at a time, but ultimately they operate together in complicated ways to shape the Court's decisions. Those who want to understand why the Court does what it does must accept the complexity of the process by which justices make their choices.

NOTES

1. *Old Chief v. United States,* 136 L. Ed. 2d 574, 595 (1997).
2. Sarah Henry, "When I Stood Before the Supreme Court," *California Lawyer,* October 1996, 48.
3. Bernard Schwartz, *Decision: How the Supreme Court Decides Cases* (New York: Oxford University Press, 1996), 14.
4. See Joan Biskupic, "Separating the Yakkers from the Silent Types on the Court," *Washington Post,* April 30, 1993, A23.
5. Joan Biskupic, "At Long Last, Seniority," *Washington Post,* March 20, 1995, A15.
6. David Savage, "Hate Speech, Hate Crimes, and the First Amendment," in *A Year in the Life of the Supreme Court,* ed. Rodney A. Smolla (Durham, N.C.: Duke University Press, 1995), 195.
7. Joan Biskupic, "Nothing Subtle About Scalia, the Combative Conservative," *Washington Post,* February 18, 1997, A4.

8. Saundra Torry, "Arguably, Counsel Fell Short of a Supreme Moment," *Washington Post,* January 20, 1997, F7. In the news story, the lawyer's name was inserted in the Rehnquist quotation for clarity. The case was *Clinton v. Jones* (1997).

9. William H. Rehnquist, *The Supreme Court: How It Was, How It Is* (New York: William Morrow, 1987), 277.

10. This discussion of the conference is based in part on Rehnquist, *The Supreme Court,* 289–295.

11. Schwartz, *Decision,* 42.

12. Rehnquist, *The Supreme Court,* 295.

13. Ruth Bader Ginsburg, "Remarks for American Law Institute Annual Dinner May 19, 1994," *Saint Louis University Law Review* 38 (Summer 1994): 887.

14. Beverly Blair Cook, "Justice Brennan and the Institutionalization of Dissent Assignment," *Judicature* 79 (July–August 1995): 17–23.

15. Antonin Scalia, "The Dissenting Opinion," *Journal of Supreme Court History,* 1994, 42.

16. *U.S. Department of Justice v. Reporters Committee for Freedom of the Press,* 489 U.S. 749, 780 (1989).

17. *Lewis v. United States,* 135 L. Ed. 2d 590, 598 (1996).

18. David G. Savage, *Turning Right: The Making of the Rehnquist Supreme Court* (New York: John Wiley & Sons, 1992), 328.

19. Joan Biskupic, "The Court of Last Resort," *Washington Post,* October 9, 1996, H5.

20. Robert L. Stern, Eugene Gressman, Stephen M. Shapiro, and Kenneth S. Geller, *Supreme Court Practice,* 7th ed. (Washington, D.C.: Bureau of National Affairs, 1993), 620–621.

21. Jeffrey Rosen, "The Agonizer," *The New Yorker,* November 11, 1996, 87. The decision process in *Casey* is also discussed in David J. Garrow, "Justice Souter Emerges," *New York Times Magazine,* September 25, 1994, 36–40; and James F. Simon, *The Center Holds: The Power Struggle Inside the Rehnquist Court* (New York: Simon & Schuster, 1995), 163–166.

22. Tony Mauro, "Solicitor General Has Subpar Season," *Legal Times,* September 4, 1995, 9.

23. Walter Murphy, *Elements of Judicial Strategy* (Chicago: University of Chicago Press, 1964), 44 n.*. See Jack Knight and Lee Epstein, "The Norm of *Stare Decisis,*" *American Journal of Political Science* 40 (November 1996): 1018–1035.

24. *Bennis v. Michigan,* 134 L. Ed. 2d 68, 80 (1996).

25. Joan Biskupic, "Court Reluctantly Affirms 'Reasonable Doubt' Jury Instruction," *Washington Post,* March 23, 1994, A3. The case was *Victor v. Nebraska* (1994).

26. See *Department of Defense v. Federal Labor Relations Authority,* 510 U.S. 487, 503, 509 (1994).

27. Cass R. Sunstein, "The Spirit of the Laws," *New Republic,* March 11, 1991, 32.

28. 18 *U.S. Code* sec. 924(c)(1). See Carlos E. Gonzales, "Reinterpreting Statutory Interpretation," *North Carolina Law Review* 74 (March 1996): 588–590.

29. Linda Greenhouse, "Justices Explore the Elusive Meaning of a Simple Word," *New York Times,* October 31, 1995, C20.

30. *Thunder Basin Coal Co. v. Reich,* 510 U.S. 200, 219 (1994). See Antonin

Scalia, *A Matter of Interpretation: Federal Courts and the Law* (Princeton, N.J.: Princeton University Press, 1997), 14–37.

31. *United States v. Mezzanatto*, 130 L. Ed. 2d 697, 711 (1995).

32. This count is based on the list in Saul Brenner and Harold J. Spaeth, *Stare Indecisis: The Alteration of Precedent on the Supreme Court, 1946–1992* (New York: Cambridge University Press, 1995), 112–121; supplemented by the lists in the annual *Supreme Court Yearbook*, written by Kenneth Jost and published by Congressional Quarterly.

33. *Maryland v. Wirtz* (1968); *National League of Cities v. Usery* (1976); *Garcia v. San Antonio Metropolitan Transit Authority* (1985).

34. Jeffrey A. Segal and Harold J. Spaeth, "The Influence of *Stare Decisis* on the Votes of United States Supreme Court Justices," *American Journal of Political Science* 40 (November 1996): 971–1003; Saul Brenner and Marc Stier, "Retesting Segal and Spaeth's *Stare Decisis* Model," *American Journal of Political Science* 40 (November 1996): 1036–1048; Donald R. Songer and Stefanie A. Lindquist, "Not the Whole Story: The Impact of Justices' Values on Supreme Court Decision Making," *American Journal of Political Science* 40 (November 1996): 1049–1063.

35. *Fulton Corporation v. Faulkner* (1996).

36. *Kansas Department of Corrections v. Brinkman* (1994).

37. Quoted in Alpheus Thomas Mason, *The Supreme Court from Taft to Burger* (Baton Rouge: Louisiana State University Press, 1979), 293.

38. Savage, *Turning Right*, 381–382. The 1991 case was *Arizona v. Fulminante*.

39. Jeffrey A. Segal and Albert D. Cover, "Ideological Values and the Votes of U.S. Supreme Court Justices," *American Political Science Review* 83 (June 1989): 557–565; Jeffrey A. Segal, Lee Epstein, Charles M. Cameron, and Harold J. Spaeth, "Ideological Values and the Votes of Justices Revisited," *Journal of Politics* 57 (August 1995): 812–823.

40. See Jeffrey Toobin, "The Burden of Clarence Thomas," *The New Yorker,* September 27, 1993, 38–51; and Jeffrey Rosen, "Moving On," *The New Yorker,* April 29–May 6, 1996, 66–73.

41. A good example is Jeffrey A. Segal and Harold J. Spaeth, *The Supreme Court and the Attitudinal Model* (New York: Cambridge University Press, 1993).

42. John A. Jenkins, "The Partisan: A Talk with Justice Rehnquist," *New York Times Magazine,* March 3, 1985, 31.

43. Savage, *Turning Right*, 260.

44. See Lee Epstein and Jack Knight, *The Choices Justices Make* (Washington, D.C.: CQ Press, 1998); and Jeffrey A. Segal, "Separation-of-Powers Games in the Positive Theory of Congress and Courts," *American Political Science Review* 91 (March 1997): 28–44.

45. The cases were, respectively, *Field v. Mans* (1995) and *Commissioner v. Lundy* (1996).

46. *Callins v. Collins*, 510 U.S. 1141 (1994). The earlier decisions were *Furman v. Georgia* (1972) and *Gregg v. Georgia* (1976).

47. Figures on agreement between Blackmun and his colleagues are taken from the annual statistics on the Supreme Court term in the November issues of *Harvard Law Review*, vols. 85–100 (1972–1987). See also "The Changing Social Vision of Justice Blackmun," *Harvard Law Review* 96 (1983): 717–736.

48. Joseph F. Kobylka, "The Judicial Odyssey of Harry Blackmun: The Dynamics of Individual-Level Change on the U.S. Supreme Court" (Paper presented at the annual conference of the Midwest Political Science

Association, Chicago, April 1992); Stephen L. Wasby, "Justice Harry A. Blackmun: Transformation from 'Minnesota Twin' to Independent Voice," in *The Burger Court: Political and Judicial Profiles*, ed. Charles M. Lamb and Stephen C. Halpern (Urbana: University of Illinois Press, 1991), 63–99.

49. Terry Eastland, "The Tempting of Justice Kennedy," *American Spectator* 26 (February 1993): 32–37.

50. *United States v. Virginia* (1996).

51. Richard A. Posner, "A Tribute to Justice William J. Brennan, Jr.," *Harvard Law Review* 104 (November 1990): 13.

52. Segal and Spaeth, "Influence of *Stare Decisis*," 983–984.

53. These figures were calculated by the author from the lists of overturnings in Congressional Research Service, *The Constitution of the United States: Analysis and Interpretation* (Washington, D.C.: Government Printing Office, 1987), 2123–2127, and *1990 Supplement* (Washington, D.C.: Government Printing Office, 1991), 265–266. These lists differ somewhat from that in Brenner and Spaeth, *Stare Indecisis*, discussed earlier.

54. See Richard Kluger, *Simple Justice: The History of Brown v. Board of Education and Black America's Struggle for Equality* (New York: Alfred A. Knopf, 1976), 582–699. The quotation is from William O. Douglas, *The Court Years 1939–1975: The Autobiography of William O. Douglas* (New York: Random House, 1980), 115.

55. See David J. Garrow, *Liberty and Sexuality: The Right to Privacy and the Making of Roe v. Wade* (New York: Macmillan, 1994), 473–599.

56. Linda Greenhouse, "Name-Calling in the Supreme Court: When the Justices Vent Their Spleen, Is There a Social Cost?" *New York Times*, July 28, 1989, B10.

57. Schwartz, *Decision*, 42.

58. Toobin, "Burden of Clarence Thomas," 43.

59. William H. Rehnquist, "Chief Justices I Never Knew," *Hastings Constitutional Law Quarterly* 3 (Summer 1976): 647.

60. Lee Epstein and Jack Knight, "Documenting Strategic Interactions on the U.S. Supreme Court" (Paper presented at the annual conference of the American Political Science Association, Chicago, August–September 1995), 33. See also Sandra L. Wood, "Bargaining and Negotiation on the Burger Court" (Paper presented at the annual conference of the American Political Science Association, San Francisco, August–September 1996).

61. J. Woodford Howard, Jr., "On the Fluidity of Judicial Choice," *American Political Science Review* 62 (March 1968): 43–56. See also Saul Brenner and Robert H. Dorff, "The Attitudinal Model and Fluidity Voting on the United States Supreme Court: A Theoretical Perspective," *Journal of Theoretical Politics* 4 (1992): 195–205.

62. Forrest Maltzman and Paul J. Wahlbeck, "Strategic Policy Considerations and Voting Fluidity on the Burger Court," *American Political Science Review* 90 (September 1996): 587.

63. Saul Brenner, "Fluidity on the Supreme Court: 1956–1967," *American Journal of Political Science* 26 (May 1982): 390.

64. Paul J. Wahlbeck, James F. Spriggs II, and Forrest Maltzman, "Marshalling the Court: Bargaining and Accommodation on the U.S. Supreme Court" (Paper presented at the annual conference of the Western Political Science Association, San Francisco, March 1996), 18–19.

65. Bernard Schwartz, *The Unpublished Opinions of the Burger Court* (New York: Oxford University Press, 1988); Schwartz, *The Unpublished Opinions of the Rehnquist Court* (New York: Oxford University Press, 1996).

66. Douglas, *The Court Years*, 18.

67. "The Court's Uncompromising Libertarian," *Time Magazine*, November 24, 1975, 69. See also Melvin I. Urofsky, "Getting the Job Done: William O. Douglas and Collegiality in the Supreme Court," in *He Shall Not Pass This Way Again: The Legacy of Justice William O. Douglas*, ed. Stephen L. Wasby (Pittsburgh: University of Pittsburgh Press, 1990), 33–37.

68. James F. Simon, *The Antagonists: Hugo Black, Felix Frankfurter and Civil Liberties in Modern America* (New York: Simon & Schuster, 1989), 249.

69. Hunter R. Clark, *Justice Brennan: The Great Conciliator* (New York: Birch Lane Press, 1995), 7.

70. Ibid.; Kim Isaac Eisler, *A Justice for All: William J. Brennan, Jr., and the Decisions That Transformed America* (New York: Simon & Schuster, 1993), esp. 189.

71. Jurek Martin and George Graham, "Almost a Law Unto Themselves," *Financial Times*, April 9, 1994, 7.

72. Alexander Wohl, "What's Left," *American Bar Association Journal* 77 (February 1991): 42.

73. Nina Totenberg, "A Tribute to Justice William J. Brennan, Jr.," *Harvard Law Review* 104 (November 1990): 37.

74. Bernard Schwartz, *A History of the Supreme Court* (New York: Oxford University Press, 1993), 318.

75. Bradley C. Canon, "Justice John Paul Stevens: The Lone Ranger in a Black Robe," in *The Burger Court*, ed. Lamb and Halpern, 373.

76. See Christopher E. Smith, *Justice Antonin Scalia and the Supreme Court's Conservative Moment* (Westport, Conn.: Praeger, 1993).

77. John C. Jeffries, Jr., *Justice Lewis F. Powell, Jr.* (New York: Charles Scribner's Sons, 1994), 534.

78. *United States v. Virginia*, 135 L. Ed. 2d 735, 787 (1996).

79. *Board of County Commissioners v. Umbehr*, 135 L. Ed 2d 843, 858 (1996).

80. Alex Kozinski, "My Pizza with Nino," *Cardozo Law Review* 12 (June 1991): 1583–1591. The quotation is on 1588.

81. Rehnquist, "Chief Justices I Never Knew," 637.

82. Forrest Maltzman and Paul J. Wahlbeck, "Hail to the Chief: Opinion Assignment on the Supreme Court" (Paper presented at the annual conference of the American Political Science Association, Chicago, August–September 1995), 11.

83. This discussion of criteria for opinion assignment is based largely on the findings for the 1953–1990 period in Maltzman and Wahlbeck, "Hail to the Chief"; and Maltzman and Wahlbeck, "May It Please the Chief? Opinion Assignments in the Rehnquist Court," *American Journal of Political Science* 40 (May 1996): 421–443.

84. David J. Garrow, "The Rehnquist Reins," *New York Times Magazine*, October 6, 1996, 68.

85. Ruth Marcus, "Alumni Brennan, Blackmun Greet Harvard Law Freshmen," *Washington Post*, September 6, 1986, 2.

86. Tony Mauro, "The Highs and Lows of the 1992 Court," *Legal Times*, December 28, 1993, 14.

87. Bernard Schwartz, *Behind Bakke: Affirmative Action and the Supreme Court* (New York: New York University Press, 1988), 99.

88. Bernard Schwartz, *The Ascent of Pragmatism: The Burger Court in Action* (Reading, Mass.: Addison-Wesley, 1990), 14.

89. Garrow, *Liberty and Sexuality*, 558.

90. Jeffries, *Justice Lewis F. Powell, Jr.*, 545.

91. This discussion of Rehnquist is based in part on Schwartz, *A History of the Supreme Court*, 364–367; Savage, *Turning Right;* David G. Savage, "The Rehnquist Court," *Los Angeles Times Magazine*, September 29, 1991, 12–16, 38, 40; and Garrow, "The Rehnquist Reins," 65–71, 82, 85.

92. Henry J. Abraham, *Justices and Presidents: A Political History of Appointments to the Supreme Court*, 3d ed. (New York: Oxford University Press, 1992), 351.

93. See Phillip J. Cooper, *Battles on the Bench: Conflict Inside the Supreme Court* (Lawrence: University of Kansas Press, 1995).

94. Richard A. Posner, *The Federal Courts: Challenge and Reform* (Cambridge, Mass.: Harvard University Press, 1996), 355.

95. Joan Biskupic, "Female Justices Attest to Fraternity on Bench," *Washington Post*, August 21, 1994, A24.

96. Scalia, "The Dissenting Opinion," 41.

97. Scott Winokur, "Justice and Balance," *San Francisco Examiner*, March 3, 1991, E-5.

98. Mary Frances Berry, *Stability, Security, and Continuity: Mr. Justice Burton and Decision-Making in the Supreme Court, 1945–1958* (Westport, Conn.: Greenwood Press, 1978), 27.

99. *Skinner v. Railway Labor Executives' Association*, 489 U.S. 602, 654 (1989).

100. Jeffrey Toobin, "Chicken Supreme," *The New Yorker*, August 14, 1995, 82.

101. See William Mishler and Reginald S. Sheehan, "The Supreme Court as a Countermajoritarian Institution? The Impact of Public Opinion on Supreme Court Decisions," *American Political Science Review* 87 (March 1993): 87–101; Helmut Norpoth and Jeffrey A. Segal, "Popular Impact on Supreme Court Decisions: Comment," *American Political Science Review* 88 (September 1994): 711–716; and Roy B. Flemming and B. Dan Wood, "The Public and the Supreme Court: Individual Justice Responsiveness to American Policy Moods," *American Journal of Political Science* 41 (April 1997): 468–498.

102. William H. Rehnquist, "Constitutional Law and Public Opinion" (Talk presented at Suffolk University School of Law, Boston, April 10, 1986), 40–41.

103. Mauro, "The Highs and Lows of the 1992 Court," 14.

104. This discussion of the mass media is based in part on Richard Davis, *Decisions and Images: The Supreme Court and the Press* (Englewood Cliffs, N.J.: Prentice-Hall, 1994).

105. Eastland, "The Tempting of Justice Kennedy." See Thomas Sowell, "Blackmun Plays to the Crowd," *St. Louis Post Dispatch*, March 4, 1994, 7B; and Robert H. Bork, "Again, a Struggle for the Soul of the Court," *New York Times*, July 8, 1992, A19.

106. Lee Epstein and Joseph F. Kobylka, *The Supreme Court and Legal Change: Abortion and the Death Penalty* (Chapel Hill: University of North Carolina Press, 1992).

107. The success rate for the 1946–1994 terms is from Lee Epstein, Jeffrey A. Segal, Harold J. Spaeth, and Thomas G. Walker, *The Supreme Court Compendium*, 2d ed. (Washington, D.C.: Congressional Quarterly, 1996), 631.

108. Kevin T. McGuire, "Explaining Executive Success in the U.S. Supreme Court" (Paper presented at the Conference on the Scientific Study of Judicial Politics, St. Louis, November 1996).

109. Gerald N. Rosenberg, "Judicial Independence and the Reality of Political Power," *Review of Politics* 54 (Summer 1992): 369–398.

110. For contrasting arguments and evidence, see Pablo T. Spiller and Rafael Gely, "Congressional Control or Judicial Independence: The Determinants of U.S. Supreme Court Labor-Relations Decisions, 1949–1988," *RAND Journal of Economics* 23 (1992): 463–492; and Segal, "Separation-of-Powers Games."

111. Juan Williams, "The Triumph of Thurgood Marshall," *Washington Post Magazine,* January 7, 1990, 19.

Chapter 5

Policy Outputs

I n the preceding chapter I examined why Supreme Court justices make their policy choices and how they do so. This
chapter focuses on the policies they choose. I begin by looking
at the Court's areas of activity and the policy areas it emphasizes.
In the next two sections I discuss the substance of the Court's
policies in those areas by examining the Court's activism and
ideological direction. In the final section, I consider explanations for historical patterns in Supreme Court policy.

Areas of Activity

The Court's Current Activity

The Emphases. During any given term, the Supreme Court resolves a broad range of issues in fields as varied as antitrust, environmental protection, and freedom of speech. In this sense
the Court's agenda is highly diverse. But the Court generally de-
votes most of its efforts to a few policy fields. To a considerable
degree, then, the Court is a specialist.

The content of the Court's agenda can be illustrated with the
cases that it heard in the 1996 term. It is useful first to describe
the issues in a fairly representative sample of cases decided during that term:

1. Whether the Fourth Amendment allows a blanket drug-
felony exception to the requirement that police officers knock
on the door of a residence and announce their identity before
attempting forcible entry. (*Richards v. Wisconsin,* 1997)

2. Whether a federal court's redistricting plan for the Georgia congressional delegation violated the Constitution because of variation in population among districts or the Voting Rights Act because of the racial composition of districts. (*Abrams v. Johnson*, 1997)

3. Whether a California law regulating wages in apprenticeship programs run by contractors on public works projects was preempted by the federal Employee Retirement Income Security Act. (*California Division of Labor Standards v. Dillingham*, 1997)

4. Whether a person who trades in securities for personal profit, and who used confidential information that was misappropriated in breach of a fiduciary duty, is guilty of securities fraud. (*United States v. O'Hagan*, 1997)

5. Whether a federal statute requiring states to operate a child support enforcement program with certain features in order to receive certain federal funds gives individuals the right to sue states for failing to comply with that requirement. (*Blessing v. Freestone*, 1997)

6. Whether a Supreme Court decision holding that judges and jurors could not take into account inappropriate aggravating circumstances in determining whether to impose the death penalty applied to a prisoner whose conviction had become final before that decision. (*Lambrix v. Singletary*, 1997)

7. Whether, under the Fourteenth Amendment, a state could prevent a parent from appealing a decision terminating her parental rights because she could not afford the fees charged for an appeal. (*M.L.B. v. S.L.J.*, 1996)

8. Whether punitive damages received in a personal injury case are subject to the federal income tax. (*O'Gilvie v. United States*, 1996)

9. Whether a federal judge's limitation of activities by protesters at abortion clinics to the areas outside "buffer zones" violated the First Amendment. (*Schenck v. Pro-Choice Network*, 1997)

10. Whether certain transactions in options to buy or sell foreign currency are exempt from regulation under the Commodity Exchange Act. (*Dunn v. Commodity Futures Trading Commission*, 1997)

TABLE 5-1

Characteristics of Decisions by the Supreme Court with Full Opinions, 1996 Term

Characteristic	Number	Percentage
Number of decisions	89	—
Cases from lower federal courts	79	89
Cases from state courts	9	10
Original cases	1	1
Federal government party[a]	33	37
State or local government party[a]	40	45
No government party	16	18
Constitutional issue present[b]	46	52
No constitutional issue	43	48
Civil liberties issue present[b]	48	54
No civil liberties issue	41	46
Criminal cases[c]	23	26
Civil cases	66	74

Note: The data are based on listings of cases in *United States Supreme Court Reports, Lawyer's Edition.* Consolidated cases decided with one set of opinions were counted once.

[a] Cases with both a federal government party and another government party were listed as federal government. Government as party includes agencies and individual government officials.

[b] Cases were counted as having constitutional or civil liberties issues if the parties raised those issues, even if the Court decided them on the basis of other issues.

[c] Includes actions brought by prisoners to challenge the legality of their convictions but excludes cases concerning rights of prisoners.

Table 5-1 provides a more systematic picture of the Court's agenda in the 1996 term by summarizing the attributes of the eighty-nine decisions with full opinions in that term. The distribution of cases by category is similar to the distribution in other recent terms.

The federal government or one of its agencies was a party in a large minority of cases, and even more often a state or local government was a party. Moreover, most of the disputes between private parties were based directly on government policy, such as regulation of labor-management relations and protection against discrimination.

There were about equal numbers of constitutional and non-constitutional cases. Observers of the Court tend to focus on its interpretations of the Constitution, which often involve fundamental issues about the structure and power of government. But the Court also acts as interpreter of federal statutes, adjudicating what are often important disputes about their meaning.

In the 1996 term, as has been true for three decades, the Court's primary area of activity was civil liberties. As in earlier discussions, the term *civil liberties* refers here to three general types of rights: procedural rights of people involved in government proceedings; the right of disadvantaged groups to equal treatment; and certain "substantive" rights, the most important of which are freedom of expression and freedom of religion.

Related to the Court's civil liberties emphasis is an interest in criminal law and procedure. In recent years more than one-quarter of the Court's decisions have fallen in this area. Some criminal cases involve statutory interpretation, but a large majority concern constitutional rights of due process.

The list of representative cases from the 1996 term illustrates two other areas in which the Court is active. Outside of civil liberties, the largest number of cases concern economic issues. While most civil liberties cases are based on constitutional questions, economic cases generally involve statutory interpretation. Most of these cases arise from government regulation of economic activity, such as labor-management relations, antitrust, and environmental protection. Issues related to tax law are also common.

Another major subject of Court activity is federalism, the division of power between federal and state governments. Federalism overlaps with other categories, and most federalism cases concern economic issues. A common issue in this category, illustrated by the *Dillingham* case (number 3 in the list above), is whether federal legislation on economic matters preempts state law.

Thus the Court deals with a wide range of matters, from the procedural rights of criminal defendants to the meaning of provisions in the federal tax laws. But the Court gives particular attention to some areas of policy. Most striking is its concentration on civil liberties. Although civil liberties cases are quite varied, the fact that half of the Court's decisions concern this single kind of issue is an indication of the Court's specialization.

Change in the Court's Agenda

Several forces shape the Court's agenda. The most direct force is the interests of the justices themselves, but also important are federal legislation, patterns of litigation, and social trends. As these forces change, so does the agenda. The Court's attention to specific categories of cases may increase or decline over several years. Over long periods, the agenda as a whole may undergo fundamental change.[1]

Changes in Specific Areas. Perhaps the most common source of specific change in the Court's agenda is a decision by the Court or a congressional statute that opens up an area of activity or expands an existing area. The legal change creates new issues that the Court ultimately chooses to resolve.

In the past few decades, the Court has issued decisions that opened up many new areas of civil liberties issues. This was true of several areas involving defendants' rights: search and seizure, questioning of suspects, and the death penalty. In each of those areas the Court had heard cases in the past, but the establishment of a new right or the raising of a new set of questions in the 1960s and 1970s encouraged litigants to bring cases to the Court and made it imperative for the Court to hear some of these cases. Because of the growing number of criminal prosecutions and the complexity of issues in criminal procedure, these areas have remained significant sources of business for the Court.

Some pieces of legislation also open up new areas. Until Congress legislated against employment discrimination, there was little basis for bringing discrimination cases to court. Then Congress did adopt several statutes prohibiting employment discrimination, the most important of which was Title VII of the Civil Rights Act of 1964. Large numbers of cases were filed in federal court under these statutes, inevitably creating questions of interpretation for the statutes. As a result, the Court has decided several dozen cases. The number of employment discrimination cases in the Court was highest from the early 1970s to the early 1980s, when many basic questions under Title VII and other statutes had to be resolved.

FIGURE 5-1

Supreme Court Decisions on Employment Discrimination and on
Employees' Pension Rights under ERISA, 1966–1995 Terms

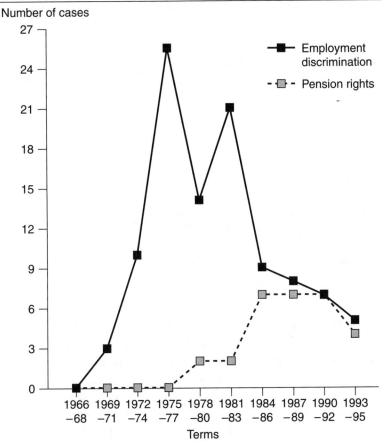

Number of cases

Source: Harold Spaeth's U.S. Supreme Court Judicial Database, updated by the author.

Note: Cases are included if the Court decided them after oral argument.

A similar process occurred with the Employee Retirement
Income Security Act (ERISA) of 1974, which gave rights to
workers regarding their pension plans. The resulting legal issues led the Court to accept a substantial number of ERISA
cases, more than thirty by now, so that the pension rights of employees are a staple of the Court's agenda. This development
and the pattern of employment discrimination cases are shown
in Figure 5-1.

TABLE 5-2

*Percentages of Supreme Court Agenda Devoted to Selected
Issue Areas, in Selected Periods, 1933–1996*

	Terms				
	1933–	1948–	1963–	1978–	1991–
Issue area	1942	1957	1972	1987	1995
Civil liberties[a]	10.0	28.9	53.3	53.1	49.8
Racial equality[b]	0.5	1.8	6.3	4.6	2.6
Criminal procedure[b]	4.8	14.2	23.4	22.6	20.4
Federal taxation	16.8	7.4	4.0	2.8	3.0
Federalism	13.9	10.8	6.2	10.6	10.3

Sources: Richard L. Pacelle, Jr., *The Transformation of the Supreme Court's Agenda From the New Deal to the Reagan Administration* (Boulder, Colo.: Westview Press, 1991), 56–57, 147, 159. Data for 1991–1995 were provided by Professor Pacelle.

Note: Only cases with opinions of at least one page in length are included.

[a] Includes due process, equality, and substantive rights such as freedom of expression and freedom of religion.
[b] Included within civil liberties category.

Of course, issues can recede from the agenda as well. As suggested already, the Court may hear an increasing number of cases in an area when fundamental questions must be resolved; after that period, the number of cases is likely to decline. That pattern is exemplified by obscenity, where the peak came in the late 1960s and early 1970s. Action by the other branches was responsible for a more dramatic decline in cases involving the military draft: when conscription ended in 1973, the small stream of selective service cases dried up.

Changes in the Agenda as a Whole. Beyond these changes in specific areas, the overall pattern of the Court's agenda may change over a period of several decades. Indeed, comparison of the Court's 1996 agenda with the agendas of the early 1930s indicates that there has been a fundamental change in the kinds of issues and cases the Court addresses. This change is documented by findings from Richard Pacelle's study of the Court's agenda from 1933 to 1996, summarized in Table 5-2. Pacelle has also illuminated the process by which this change occurred, and the discussion that follows is based primarily on his analysis.

In the 1930s, issues of procedural due process constituted a small proportion of the Court's agenda, and other civil liberties issues were barely present. Far more numerous were cases that concerned economic issues, arising primarily from government economic policies. Also important but clearly secondary were cases about federalism.

By the 1960s, civil liberties had replaced economics as the Court's primary concern, and this broad category has remained dominant since then. Most categories of economic cases, including challenges to federal taxes and state regulatory policies, have declined precipitously in number. Federal economic regulation has become a much smaller component of the agenda, though the number of cases arising in such areas as securities and environmental regulation has actually increased. Federalism cases are also less common than they were in the 1930s, but this category has had something of a resurgence since the 1970s. Federalism aside, the major trend is clear: the Court has evolved from an institution concerned primarily with economic issues to one that gives attention primarily to individual liberties.

Many forces contributed to this change in the Court's agenda, ranging from public opinion to federal legislation. But actions by the Court itself had the most direct effect. Perhaps most important, the justices were increasingly interested in protecting civil liberties and thus in hearing challenges to government policies that allegedly infringed on liberties. Because they had to make room on the agenda for civil liberties cases and because they were less interested in scrutinizing economic policies, the justices gave more limited attention to fields other than civil liberties.

But the shift in emphasis from economics to civil liberties was gradual rather than swift. The Court had to continue addressing important economic issues, particularly those that had caused conflicts between lower courts. Litigants also needed time to respond to the Court's growing support for civil liberties by bringing additional cases to the Court. And massive change in the agenda inevitably takes time; the Court could not have moved simultaneously into all the diverse areas of civil liberties that have occupied a place on its agenda since the 1960s. Of course, the shift was not total: the Court decides a great many cases that concern economic issues, even while its agenda emphasizes civil liberties.

A Broader View of the Agenda

If the Supreme Court's current agenda differs from the agendas of previous Courts, it also differs from those of other policy makers. In turn, those differences provide some perspective on the Court's role.

Comparison with Other Institutions. In some respects, the Supreme Court's agenda is similar to that of other appellate courts, particularly state supreme courts and federal courts of appeals. To a considerable extent, all of these courts focus on government parties and government policy. Criminal cases are prominent on the agendas of virtually all appellate courts. Except for the rights of criminal defendants, however, civil liberties issues are relatively rare in lower appellate courts. The Supreme Court stands alone in the prominence of issues involving rights to equal treatment and freedom of expression.

Like the Court, the president is something of a specialist. But the president's agenda has its own emphases: foreign policy and maintenance of the nation's economic health. In contrast, the Court makes few decisions about foreign policy, and its decisions on economic policy barely touch the function of managing the economy.

In contrast, Congress is something of a generalist, spreading its activity across a large set of issues. One result is that the congressional agenda covers virtually all the types of policy that the Supreme Court deals with. But some of the issues that are central to the Court, especially in civil liberties, receive much less attention from Congress. And Congress gives considerable attention to many areas, ranging from foreign policy to agriculture, that are less important to the Court.

The Court's Position. These comparisons of agendas underline the limited range of the Court's work. Its jurisdiction is very broad, but the bulk of its decisions are made in a few policy areas.

The Court's specialization affects its role in policy making. Even in civil liberties, the Court can address only a small portion of the policy issues that arise. But by deciding as many cases as it does in this area, the Court maximizes its opportunities to shape law and public policy on civil liberties.

In contrast, the Court's relative lack of activity in several major areas of policy severely limits its potential impact in those fields. It cannot have much effect on development of the law in such fields as contracts and personal injuries. The Court today has little impact on government management of the economy and even less impact on foreign policy;[2] many people consider these the two most important areas of government policy.

These realities should give pause to those who believe that the Supreme Court is the most important policy maker in the United States. Without question the Court is an important policy maker, but it should not be regarded as preeminent when the range of its activities is so limited. It could not possibly be dominant as a policy maker except in federalism, civil liberties, and some limited areas of economic policy. For reasons that are discussed in the rest of this chapter and in Chapter 6, even here the Court's dominance is far from certain.

Supreme Court Activism: Judicial Review

Ultimately, the Supreme Court's role as a policy maker depends less on the issues that it addresses in its decisions than on the content of those decisions. One major characteristic of that content is activism.

Of the various forms of judicial activism, perhaps the most important are rulings that conflict with policies of the other branches. This form of activism is often gauged by the Court's use of judicial review, its power to overturn acts of other policy makers on the ground that they violate the Constitution. The Court intervenes in the policy-making process most directly and most clearly through its use of judicial review. And judicial review, unlike some other forms of activism, is easy to measure. For those reasons it is a good focus for analysis of activism.

Overturning Acts of Congress

The most familiar use of judicial review comes in decisions holding that federal statutes are unconstitutional. Such rulings represent a striking assertion of power by the Court. When the

Court overturns a federal law on constitutional grounds, it directly negates a decision by another branch of the federal government.

There is sometimes disagreement about whether a statute actually has been struck down by the Court. By one count, however, by the end of 1996 the Court had overturned 135 federal laws completely or in part.[3] This number in itself is significant. On the one hand, it indicates that the Court has made fairly frequent use of its review power—on average, more than once every two years. On the other hand, the laws struck down by the Court constitute a minute fraction of the more than sixty thousand laws that Congress has adopted. A closer look at these decisions provides a better sense of their significance.[4]

One question is the importance of the statutes that the Court has overturned. The Court has struck down some statutes of major significance. Among these were the Missouri Compromise of 1820, concerning slavery in the territories, which the Court declared unconstitutional in the *Dred Scott* case in 1857; the laws prohibiting child labor that were struck down in 1918 and 1922; and the New Deal economic legislation that was overturned in 1935 and 1936.[5] In contrast, many of the Court's decisions declaring statutes unconstitutional have been unimportant to the policy goals of Congress and the president, either because the statutes were minor or because they were struck down only as they applied to particular circumstances.

A related question is the timing of judicial review. The Court's decisions striking down federal statutes fall into three groups of nearly equal size: those that came no more than four calendar years after a statute's enactment, those that came five to twelve years later, and those that occurred at least thirteen years later. Congress sometimes retains a strong commitment to a statute from an earlier period. But often it collectively cares little if an older law is overturned: the statute becomes less relevant over time, or the collective point of view in Congress becomes less favorable to the provision in question. For that reason, many of the decisions that struck down older statutes were unlikely to arouse much concern in the legislative branch.

Thus the Court's frequent use of its power to invalidate congressional acts is somewhat misleading. Any decision that strikes down a federal statute might seem likely to bring about a major

TABLE 5-3

Number of Federal Statutes Held Unconstitutional by the Supreme Court, 1790–1996

Period	Number	Period	Number
1790–1799	0	1900–1909	9
1800–1809	1	1910–1919	6
1810–1819	0	1920–1929	15
1820–1829	0	1930–1939	13
1830–1839	0	1940–1949	2
1840–1849	0	1950–1959	5
1850–1859	1	1960–1969	16
1860–1869	4	1970–1979	20
1870–1879	7	1980–1989	16
1880–1889	4	1990–1996	11
1890–1899	5	Total	135

Source: Congressional Research Service, *The Constitution of the United States of America: Analysis and Interpretation* and *1990 Supplement* (Washington, D.C.: Government Printing Office, 1987, 1991), updated by the author.

conflict between the Court and Congress, but that is not necessarily the case. Conflict is most likely when the Court invalidates an important congressional policy within a few years of its enactment, but most of the time those criteria are not met.

Another way to gauge the significance of judicial review is in terms of the historical pattern of its use. As Table 5-3 shows, the Court has not overturned federal statutes at a consistent rate. It struck down only two statutes before 1865. But at that point the Court began to exercise its judicial review power more actively, overturning thirty-five federal laws between 1865 and 1919. Two more increases, even more dramatic, followed: the Court struck down fifteen federal laws during the 1920s, and twelve from 1934 through 1936. Over the next quarter century, the Court employed this power sparingly. But from 1963 through 1996 it overturned sixty-three statutes, far more than in any previous period of the same length and nearly half of the total for the Court's entire history.

The years 1918 to 1936 were the period of greatest conflict between the Court and Congress. During that period the Court overturned twenty-nine provisions. More important, much of the legislation that the Court declared unconstitutional in this period was significant. Between 1918 and 1928, the Court struck down two child labor laws and a minimum wage law, along with several less important statutes. Then, between 1933 and 1936, a majority of the Court engaged in a frontal attack on the New Deal program, an attack that ended with the Court's retreat in 1937.

Although the Court overturned legislation from 1963 to 1996 at a record pace, few of the laws it struck down were of major importance, and many were fairly old. Typically, the Court invalidated a minor law or an unessential provision of a major law.

Some of the provisions struck down since 1963 clearly *were* important. The Court invalidated some major provisions of the Federal Election Campaign Act concerning campaign finance in *Buckley v. Valeo* (1976) and in several later decisions. In *Immigration and Naturalization Service v. Chadha* (1983), the Court struck down a relatively minor provision of an immigration law, but its ruling indicated the general invalidity of the legislative veto, a widely used mechanism for congressional control of the executive branch. And, moving beyond 1996, in *City of Boerne v. Flores* (1997) the Court struck down the Religious Freedom Restoration Act of 1993, designed to expand protections of religious practices against government regulation, and in doing so limited congressional power to enforce the Fourteenth Amendment. But in general, the legislation overturned by the Court since the early 1960s has not been nearly as significant as the economic legislation that it held to be unconstitutional in the 1930s.

During other periods, the Court struck down major pieces of legislation, sometimes with considerable impact on politics and federal policy.[6] But these decisions were sporadic. Only in the period from 1918 through 1936 did the Court use its power to review federal legislation in a sustained way to disturb a major line of federal policy.

Overturning State and Local Laws

The Supreme Court's exercise of judicial review over state and local laws has less of an activist element than does its use of that power over federal laws. When the Court strikes down a state law, it does not put itself in conflict with the other

TABLE 5-4
Number of State Laws and Local Ordinances
Held Unconstitutional by the Supreme Court, 1790–1996

Period	Number	Period	Number
1790–1799	0	1900–1909	40
1800–1809	1	1910–1919	118
1810–1819	7	1920–1929	139
1820–1829	8	1930–1939	93
1830–1839	3	1940–1949	57
1840–1849	9	1950–1959	61
1850–1859	7	1960–1969	149
1860–1869	23	1970–1979	193
1870–1879	36	1980–1989	162
1880–1889	46	1990–1996	45
1890–1899	36	Total	1,233

Source: Congressional Research Service, *The Constitution of the United States of America: Analysis and Interpretation* and *1990 Supplement* (Washington, D.C.: Government Printing Office, 1987, 1991), updated by the author.

branches of the federal government. Indeed, it may be supporting their powers over those of the states. Still, by striking down a state or local law, the Court invalidates the action of another policy maker. For that reason, this form of judicial review is significant.

From 1790 to 1996, by one count, the Court overturned 1,233 state statutes and local ordinances. Most were struck down on the ground that they directly violated the Constitution, some because they were superseded by federal law under the constitutional principle of federal supremacy. That is about ten times the number of federal statutes struck down by the Court (see Table 5-3). The disparity is even greater than these figures suggest, because many of the Court's decisions overturning particular state and local laws also applied to similar laws in other states.

As shown in Table 5-4, the rate with which the Court invalidates state and local laws has increased tremendously over time. One jump came in the 1860s, another early in this century. As with federal statutes, the highest rate of decisions striking down state and local laws has come since 1960. In that period, the

Court has declared unconstitutional an average of fifteen such laws per year.

While the Court struck down relatively few state laws before 1860, its decisions during that period were important because they limited state powers under the Constitution. For instance, under John Marshall (1801–1835) the Court weakened the states with decisions such as *McCulloch v. Maryland* (1819), which denied the states power to tax federal agencies, and *Gibbons v. Ogden* (1824), which narrowed state power to regulate commerce.

The state and local laws overturned by the Court in more recent periods have been a mixture of the important and the minor. In the aggregate, the Court's decisions have been sufficiently important to give it a significant role in shaping state policy. During the late nineteenth century and the first third of the twentieth, the Court struck down a great deal of important state economic legislation, including many laws regulating business practices and labor relations. The net effect was to turn back much of a major tide of public policy.

The Court's decisions since the mid-1950s have also impinged on important elements of state policy. A series of rulings helped to break down the legal basis of racial segregation and discrimination in southern states. In 1973 the Court overturned the broad prohibitions of abortion that existed in most states, thereby requiring a general legalization of abortion. And through a long series of decisions, the Court has limited state power to regulate the economy in areas that Congress has preempted under its constitutional supremacy. In doing so, the Court has shifted power further toward the federal government and away from the states.

Other Targets of Judicial Review

The Supreme Court can declare unconstitutional any government policy or practice, not just laws enacted by legislative bodies. In recent years the Court has overturned such actions as a state jury's imposition of a death sentence, a county board's termination of a trash hauler's contract in retaliation for criticism of the board, and a federal court injunction that imposed certain limits on picketing at an abortion clinic.[7] The number of nonstatutory policies and practices that the Court has struck down is probably much larger than the 1,400 laws it has over-turned.

One area of special importance is the Court's scrutiny of criminal procedure. Since the 1960s, the Court has been active in assessing the legality of police investigations and trial pro-cesses, especially in state proceedings. In large numbers of cases, it has held that particular procedures violated constitu-tional protections of defendants' rights. By playing this role, the Court has had a major impact on the criminal justice process.

Also of particular interest is the Court's scrutiny of orders and other actions by the president. Decisions of presidents, or of of-ficials acting on their behalf, can be challenged on the grounds that they are unauthorized by the Constitution or that they di-rectly violate a constitutional rule. It is difficult to say how fre-quently the Court strikes down presidential actions as unconsti-tutional, because it is often unclear whether an action by the executive branch should be considered "presidential." But such decisions by the Court seem to be relatively rare.[8]

The Court has invalidated a few major actions by presi-dents, however. In *Ex parte Milligan* (1866), it held that Presi-dent Lincoln had lacked the power to suspend the writ of habeas corpus for military prisoners during the Civil War. And in *Youngstown Sheet and Tube Co. v. Sawyer* (1952), it declared that President Truman had acted illegally when he ordered the fed-eral government to seize major steel mills whose workers were on strike during the Korean War. Those two decisions under-line the importance of the Court's power to scrutinize presi-dential actions.

Judicial Review: The General Picture

The Supreme Court's record in using judicial review is un-even. The extent of activism has varied during the Court's his-tory, with a general increase over time. One reason for that in-crease is growth in the level of government activity, including the number of statutes; there are more policies and practices to challenge. The use of judicial review has also differed between levels of government. The Court has overturned considerably more state and local policies than federal policies, and it has done more to limit the freedom of action of state and local gov-ernments on important issues.

Taken as a whole, the Court's record is ambiguous. Certainly the justices have made considerable use of the power of judicial review. By striking down many government decisions, including some important ones, the Supreme Court has established itself as a major participant in the policy-making process.

From another perspective, however, the Court's use of judicial review seems limited. The Court generally has been quite selective in employing its power to strike down laws. Partly as a result, the great majority of public policies at all levels of government have continued without Court interference. While judicial review allows the Court to play a major role in policy making, it certainly has not made the Court the dominant national policy maker.

Statutory Interpretation

Only a minority of the Supreme Court's decisions determine whether some government practice is unconstitutional. Most of the Court's work involves the interpretation of federal statutes. Statutory interpretation can involve activism in at least two senses.

First, the Court's statutory decisions often involve the question of whether the executive branch has interpreted a provision correctly in adopting a regulation or carrying out a practice. If the Court concludes that an administrative agency has erred, it strikes down the agency's action as unauthorized by statute. For example, a federal statute requires compensation of military veterans who are injured as the result of medical treatment given to them as veterans. For sixty years the Department of Veterans Affairs and its predecessor had interpreted this statute to say that compensation was due only if the injury was the fault of the Department or resulted from an accident during medical treatment. In *Brown v. Gardner* (1994), the Court held that these agencies had interpreted the law incorrectly throughout the sixty years. (Until 1988, these administrative decisions could not be challenged in court.)

Second, the Court sometimes puts its own stamp on a statute through its interpretations of that statute over the years. One example is Title VII of the Civil Rights Act of 1964, the major federal law prohibiting discrimination in employment. Until the late 1980s, the Court's interpretations of Title VII had the primary theme of broadening it as a protection of racial minority groups and women. Among other things, the Court ruled that an employer's practices could violate Title VII even if there was no intent to discriminate, that Title VII did not prohibit affirmative action, and that sexual harassment constituted discrimination under the statute.[9] During certain periods the Court has played the same kind of role in fields such as labor-management relations, antitrust, and environmental protection. Even when the Court's shaping of a statute does not lead to conflict with other policy makers, the Court is often asserting itself as an independent policy maker through its interpretations of statutory language.

The Direction of Policy

The Supreme Court's activism is a gauge of the Court's importance in making public policy, but just as important is the *content* of that activism—and of the Court's policies as a whole. This section examines patterns in the content of the Court's policies in the past century, giving special attention to their ideological direction and their beneficiaries.

The 1890s to the 1930s

Scrutinizing Economic Regulation. In 1915 the Supreme Court decided *South Covington & Cincinnati Street Railway Co. v. City of Covington.* The company, which ran streetcars between Covington, Kentucky, and Cincinnati, Ohio, challenged several provisions of a Covington ordinance regulating its operations. The Court struck down some provisions on the ground that they constituted a burden on interstate commerce between Ohio and Kentucky. The Court also declared invalid a regulation stipulating that the temperature in the cars never be permitted to go below fifty degrees Fahrenheit: "We therefore think . . . this feature of the ordinance is unreasonable and cannot be sustained"—apparently on the ground that the regulation violated the Fourteenth Amendment by depriving the company of its property without due process of law.

The *South Covington* case illustrates some important characteristics of the Court's decisions during the period from the 1890s to the late 1930s. In that period the Court dealt primarily with economic issues, particularly government policies that affected private businesses. Most important, it ruled on challenges to growing government regulation of business practices.

The Court frequently ruled in favor of government in these cases, rejecting most challenges to federal and state policies and giving broad interpretations to some government powers. But the Court also established important limits on government regulatory powers under the Constitution, and over time it created increasingly strong barriers to regulation. This development is reflected in the number of laws involving economic policy that the Court struck down each decade: 44 from 1900 to 1909, 112 from 1910 to 1919, and 133 from 1920 to 1929.[10] The Court attacked government regulation most directly in the mid-1930s, when it declared unconstitutional most of the major statutes in President Roosevelt's New Deal program to deal with the Great Depression.

The theme of limiting government regulatory powers was reflected in the Court's constitutional doctrines. At the national level, the Court gave narrow interpretations to congressional powers over taxation and interstate commerce. In contrast, the Court read the general limitation on federal power in the Tenth Amendment broadly as a bar to some federal action on the ground that it interfered with state prerogatives. At the state level, the Court ruled in 1886 that corporations were "persons" whose rights were protected by the Fourteenth Amendment.[11] Further, it interpreted the Fourteenth Amendment requirement that state governments provide "due process of law" in making decisions as an absolute prohibition of regulations that interfered unduly with the liberty and property rights of businesses. The Court's ruling against the Covington temperature rule was one of many such decisions.

The Court's Beneficiaries. The business community benefited from the Court's policies during this period, and major corporations benefited the most. Much of the regulatory legislation that the Court overturned or limited was aimed at the activities of large businesses, because legislators believed that these businesses abused their great economic power. The railroads were the most prominent example. In the decade from 1910 to 1919, the Court overturned forty-one state laws in cases brought by railroad companies. Thus major corporations such as railroads might be considered the clientele of the Court from the 1890s to the 1930s.

Large corporations did not simply benefit from the Court's policies, they helped to bring them about.[12] Beginning in the late nineteenth century, the corporate community employed much of the best legal talent in the United States to challenge the validity of regulatory statutes, and the effective advocacy of these attorneys laid some of the groundwork for the Court's policies favoring business.

The corporate interests that brought their claims to the Supreme Court came to the judiciary because of their defeats elsewhere in government. Congress and the state legislatures were not uniformly unfriendly to business interests, but there was strong legislative support for regulation of private enterprise. In accepting the business position so frequently, the Court served as a court of last resort for corporations in a political sense as well as the legal sense.

Civil Liberties: A Limited Concern. Civil liberties as I have defined them were a minor concern of the Court between 1890 and the mid-1930s. Only occasionally did it hear cases dealing with issues such as the procedural rights of criminal defendants and discrimination against disadvantaged groups.

The Court issued a number of specific decisions that favored civil liberties in this period.[13] But the justices gave individual rights far less protection than they accorded the economic rights of businesses. The absence of wholehearted support for racial equality was exemplified by *Plessy v. Ferguson* (1896), in which the Court upheld the legitimacy of racial segregation by ruling that state governments could mandate "separate but equal" facilities for different racial groups. In 1908 the Court held that only a limited set of the procedural rights for criminal defendants in the Bill of Rights were "incorporated" into the due process clause of the Fourteenth Amendment and thus were applicable to proceedings in state courts.[14] Late in that era, the Court ruled that the due process clause protected freedom of speech and freedom of the press from state violations. But in a series of decisions it held that the federal government could prosecute people whose expressions allegedly endangered military recruitment and other national security interests.[15]

Overview. In ideological terms, the Court of this period was predominately conservative. It interpreted the law in ways that protected advantaged interests in society, such as business corporations. It did little to protect disadvantaged groups, such as racial minorities.

This conservatism was not new; the dominant themes of the Court's work in earlier periods were also conservative. The Court provided considerable support for the rights of property holders and much less support for liberal values such as civil liberties.

Thus, an observer of the Supreme Court during this era had good reason to conclude that the Court was a fundamentally conservative institution. Indeed, this was the position of two distinguished observers as late as the early 1940s. Henry Steele Commager argued in 1943 that, with one possible exception, the Court had never intervened on behalf of the underprivileged; indeed, it frequently had blocked efforts by Congress to protect the underprivileged.[16] Two years earlier, Attorney General and future Supreme Court justice Robert Jackson reached this stark conclusion: "Never in its entire history can the Supreme Court be said to have for a single hour been representative of anything except the relatively conservative forces of its day."[17]

1937 to 1969

At the beginning of 1937, the Court's conservatism seemed to be deeply rooted. But later that year the Court began a shift in its direction that one historian has called "the Constitutional Revolution of 1937." That revolution, he said,

altered fundamentally the character of the Court's business, the nature of its decisions, and the alignment of its friends and foes. From the Marshall Court to the Hughes Court, the judiciary had been largely concerned with questions of property rights. After 1937, the most significant matters on the docket were civil liberties and other personal rights. . . . While from 1800 to 1937 the principal critics of the Supreme Court were social reformers and the main supporters people of means who were the principal beneficiaries of the Court's decisions, after 1937 roles were reversed, with liberals commending and conservatives censuring the Court.[18]

Acceptance of Government Economic Policy. In the first stage of the revolution, the Court abandoned its opposition to government intervention in economic matters. That step came quickly. In a series of decisions beginning in 1937, majorities accepted the constitutional power of government—particularly the federal government—to regulate and to manage the economy. The culmination of this shift was a 1942 decision in which the Court held that federal power to regulate interstate commerce extended so far that it applied to a farmer growing wheat for his own livestock.[19]

This collective change of heart proved to be of long duration. The Court consistently upheld major economic legislation against constitutional challenge, striking down only one minor provision of federal law regulating business in the period from the 1940s through the 1960s.[20] Supporting federal supremacy in economic matters, the Court struck down many state laws on the ground that they impinged on the constitutional powers of the federal government or that they were preempted by federal statutes. But in other respects state governments were also given more freedom to make economic policy.

The Court continued to address nonconstitutional economic issues involving interpretations of federal statutes. In some instances it overrode decisions of regulatory agencies such as the Interstate Commerce Commission and the National Labor Relations Board, holding that those decisions misinterpreted statutes. Some of these interventions were significant, but the Court did not challenge the basic economic programs of the federal government.

Support for Civil Liberties. In a 1938 decision, *United States v. Carolene Products Co.,* the Court signaled that there might be a second stage of the revolution. This was simply one of many cases in which the Court upheld federal economic policies. But in what would become a famous footnote, Justice Harlan Stone's opinion for the Court argued that the Court was justified in taking a tolerant view of government economic policies while it gave "more exacting judicial scrutiny" to policies that infringed on civil liberties.

This second stage took much longer to develop than the first stage. In the 1940s and 1950s the Court gave more attention and support to civil liberties than it had in earlier eras, but it did not make a strong and consistent commitment to the expansion of individual liberties. This stage of the revolution finally came to full fruition in the 1960s. In that decade civil liberties issues dominated the Court's agenda for the first time and the Court's decisions expanded liberties in many fields, from civil rights of racial minority groups to procedural rights of criminal defendants to freedom of expression.

As in the preceding era, the Court's policy position was reflected in the constitutional doctrines it adopted. Departing from its earlier view, the Court of the 1960s ruled that nearly all the rights of criminal defendants in the Bill of Rights were incorporated in the Fourteenth Amendment and thus applied to state proceedings. In interpreting the equal protection clause of the Fourteenth Amendment, the Court held that some government policies challenged as discriminatory would be given "strict scrutiny," if the groups treated differently were especially vulnerable or if the rights that the policies affected were especially important. And *Griswold v. Connecticut* (1965) created a new constitutional right to privacy, with opinions that based this right on several provisions of the Constitution.

The Court's direction after 1937 is illustrated by the pattern of decisions declaring laws unconstitutional. Figure 5-2 shows the number of economic statutes and statutes limiting civil liberties that the Court overturned in successive decades, from 1900 to the 1990s. The number of economic laws that the Court struck down declined precipitously between the 1920s and the 1940s and remained relatively low in the 1950s and 1960s. In contrast, the number of statutes struck down on civil liberties grounds became significant in the 1940s and 1950s and increased sharply in the 1960s. That increase reflected the Court's increasing liberalism. The reversal of these trends in the 1980s is also noteworthy; I discuss its implications later in this section.

The Court's Beneficiaries. The groups that benefited most from the Court's policies, of course, were those that brought civil liberties claims to the Court. Among them were socially and economically disadvantaged groups, criminal defendants, and people who took unpopular political stands. In 1967, during the Court's most liberal period, an unsympathetic editorial cartoonist depicted the Court as a Santa Claus whose list of gift recipients included Communists, pornographers, extremists, drug pushers, criminals, and perverts.[21] Whatever one may think of this characterization, it underlines the change in the Court.

FIGURE 5-2
*Number of Economic and Civil Liberties Laws
(Federal, State, and Local) Overturned by the
Supreme Court by Decade, 1900s–1990s*

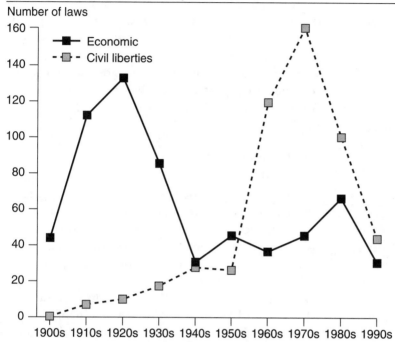

Source: Congressional Research Service, *The Constitution of the United States of America: Analysis and Interpretation* and *1990 Supplement* (Washington, D.C.: Government Printing Office, 1987, 1991), updated by the author.

Note: Civil liberties category does not include laws supportive of civil liberties. The figures for the 1990s are based on the actual numbers for 1990–1996, multiplied by 1.43 to create a ten-year "rate" for that decade.

The segment of the population that the Court supported most strongly was black citizens, particularly in the fields of education and voting rights. The Court also made great efforts to protect the civil rights movement when it came under attack by southern states in the late 1950s and 1960s. Like the Court's policies favoring corporations in an earlier era, this support reflected effective litigation efforts, particularly by the Legal Defense Fund of the NAACP.

The Court did not support all the civil liberties claims brought to it, but it was usually more favorable to liberties than the other branches of government. Congress did not adopt a strong civil rights bill attacking racial discrimination until 1964, ten years after *Brown v. Board of Education.* The Court's support for some other liberties diverged even more from the positions of the other branches. The procedural rights of criminal defendants had few advocates in the executive and legislative branches. Political activities of leftist political groups such as the Communist party were attacked a good deal by Congress. As it had done when it favored business interests, the Court provided relief for groups that fared less well elsewhere in government.

The Burger and Rehnquist Courts

In the three decades since 1969, the Supreme Court's policies have had a clear trend but not a clear theme. The trend has been one of increasing conservatism, both in civil liberties and in other fields. But there has been no theme comparable to the Court's opposition to government regulation of the economy early in this century or its championing of individual liberties in the 1960s.

Thus it is difficult to characterize the Court under chief justices Warren Burger and William Rehnquist. That difficulty is reflected in the disagreement among commentators about how conservative the Court has become. Some depict the Court as highly conservative, but others argue that it remains relatively liberal—far *too* liberal, as some conservatives see it.

In civil liberties, the Court generally has narrowed legal protections for individual liberties, and this has been particularly true of the Rehnquist Court. This shift in the balance between individual liberties and other values is reflected in the declining rate of success for parties bringing civil liberties claims, shown in Table 4-4 (page 161). It is also reflected in the numbers of laws struck down on the ground that they violated constitutional protections of civil liberties, shown in Figure 5-2. That number actually increased in the 1970s, to the highest level for any decade, but after that it declined dramatically. Even today, however, the Court frequently supports civil liberties claims and adopts some doctrines that expand protection for individual rights.

The reduction in support for civil liberties came most quickly and has gone the furthest in the area of defendants' rights. Beginning in the early 1970s, the Court narrowed the *Miranda* rules for police questioning of suspects and the *Mapp* rule disallowing the use of evidence obtained through illegal searches. It was the Burger Court that struck down existing death penalty laws in *Furman v. Georgia* (1972). But in *Gregg v. Georgia* (1976) the Court approved some of the new laws that states enacted, and over time it became increasingly willing to accept the use of capital punishment. The Court's current stance in criminal justice is symbolized by its decision in *United States v. Watts* (1997), which held that a federal judge could lengthen a convicted defendant's sentence for an additional offense even though the jury had acquitted the defendant of that offense.

On issues of racial equality, the Court moved in a conservative direction more slowly and unevenly. The Burger Court limited the use of the Fourteenth Amendment to protect civil liberties against violations by private institutions connected to government. But it held that Northern-style school segregation could be unconstitutional and approved the use of affirmative action in employment and school admissions. By and large, it gave broad interpretations to federal laws against discrimination. In the late 1980s, however, the Rehnquist Court began to adopt narrower interpretations of those laws. And in *Adarand Constructors v. Pena* (1995) it gave government a heavy burden of proof in justifying programs that favor businesses owned by members of racial minority groups. That decision seemed to indicate a decreasing sympathy for affirmative action programs in general.

On sex discrimination, it was the Burger Court that first struck down laws under the equal protection clause on the ground that they discriminated against women. In this area, the Court has continued to provide considerable support for equality. This position is reflected in *United States v. Virginia* (1996), in which the Court required that the Virginia Military Institute admit female students.

Freedom of expression is the only area in which the Court has directly overruled major Warren Court decisions favoring civil liberties—specifically, in standards determining obscenity.[22] The Court has narrowed some other First Amendment protections as well. But it has limited government power to regulate commercial speech such as liquor advertising. And it has supported rights of individuals to political expression by overruling government actions such as a state law against the distribution of anonymous campaign literature.[23]

In the economic arena, the Burger and Rehnquist Courts have taken more conservative positions than the Warren Court in interpreting federal regulatory statutes. For example, the Court established rules that strengthened the position of companies charged with violations of the antitrust laws, moving away from Warren Court rules that certain business practices are automatically illegal.[24] In labor-management law the Court has given more support to employers, and it has interpreted environmental laws narrowly for the most part. But the Court has not been uniformly favorable to the business community in these areas.

In the early twentieth century, the primary mark of the conservative Court was its narrow interpretations of government powers to regulate economic activity. The Burger Court did not disturb the broader interpretation of those powers that had prevailed since 1937. The Rehnquist Court has taken some limited steps in that direction. It has expanded property owners' rights to compensation when government regulates the use of their property.[25] Its decision in *United States v. Lopez* (1995), striking down a federal law that prohibited guns in and around schools, suggested that the Court might give a narrower interpretation to congressional power over interstate commerce. But the Court has not substantially limited government power over the economy. Similarly, it has shown greater support for the states in state-federal conflicts, generally regarded as a conservative position, but it has not altered the federal-state balance dramatically.

Thus the record of the Burger and Rehnquist Courts is complex. But the changes in the Court's policies since 1969, like earlier changes, make it clear that the Court's ideological position can evolve over time. The Court was generally a conservative institution until the late 1930s, it then became a liberal supporter of civil liberties, and its position now is one of moderate conservatism.

This history raises questions of explanation. What accounts for patterns in the Court's policies, and how can we understand changes in those patterns? The next section addresses those questions.

Explaining the Court's Policies

Of all the forces that shape Supreme Court decisions, two are particularly useful in explaining broad patterns of policy: the Court's environment and the policy preferences of its members.

The Court's Environment

Freedom from External Pressures. The life terms of Supreme Court justices give them considerable freedom from the other branches of government and from the general public. That freedom is the most important characteristic of the Court's relationship with its political and social environment.

The Court's freedom is reflected in some of the positions that it takes in individual decisions. It is not difficult to identify Supreme Court decisions that legislators would not have made because they ran strongly counter to public opinion. Congress could never adopt a resolution supporting the right of people to burn flags as an act of political protest. No state legislature could enact a statute that prohibits members of the clergy from offering prayers at public school graduations.

More important, the Court has adopted broad lines of policy that ran counter to the majority view in the general public and elsewhere in government. To a considerable degree, it resisted the widespread support for regulation of business in the early twentieth century. More recently the Court greatly expanded the procedural rights of criminal defendants. No elected body, even a court, could have adopted so many rules favoring so unpopular a segment of society.

Minimum Levels of Support. As much autonomy as the Supreme Court enjoys, it is not completely free from its environment. Tides of public opinion can carry the justices along, in part by reshaping their own opinions. Members of the Court are especially subject to influence from the segments of society whose judgment is most important to them.

Perhaps the most important effect of the environment is that the Court is unlikely to take a sustained position that lacks significant support outside the Court. In the absence of such support the justices might perceive that they would make themselves vulnerable to attacks from the other branches, even that they were threatening the Court's legitimacy. On a quite different level, a position for which there was little support might be difficult for the justices themselves to take seriously.

There is a more concrete reason why some minimum level of support is necessary. The Court acts on the litigation that comes to it, and litigation on a set of issues usually requires considerable activity by interest groups. That much activity is unlikely to occur on behalf of a policy position that has little support in society. It was not until the re-emergence of the women's movement in the late 1960s that the Court began to receive many cases challenging laws that treated men and women differently.

In most respects, the Court's two distinctive policy positions in the twentieth century had only minority support in society, but a level of support that was sufficient for the Court to adopt these positions. The Court's resistance to government regulation of the economy before 1937 was actively supported by most of the business community and much of the legal profession. The Court received considerable praise for its economic decisions from respected individuals and groups. And corporations and their representatives brought to the Court a steady flow of litigation and strong legal arguments against government economic policies.

The Court's expansions of civil liberties from the 1940s to the 1970s also had meaningful support. The NAACP, the ACLU, and a variety of other groups brought civil liberties cases to the Court and argued for broad interpretations of legal protections for civil liberties. Many legal commentators and a significant minority of political and social leaders viewed this line of policy favorably.

Early in the twentieth century, little of this support for civil liberties existed. At that time it would have been very difficult for the Court to take strong positions favoring racial equality or the rights of criminal defendants. For the same reason, the Court today would find it difficult to limit government power over the economy as much as it did in the 1920s and 1930s even if most of the justices wanted to do so; there simply is too little public support for that position. Societal opinion creates subtle boundaries on the range of policies the Court can adopt.

Congressional Influence. Congressional power over the Court produces a more concrete constraint. Congress often can limit the impact of the Court's decisions, and it can override statutory decisions completely. To a degree, the justices may take those powers into account when they decide cases.

Probably more important in influencing broad lines of Court policy are congressional powers over the Court as an institution. Congress controls the Court's budget, and it can change the Court's jurisdiction. Congress seldom employs these powers to attack the Court, but its members frequently threaten to do so. Moreover, strong criticism from members of Congress might affect the Court's standing with the public. Thus justices have an incentive to minimize direct conflicts with Congress.

Occasionally congressional criticism and the threat that Congress will use its powers against the Court have a very evident impact on Court policy. This was the case with the Court's retreats from opposition to the New Deal in 1937 and from some of its expansions of civil liberties in the late 1950s. Even when there is no direct threat, however, justices may choose not to oppose the direction of national policy in order to avoid incurring congressional wrath.

This caution is probably reflected in the Court's limited use of judicial review at the national level. As we have seen, only between 1918 and 1936 did the Court overturn a set of major congressional policies. But the Court has been far more active in striking down state and local laws. One reason for this difference is that Congress has much more power to attack the Court as an institution than do state and local policy makers.[26]

Policy Preferences and the Appointment Power

The Importance of Policy Preferences. The Court's freedom from external pressures, though far from total, is substantial. As a result, the justices' positions reflect primarily their own judgments about the choices they face. Those judgments are based in part on their assessments of cases in legal terms. But because the questions before the Court seldom have clear legal answers, justices' policy preferences are the strongest determinant of the positions they take.

From this perspective, a great deal about patterns of Supreme Court policy can be explained quite simply. During any given period in the Court's history, its policies have reflected the collective preferences of its members. Most of the justices who served from the 1890s to the 1930s were political conservatives. As conservatives, they accepted government restrictions on civil liberties but were skeptical of economic policies that infringed on the freedom of business enterprises. In contrast, the justices who came to the Court from the late 1930s to the late 1960s were predominately liberals who supported government management of the economy and, in most instances, broader protections of civil liberties.

This explanation is not entirely satisfying, because it does not tell why certain preferences predominated on the Court during particular periods. One reason is that some national values were dominant during the periods in which justices were developing their attitudes. Another is that the justices came from backgrounds that instilled particular values in them; thus, the higher status backgrounds that predominated during most of the Court's history may have produced a sympathy for the views and interests of those segments of society. Further, the prevailing ideology in elite segments of the legal profession shapes the views of its members, including future Supreme Court justices. But the most direct source of the Court's collective preferences is the decisions that presidents make in appointing justices.

The Impact of Appointments. It stands to reason that the predominant pattern of Supreme Court policy at any given time reflects the appointments that presidents make. If a series of appointees is politically conservative, the Court is likely to become a conservative body. And because vacancies occur on the Court with some frequency—on the average, once every two years—most presidents can have a significant impact on the Court's direction.

Robert Dahl argued that for this reason, "the policy views dominant on the Court are never for long out of line with the policy views dominant among the lawmaking majorities of the United States."[27] In Dahl's judgment, the president's power to make appointments has limited the number of major federal statutes overturned by the Court: justices generally take the same view of policy as members of Congress and the president, so they seldom upset the policies of these branches. I think there is much to Dahl's argument. But the appointment power produces only imperfect control by "lawmaking majorities" because of several complicating factors.

One factor is time lag. Most justices serve for many years, so the Court nearly always reflects the views of past presidents and Senates at least as much as those of the current president and Senate. For this reason Fred Rodell suggested that the aphorism, "the Supreme Court follows the election returns" be amended to refer to the returns "of ten or twelve years before."[28]

The lag varies, chiefly because presidents have differing opportunities to make appointments. President Nixon could select four justices during his first term in office, while Franklin Roosevelt and Jimmy Carter made none in the four years after they took office. Roosevelt's bad luck in this respect led to his conflict with the Court over its handling of New Deal legislation. Had he been able to replace two conservative justices early in his first term, the Court probably would not have acted as a major roadblock to his program. Carter's luck was even worse; the absence of vacancies during his term, combined with his failed reelection bid in 1980, made him the first president to serve at least four years without appointing any justices. As a result, he had no opportunity to make the Court more liberal. Of course, a president's influence on the Court's direction depends only in part on the number of appointments to be made. It also depends on the ideological configuration of the Court and on which members leave it.

Another complicating factor is the deviation of justices from presidential expectations. Presidents usually get most of what they want from their appointees, but this is not a certainty. The unprecedented liberalism of the Court in the 1960s resulted largely from Eisenhower's miscalculations in nominating Earl Warren and William Brennan. The Court of the 1990s would be more conservative if Anthony Kennedy and David Souter had not deviated from the expectations of the Republican presidents who chose them.

For these reasons, Dahl's argument is valid only as a statement of a general tendency. The process of appointment does limit the Court's disagreement with the policies of Congress and the president. But the lag that is inherent in the selection process weakens the link between the Court and current lawmaking majorities.

It is also worth underlining the element of chance in shaping the Court's general direction. Chance plays a part in the timing of Court vacancies and in the performance of justices relative to their appointers' expectations. For that matter, the identity of

the president who fills vacancies on the Court sometimes reflects chance; the close victories of John Kennedy in 1960 and
Richard Nixon in 1968 were hardly inevitable.

The two policy orientations that prevailed on the Supreme
Court between the 1890s and the 1960s reflected the existence
of strong lawmaking majorities during two periods: the conservative Republican governments that dominated much of
the period from the Civil War to the Great Depression, and the
unprecedented twelve-year tenure of Franklin Roosevelt. But
these orientations also reflected patterns of resignations and
deaths, unexpected behavior on the part of justices, and other
factors that were a good deal less systematic. Thus, to take one
example, it is possible to imagine a different sequence of events
in which the Court never became a strong supporter of civil liberties.[29] The forces that shape the Court's policy positions, like
so much about the Court, are highly complex.

Conclusion

In this chapter I have examined a wide range of subjects concerning the Supreme Court's policy outputs. A few conclusions
merit emphasis.

First, in some periods the Court's policy making has had fairly
obvious themes. During the first part of the twentieth century,
the dominant theme was scrutiny of government economic
policies. Later, the primary theme was scrutiny of practices that
infringed on individual civil liberties. In each instance, the
theme was evident in both the Court's agenda and the content
of its decisions.

Second, these themes and the Court's work as a whole reflect
both the justices' policy preferences and the influence of the
Court's environment. In large part the Court's policies are what
its members would like them to be. But the Court is subject to
environmental influences that limit the divergence between
Supreme Court decisions and the policies adopted by the other
branches of government. In a different way, the president's appointment power establishes a direct link between the justices'
policy preferences and their political environment.

Finally, the Court's role as a policy maker—though clearly
significant—is a limited one. The Court gives considerable attention to some areas of policy, but there are several major pol-

icy areas that it scarcely touches. Some critical matters, such as foreign policy, are left almost entirely to the other two branches. Even in the areas that the Court gives the most attention, it seldom disturbs the basic features of national policy.

The significance of the Supreme Court as a policy maker ultimately depends on the impact of its decisions, which is the subject of Chapter 6. After examining the effect of the Court's decisions, we can make a more comprehensive assessment of the Supreme Court's role in the policy-making process.

NOTES

1. This discussion of agenda change is drawn in part from Richard L. Pacelle, Jr., *The Transformation of the Supreme Court's Agenda from the New Deal to the Reagan Administration* (Boulder, Colo.: Westview Press, 1991); and Pacelle, "The Dynamics and Determinants of Agenda Change in the Rehnquist Court," in *Contemplating Courts*, ed. Lee Epstein (Washington, D.C.: CQ Press, 1995), 251–274. Numbers of cases involving particular issues or statutes were calculated from data in the U.S. Supreme Court Judicial Database created by Harold Spaeth, updated by the author.
2. On the Court and foreign policy, see Thomas M. Franck, *Political Questions/Judicial Answers: Does the Rule of Law Apply to Foreign Affairs?* (Princeton, N.J.: Princeton University Press, 1992).
3. Because of ambiguities, different observers have obtained different numbers of laws overturned. The numbers of federal and state laws struck down by the Court that are presented in this chapter are based on data in Congressional Research Service, *The Constitution of the United States of America: Analysis and Interpretation* and *1990 Supplement* (Washington, D.C.: Government Printing Office, 1987, 1991), updated by the author. There are two unusual features of the compilation of laws struck down in the book by the Congressional Research Service. First, although the count is of statutes, when the Court overturned different sections of the same statute in different decisions, the book counts these as two different statutes. The second unusual feature concerns decisions that nullify state laws on the ground that they are preempted by federal laws: apparently most, but not all, of these decisions are treated as declarations that the state law is unconstitutional. In updating the list in the book, I included all state laws that the Court held to be preempted.
4. The distinctions made in the paragraphs that follow are drawn chiefly from Robert A. Dahl, "Decision-Making in a Democracy: The Supreme Court as a National Policy-Maker," *Journal of Public Law* 6 (Fall 1957): 279–295.
5. *Scott v. Sandford* (1857); *Hammer v. Dagenhart* (1918); *Bailey v. Drexel Furniture Co.* (1922). Decisions overturning New Deal economic legislation include *United States v. Butler* (1936) and *Schechter Poultry Corp. v. United States* (1935).
6. See William Lasser, "The Supreme Court in Periods of Critical Realignment," *Journal of Politics* 47 (1985): 1174–1187.
7. The cases were, respectively, *Tuggle v. Netherland* (1995); *Board of County Commissioners v. Umbehr* (1996); and *Schenck v. Pro-Choice Network* (1997).

8. Glendon A. Schubert, Jr., *The Presidency in the Courts* (Minneapolis: University of Minnesota Press, 1957); Robert Scigliano, "The Presidency and the Judiciary," in *The Presidency and the Political System*, 3d ed., ed. Michael Nelson (Washington, D.C.: CQ Press, 1990), 471–499.

9. The major cases were, respectively, *Griggs v. Duke Power Company* (1971); *United Steelworkers of America v. Weber* (1979); and *Meritor Savings Bank v. Vinson* (1986).

10. To obtain these figures and others to be presented later in the chapter, I categorized decisions that struck down laws according to whether they pertained to economics, civil liberties, or other subjects. The criteria that I used were necessarily arbitrary; other criteria would have resulted in slightly different totals.

11. *Santa Clara County v. Southern Pacific Railroad Co.* (1886).

12. Benjamin Twiss, *Lawyers and the Constitution* (Princeton, N.J.: Princeton University Press, 1942).

13. John Braeman, *Before the Civil Rights Revolution: The Old Court and Individual Rights* (Westport, Conn.: Greenwood Press, 1988).

14. *Twining v. New Jersey* (1908).

15. See *Schenck v. United States* (1917).

16. Henry Steele Commager, "Judicial Review and Democracy," *Virginia Quarterly Review* 19 (Summer 1943): 428.

17. Robert H. Jackson, *The Struggle for Judicial Supremacy* (New York: Alfred A. Knopf, 1941), 187.

18. William E. Leuchtenburg, *The Supreme Court Reborn: The Constitutional Revolution in the Age of Roosevelt* (New York: Oxford University Press, 1995), 235.

19. *Wickard v. Filburn* (1942).

20. *United States v. Cardiff* (1952).

21. *San Francisco Examiner,* December 14, 1967, 42.

22. *Miller v. California* (1973).

23. See, respectively, *44 Liquormart, Inc. v. Rhode Island* (1996) and *McIntyre v. Ohio Elections Commission* (1995).

24. Martin Shapiro, "The Supreme Court from Early Burger to Early Rehnquist," in *The New American Political System*, 2d ed., ed. Anthony King (Washington, D.C.: AEI Press, 1990), 69–70.

25. *Lucas v. South Carolina Coastal Council* (1992); *Dolan v. City of Tigard* (1994).

26. See William Lasser, *The Limits of Judicial Power: The Supreme Court in American Politics* (Chapel Hill: University of North Carolina Press, 1988), 262–270.

27. Dahl, "Decision-Making in a Democracy," 285.

28. Fred Rodell, *Nine Men* (New York: Random House, 1955), 9. The original aphorism was coined by author Finley Peter Dunne and put in the mouth of his character Mr. Dooley in 1901. See Finley Peter Dunne, *Mr. Dooley on Ivrything and Ivrybody,* selected by Robert Hutchinson (New York: Dover Publications, 1963), 160.

29. Lawrence Baum, "On the Unpredictability of the Supreme Court," *P.S.: Political Science & Politics* 25 (December 1992): 683–688.

Chapter 6

The Court's Impact

I n two decisions in 1962 and 1963, the Supreme Court ruled
that prayer and Bible reading exercises in public schools violate the constitutional prohibition of an establishment of religion.[1] These decisions seemed to resolve the issue of organized
religious observances in public schools.

As it turned out, the Court did not resolve that issue. While
many school districts eliminated the practices that the Court
had held unconstitutional, many others retained them. Some
states enacted laws that were intended to get around the Court's
rulings, such as a requirement of a "moment of silence" that
could be used by teachers as an occasion for prayer. Other states
simply mandated prayer in contradiction of the Supreme
Court. When noncompliant districts and state governments
were taken to court, federal judges generally struck down practices that conflicted with the Court's decisions. But one Alabama district judge announced in an opinion that the Supreme
Court had "erred" and refused to apply its rulings.[2]

Opposition extended to Congress.[3] Members denounced the
Court for its school prayer rulings. Over the years, several hundred resolutions were introduced to overturn the Court's decisions through a constitutional amendment. Other proposals
would have eliminated the Court's jurisdiction to hear cases in
this field.

The controversy has continued in the 1990s. New disputes
arose over religious observances at school graduations and
athletic events, and there are signs that compliance with the
Court's decisions has declined.[4] After the 1994 elections, when

the Republican party gained majorities in both houses of Congress, there was a renewed drive for a constitutional amendment on school prayer. In 1997 a resolution for a "religious freedom amendment" was introduced in the House.[5] One effect of the draft amendment would be to allow organized prayers in schools so long as the prayers were not initiated or designated by "the government." The prospects for this proposal were uncertain, but its introduction with 116 cosponsors underlined the fact that the school prayer issue is far from settled thirty-five years after the Supreme Court seemingly resolved it.

The Supreme Court is the highest interpreter of federal law, and people often think of it as the final arbiter of the issues it addresses. But as the school prayer controversy illustrates, this image of the Court is misleading. It is more useful to think of the Court as one of many institutions that participate in a fluid process of policy making.

Often the Court's decisions decide only one aspect of an issue or offer general guidelines that other policy makers have to fill in. Even when the Court seems to rule decisively on an issue, other institutions may limit the impact of that ruling or negate it altogether. Congress and the president can write a new statute to override the Court's interpretation of an old one. Congress and the states can amend the Constitution to overcome a constitutional decision. Judges and administrators can choose not to carry out a Supreme Court policy fully. And the Court's ultimate impact on society is mediated by the actions of other institutions in and out of government. The Court may influence the strength of the labor movement or the status of women, but so do many other forces—including some that are likely to be far more powerful than the Court.

This chapter explores the impact of Supreme Court decisions. I begin by looking at what happens to the litigants themselves. The remainder of the chapter examines the broader effects of the Court's policies: their implementation, responses to them by legislatures and chief executives, and their effects on society as a whole.

Outcomes for the Parties

Whatever else it does, a Supreme Court decision affects the parties in the case. But the Court's ruling does not always determine the final outcome for the two sides. A great deal can happen to the parties after the Court rules in their case.

If the Court affirms a lower court decision, that decision usually becomes final. If the Court reverses, modifies, or vacates a decision, the case may be handled in either of two ways. Sometimes the Court simply returns the case to the lower court—usually a federal court of appeals or state supreme court—to reach a new decision dictated by the Court's ruling. More often, the Court remands (sends back) the case to the lower court for reexamination. In doing so, it directs that the case be given "further proceedings consistent with this opinion," or the like. Sometimes the court to which the case was remanded then sends it to the original trial court for retrial. This is a common path when the Court overturns a criminal conviction because of procedural errors.

When it remands a case, the Court often gives the lower court considerable leeway in its reconsideration of the case. As a result, that court may rule in favor of the same party as in its original decision, the decision that was overturned by the Supreme Court. Such a result is not necessarily illegitimate; the judges may have taken the Court's ruling into account but concluded that the same outcome was still justified. In criminal cases, for instance, there is often enough evidence of guilt for a conviction even after questionable evidence is excluded or improper procedures are corrected.

But lower court judges occasionally respond to remands in questionable ways, using the leeway that the Supreme Court provides to reach a result that conflicts with the Court's intent. A litigant who feels that a lower court has failed to follow the Supreme Court's directions after a remand can bring the case back to the Court for a second ruling. The Court may then reach a final decision itself, or it can issue a decision and remand the case again with more specific instructions to the lower court. It took the latter step in *Burden v. Zant* (1991, 1994). After a federal court of appeals failed to follow the

Court's instructions in its remand, the losing litigant—a criminal defendant—brought the case back to the Court. The Court then reached a second decision that indicated more forcefully what the court of appeals should do. In taking this action, the Court employed another tool available to it, criticizing the court of appeals with the statement that its decision "was grounded on manifest mistake."[6]

A more extreme step is to issue a writ of mandamus to the lower court, ordering it to take specified action in the case. If the writ is disobeyed, the judges can be cited for contempt of the Supreme Court. But the Court is very reluctant to take these steps. Indeed, it has never held a judge in contempt. Lower court judges who strongly oppose the Court's position in a case can refuse to comply with the terms of the remand, knowing that they will have ample warning if the Court contemplates the use of strong measures to deal with their resistance.

Faced with continued resistance, either the Supreme Court or the litigant it seeks to benefit may give up, leaving the lower court triumphant. In *Florida ex rel. Hawkins v. Board of Control* (1954, 1956, 1957), the Florida Supreme Court refused to order the admission of a black applicant to the all-white University of Florida Law School despite two Supreme Court decisions asking that the Florida court reconsider its position—the second decision virtually demanding that the Florida court order the applicant's admission. As a result, Virgil Hawkins never gained entrance to the University of Florida—though the law school's legal aid clinic was named after him in 1989.[7]

The Court was more successful in 1992, in a brief but intense conflict with the Ninth Circuit Court of Appeals in San Francisco. On the night that California was to carry out its first execution in twenty-five years, judges on the court of appeals issued four orders to stay the execution, each of which was vacated by the Supreme Court. The Court's final ruling prohibited any federal court from issuing further stays in the case except on the Court's own order, and the execution was carried out.[8]

The ultimate outcome for the parties is often determined outside of court. Sometimes the parties settle the case, with the Court's decision serving as leverage for the party that it favored. This was the case, for instance, in *Harris v. Forklift Systems*

(1993), in which the Court ruled in favor of an employee's sexual harassment claim. Two years later, the employee won a settlement from her former employer.[9]

Occasionally the other branches of government intervene on behalf of a party. A 1989 New York statute created a school district for a religious enclave, so that children from the enclave could receive publicly funded special education services while remaining separate from students outside the group. In *Board of Education v. Grumet* (1994), the Supreme Court held that the statute violated the constitutional prohibition of an establishment of religion. New York's governor and legislature then acted quickly to adopt a new statute, which was designed to meet the Court's objections to the 1989 law while maintaining the same separate district. In 1997 New York's highest court ruled that the new statute was also unconstitutional. But three months later the state enacted a third statute creating a special district for the enclave, one worded in a way that supporters hoped would garner court approval.[10]

It is not unusual for a case to take a long time to be resolved. Even if further action is confined to the courts, it is often several years before proceedings are completed. After the Supreme Court's decision in *Hazen Paper Company v. Biggins* (1993), an age discrimination case, the case went through a series of proceedings in the lower federal courts. A 1997 court of appeals decision noted that the case

has returned to us after a first trial, a panel decision, Supreme Court review, a further panel decision, an en banc order directing a further trial on one count, and then a second trial, followed now by the instant appeal. We hope that this opinion will bring the matter to a close, for a decade of litigation about a single, narrow event is enough.[11]

Implementation of Supreme Court Policies

More important than the outcome of a case for the litigants are the broader effects of the legal rules that the Supreme Court lays down in its opinions. Like statutes or presidential orders, these rules have to be implemented—put into effect—by administrators and judges. Judges' task is to apply the Court's interpretations of law whenever they are relevant to a case. For administrators, ranging from cabinet officers to police officers, the task is to follow the requirements that the Court creates for the way they carry out their work.

The responses of judges and administrators to the Court's rules of law can be examined in terms of their compliance and noncompliance with these rules. But the Court's decisions may evoke responses ranging from complete rejection to enthusiastic acceptance and extension, and the concept of compliance does not capture all the possible variations.

The Effectiveness of Implementation

Implementation is an imperfect process. People sometimes assume that when Congress enacts a statute, other policy makers automatically do what is required to make the statute effective. In reality, implementation of statutes is far from automatic. Indeed, congressional policies frequently fail to achieve their objectives because they are carried out poorly. The same is true of Supreme Court decisions: judges and administrators do not necessarily carry them out fully, so they may create a gap between the Court's goals and the actual results.

This does not mean that implementation always works badly. Any policy maker is likely to have a mixed record in getting its policies put into effect. This certainly is true of the Supreme Court. Some of the Court's decisions are carried out more effectively than others, and specific decisions are implemented better in some places or situations than in others.

On the whole, the Court seems to achieve considerable success in getting its policies carried out by lower courts, especially appellate courts. When the Court takes a new doctrinal position, judges generally do their best to follow its lead. One example is *Employment Division v. Smith* (1990), in which the Court narrowed constitutional protection for religious practices that conflict with federal and state laws. After the Court's decision, lower courts ruled in favor of those practices considerably less often.[12] Even on issues as controversial as abortion, judges usually apply the Supreme Court's rulings as well as they can.

Certainly outright refusal to follow the Court's doctrines is unusual. The disobedience of an Alabama federal judge on school prayer, discussed at the beginning of the chapter, received considerable attention because it was so rare. More common is what might be called implicit noncompliance, in which a court purports to follow the Supreme Court's lead but actually evades the implications of the Court's rulings for the case in question. To take one example, lower federal courts have engaged in some implicit noncompliance with the Court's decisions on the administration of public welfare programs.[13]

Implementation problems seem more common among administrators than among judges. Problems at the federal level are illustrated by the long period in which the Patent and Trademark Office failed to carry out Supreme Court rulings on the standards to be used in awarding or denying patents to applicants. At the state level, major examples include school religious exercises, discussed earlier, and school desegregation and police investigations, to be considered shortly.

There have also been widespread implementation problems on procedural matters in state trial courts, which resemble administrative agencies in some respects. Many courts have complied only in part with several of the Warren and Burger Court decisions on criminal procedure, such as the ruling that juvenile defendants are entitled to basic procedural rights. The Court's decision in *Tate v. Short* (1971), holding that an indigent person cannot be sentenced to jail because of inability to pay a fine, has been subverted by judges who fail to inquire into a defendant's ability to pay.[14]

Two Case Studies of Implementation

School Desegregation. Before the Supreme Court's 1954 decision in *Brown v. Board of Education,* separate schools for black and white students existed throughout the Deep South and in most districts of border states such as Oklahoma and Maryland. The Court's decision required that these dual school systems be eliminated. Full desegregation in the border states took time, but considerable compliance with the Court's ruling came within a few years. In contrast, policies in the Deep South changed very slowly. As late as 1964–1965, there was no Deep South state in which even 10 percent of the black students went to school with any white students—a minimal definition of desegregation.[15] This resistance requires a closer look.

Judges and school officials in the Deep South responded to the *Brown* decision in an atmosphere hostile to desegregation. Visible opinion among white citizens was strongly opposed to desegregation; the opinion of black citizens was far less important because a large proportion of them were prevented from voting. Throughout the South, public officials encouraged resistance to the Supreme Court. In 1956, ninety-six southern members of Congress signed a "Southern Manifesto" that attacked the *Brown* decision. Governors and legislatures expressed a strong distaste for desegregation and took official action to prevent it. Governor Orval Faubus of Arkansas, for instance, intervened to block desegregation in Little Rock in 1957.

In this atmosphere school officials generally sought to maintain the status quo. Most administrators personally favored segregation and did everything possible to preserve it. Those administrators who wanted to comply with the Court's ruling were deterred from doing so by pressure from state officials and local citizens.

In places where the schools did not act on their own, parents could file suits in the federal district courts to challenge the continuation of segregated systems. In many districts no suits ever were brought; one reason was fear of retaliation.

Even where suits were brought, their success was hardly guaranteed. In its second decision in *Brown* in 1955, the Supreme Court gave federal district judges substantial freedom to determine the appropriate schedule for desegregation in a school district. Many judges themselves disagreed with the *Brown* decision, and all felt local pressure to proceed slowly if at all. As a result, few demanded speedy desegregation of the schools, and many supported school officials in resisting change. In Dallas, for instance, two district judges struggled mightily to maintain segregation.

Some judges did support the Court wholeheartedly, but they found it difficult to overcome delaying tactics by school administrators and elected officials. In New Orleans, Judge J. Skelly Wright worked hard to bring about desegregation, but the Louisiana governor and legislature fought his efforts with considerable success.

After a long period of resistance, officials in the southern states began to comply. In the second decade after *Brown*, most dual school systems in the South were finally dismantled. Although school segregation was not eliminated altogether, the

TABLE 6-1

Percentage of Black Elementary and Secondary Students Going to School with Any Whites, in Eleven Southern States, 1954–1973

School year	Percentage	School year	Percentage
1954–1955	0.001	1964–1965	2.25
1956–1957	0.14	1966–1967	15.9
1958–1959	0.13	1968–1969	32.0
1960–1961	0.16	1970–1971	85.6
1962–1963	0.45	1972–1973	91.3

Sources: Southern Education Reporting Service, *A Statistical Summary, State by State, of School Segregation-Desegregation in the Southern and Border Area from 1954 to the Present* (Nashville: Southern Education Reporting Service, 1967) (for 1954–1967); U.S. Bureau of the Census, *Statistical Abstract of the United States* (Washington, D.C.: Government Printing Office, 1971 and 1975) (for 1968–1973).

Note: The states are Alabama, Arkansas, Florida, Georgia, Louisiana, Mississippi, North Carolina, South Carolina, Tennessee, Texas, and Virginia.

proportion of black students attending school with whites increased tremendously, as shown in Table 6-1.

The initial and key impetus for this change came from Congress. The Civil Rights Act of 1964 allowed federal funds to be withheld from institutions that practiced racial discrimination. In carrying out that provision, the Department of Health, Education, and Welfare required that schools make a "good-faith start" toward desegregation in order to receive federal aid. Faced with a threat to important financial interests, school officials felt some compulsion to go along. The 1964 act also allowed the Justice Department to bring desegregation suits where local residents were unable to do so, and this provision greatly increased the potential for litigation against school districts that refused to change their policies. This congressional action was reinforced by the Court, whose decisions in 1968 and 1969 demanded effective desegregation without further delay.[16]

In the 1970s the Court turned its attention to the North. In many northern cities, a combination of housing patterns and school board policies had created a situation in which white and nonwhite students generally went to different schools. In a Denver case, *Keyes v. School District No. 1* (1973), the Court held that segregation caused by government in such cities violated the Fourteenth Amendment and required a remedy. In a series of decisions over the next decade, the Court spelled out rules with which to identify constitutional problems and to devise remedies for northern-style segregation.

On the whole, federal district judges in the North supported the Court more than their southern counterparts. Many were willing to order sweeping remedies for segregation in the face of strong local opposition to those remedies, particularly busing. One judge ordered the imposition of higher property taxes to pay for school improvements that might facilitate desegregation in Kansas City. Another held a city in New York State and some of its council members in contempt for failing to approve new public housing for a similar purpose.[17] Ironically, the Court found some of these remedies *too* sweeping.

Few northern school districts took significant steps to eliminate segregation until they were faced with a court order or pressure from federal administrators. For the most part, however, northern districts complied with desegregation orders rather than resisting. Compliance was increased by the willingness of some district judges to supervise school desegregation directly and closely.

Congress did not support northern desegregation. Beginning in 1968 it enacted several legal provisions to prohibit federal agencies from taking action to require school busing for desegregation, and it took some limited and ineffective steps to limit the issuance of busing orders by federal courts. Presidents differed in their use of litigation and financial pressure to support desegregation. The Reagan administration sought to restrict the scope of court-imposed remedies for segregation.

The record of implementation in school desegregation is complex. In the Deep South, the Court's decisions ultimately were implemented, but only with considerable help from the other two branches. In the border states, the Court achieved substantial change even before receiving outside assistance. In the North, the Court was able to bring about major changes in school practices despite some opposition from the other branches.

Police Investigation. The Warren Court imposed substantial procedural requirements on the police in two areas of criminal investigation, issuing a landmark decision in each. In search and seizure, *Mapp v. Ohio* (1961) extended to the states the "exclusionary rule," under which evidence illegally seized by the police cannot be used against a defendant in court. The *Mapp* decision thus provided an incentive for police to follow rules for legal searches that the Court established in other decisions. In the area of interrogation, *Miranda v. Arizona* (1966) required that suspects be given a series of warnings before police questioning if their statements were to be used as evidence. How have judges and police officers responded to those rules?

Lower court responses to *Mapp* and *Miranda* have been mixed. Some state supreme courts criticized the decisions and interpreted them narrowly. At the trial level, many judges who sympathize with the police are reluctant to exclude evidence from trials on the basis of Supreme Court rules. But some lower court judges have applied the Court's rulings vigorously.

While the basic rules of *Mapp* and *Miranda* remain standing, the Burger and Rehnquist Courts have narrowed their protections of suspects. Many lower courts have followed this new direction enthusiastically. But some state supreme courts that support the rulings of the 1960s have found a legitimate means to establish broader protections of procedural rights by declaring that rights denied by the Court under the U.S. Constitution are protected independently by state constitutions. The most important example concerns the Court's ruling in *United States v. Leon* (1984). In *Leon,* the Court held that evidence seized on the basis of a search warrant that had been improperly issued could be used in court if the officers engaging in the search had a "good faith" belief that the warrant was justified. At least nine state supreme courts have held that there is no good faith exception to the search rules in their own constitutions.[18]

Inevitably, *Mapp* and *Miranda* were unpopular in the law enforcement community. Most police officers want maximum freedom for their investigative activities and resent court decisions that impose constraints on them. But they also want their evidence to stand up in court. The result has been a complex pattern of police behavior.

In the case of police questioning, it appears that literal compliance with the *Miranda* rules gradually has become standard practice. For instance, a scholar who observed nearly two hundred interrogations in three California cities in the 1990s found no instances in which detectives were required to provide *Miranda* warnings and failed to do so.[19]

Despite the warnings, most suspects waive their rights and answer questions. One reason is that police officers structure the situation to induce a waiver. One common approach is exemplified by this statement from a detective to a suspect:

> In order for me to talk to you specifically about the injury with [the victim], I need to advise you of your rights. It's a formality. I'm sure you've watched television with the cop shows right and you hear them say their rights and so you can probably recite this better than I can, but it's something I need to do and we can get this out of the way before we talk about what's happened.[20]

Officers sometimes continue to question suspects who have invoked their right to remain silent or to wait for a lawyer. Civil rights lawyers in 1995 presented an excerpt from a training manual used in Los Angeles and Santa Monica in which detectives were encouraged to undertake this practice.[21] Although information obtained through such questioning cannot be admitted directly in court, under a 1971 Supreme Court decision that evidence can be used to impeach a defendant's testimony.[22]

This noncompliance indicates that police officers find *Miranda* to be a hindrance despite the high rate of waivers by suspects. But the Court's ruling serves them well in other respects. Most suspects are still willing to talk, and departments that have suspects sign a form in which they waive their *Miranda* rights have a very strong defense against claims of improper practices.

By threatening that evidence would be excluded from court proceedings, *Mapp* gave police officers an incentive to comply with the body of judicial rules for searches and seizures. Prior to that time, according to one scholar, officers "*systematically* ignored the requirements of the Fourth Amendment because there was no reason to pay attention to it."[23] In effect, then, *Mapp* was an effort to bring about a revolution in police practices.

In those terms, *Mapp* has been partially successful. It produced significant changes in police behavior, including a substantial increase in the use of search warrants in some departments.[24] It appears, as we would expect, that *Mapp*'s effects have increased over time as police adjusted to it. Sociologist Jerome Skolnick observed police search practices in one large city in the 1960s and then in the 1980s, and he concluded that compliance with legal rules "improved significantly."[25]

But compliance is far from perfect. Studies indicate that in a relatively small but significant number of cases, prosecutors drop charges because of illegally seized evidence or judges grant motions to suppress illegal evidence. Such actions occur most often in cases involving "search-intensive" crimes such as drug offenses.[26] Some noncompliance is inadvertent, reflecting the complexity and ambiguity of the body of rules that police are asked to follow in searches and seizures. According to one judge, "the law is so muddy that the police can't find out what they are allowed to do even if they wanted to."[27] Intentional noncompliance reflects the conflict that police officers often perceive: if they follow the applicable legal rules, they cannot obtain evidence that they see as critical.

Explaining the Implementation Process

The effectiveness of implementation for Supreme Court policies depends on several conditions: communication of those policies to relevant officials, the motivations of those officials to follow or resist the Court's policies, the Court's authority, and the sanctions it can use to deter noncompliance.

Communication. Judges and administrators can carry out Supreme Court decisions well only if they know what the Court wants them to do. The communication process begins with the Court's opinions. Ideally, an opinion would state the Court's legal rules with sufficient precision and specificity that an official who reads the opinion would know how to apply those rules to any other case or situation. Frequently, however, opinions fall far short of that ideal: there is considerable ambiguity in the Court's messages.

Much of this ambiguity is unavoidable. The Court's opinions proclaim general legal principles in the context of specific cases. Opinions cannot cover all contingencies that arise in other cases or situations.

Additional ambiguity stems from the Court's decision-making process. The justice who writes an opinion for the Court may take equivocal or inconsistent positions on an issue, com-

promising on language to obtain agreement from other justices. The existence of multiple opinions in a case can also
create confusion, particularly when concurring or dissenting
opinions "interpret" the majority opinion. Of course, confusion
is almost guaranteed when the Court fails to produce a majority opinion.

Because of the Court's ambiguity, lower courts frequently di-
verge in their interpretation and application of its rulings. This
divergence is symbolized by a 1994 decision of one federal court
of appeals, which split 7–6 in its reading of a Court decision on
entrapment of suspects in criminal cases. Viewing the disarray
in his court, one dissenter asked the Supreme Court to revisit
the issue and clarify its position.[28]

Sometimes the Court does use a series of decisions on an issue to provide clarity. But if the Court is inconsistent, multiple
decisions can increase confusion rather than alleviate it. Inconsistency is most likely when the Court's collective views change
over time, as they often do.

Officials who are uncertain about what the Court wants may
not carry out the Court's intent properly even if they would like
to do so. When officials do *not* want to carry out the Court's intent, ambiguity gives them leeway to interpret decisions as they
see fit. Thus the Court's vague timetable for school desegregation gave southern judges and school administrators an excuse
to delay segregation.

Whether the Court's position on an issue is clear or ambiguous, its decisions must be transmitted to relevant judges and
administrators. This is not an automatic process. Even judges
seldom monitor the Supreme Court's output systematically to
identify relevant decisions. Instead, decisions come to the attention of officials through other channels.

One channel is the mass media. A few Supreme Court decisions are sufficiently interesting that they receive heavy publicity in newspapers and on television. But most decisions garner
much less attention from the mass media. Americans collectively get more news from television than from any other
source, but only a minority of decisions get any coverage on the
network news programs. And that coverage is typically quite
limited and sometimes misleading.[29]

Attorneys communicate decisions to some officials. Through
their arguments in court proceedings and administrative hear-

ings, lawyers bring favorable precedents to the attention of judges and administrators. Staff lawyers in administrative agencies often inform agency personnel of relevant decisions. But most kinds of administrators, such as teachers and public welfare workers, lack that source of information.

Another channel of information is professional hierarchies. State trial judges often become aware of the Court's decisions when they are cited by state appellate courts. Police officers learn of decisions from departmental superiors. Here, too, there is considerable potential for misinformation, especially when the communicator disagrees with a decision. Many state supreme courts and most police officials conveyed negative views of liberal criminal justice decisions by the Warren Court when they informed their subordinates of those decisions.

Effective communication of decisions depends on the receivers as well as on the channels of transmission. Legally trained officials are the most capable of understanding decisions and their implications. Police officers and other non-lawyers who work regularly with the law also have some advantage in interpreting decisions. On the whole, administrators who work outside the legal system have the greatest difficulty in interpreting what they learn about Supreme Court rulings.

Where transmission problems exist, they have an obvious and significant impact. Policy makers who do not know of a decision cannot implement it. By the same token, those who misunderstand the Court's requirements will not follow them as intended. As noted earlier, the Court's rules for searches and seizures are complex and ambiguous. In one study, police officers did "slightly better than chance" in answering questions based on six Court decisions about the legality of searches.[30] Based on that finding, we would not expect officers to follow the Court's rules for searches perfectly. In sum, effective transmission of the Court's policies, like clarity in the policies themselves, is needed for their effective implementation.

Motivations for Resistance. If policy makers know of a Supreme Court policy that is relevant to a choice they face, they must decide what to do with that policy. As we would expect, officials are likely to carry out a policy faithfully if they think it is a good policy and that they will benefit from doing so. But if that policy conflicts with their policy preferences or their self-interest, they may resist the Court's lead.

When appellate judges fail to implement Supreme Court decisions fully, the most common reason is a conflict between those decisions and their policy preferences. When the Court adopts a new policy, lower court judges may conclude that it has made a serious mistake. Those judges sometimes rebel against the Court's policy, though their rebellion is usually quiet.

Disagreement about judicial policy tends to follow ideological lines. That tendency is illustrated by conflict between the Supreme Court and the Ninth Circuit Court of Appeals in San Francisco. For the last two decades the Ninth Circuit generally has been the most liberal court of appeals. Although it has become more conservative over that period, the Ninth Circuit as a whole remains more liberal than the Supreme Court, and some of its three-judge panels that hear specific cases are far more liberal than the Court. Largely as a result, the Ninth Circuit sometimes takes positions that are at least arguably inconsistent with those of the Supreme Court. In a 1996 decision, for instance, Justice Ginsburg wrote that the Ninth Circuit "did not attend to this Court's reading of [a federal statute] in a controlling decision."[31]

Of course, trial judges and administrators may also disagree with Supreme Court decisions. A great many teachers and school administrators disapprove of the Court's decisions limiting religious observances in public schools. Similarly, most police officers regard decisions that limit their investigative powers as bad policy. This disagreement is a major source of noncompliance and partial compliance with both sets of decisions.

Supreme Court policies may conflict with officials' self-interest if they threaten existing practices that serve important purposes. Elected administrators who solidify their political strength by giving government jobs to supporters can be expected to resist Court decisions that limit their power to make such hirings.[32] In 1972 the Supreme Court ruled that mayors could not serve as judges in traffic court if their towns receive a substantial portion of their revenue from traffic fines. But precisely because they *do* benefit enormously from that revenue, some Ohio towns have ignored the Court's decision.[33]

Elected officials sometimes have good reason not to carry out highly unpopular decisions. In recent years conservative groups have enjoyed some success in campaigning against elected judges who give broad interpretations to the rights of criminal defendants. For that reason, judges may avoid following Supreme Court policies that require such broad interpretations. For the same reason, school board members in conservative areas are unlikely to take strong stands against school prayers.

Because their positions are secure, federal judges might seem to be immune from these political concerns. But they too may wish to avoid incurring public wrath. Full adherence to *Brown v. Board of Education* would have made the lives of district judges less pleasant because of the reactions of their friends and neighbors. J. Skelly Wright of Louisiana, who did adhere to *Brown,* found that his life was greatly affected. "You never know whether people really want to talk with you and I don't see a lot of people anymore."[34] Wright also had to endure public attacks, including a demonstration in which white parents and children from integrated New Orleans schools brought an effigy of Wright in a coffin into the state capitol, to the applause of legislators.[35]

Wright and a few other judges were willing to accept the costs of supporting the Supreme Court, and several northern federal judges ordered school desegregation despite the prospect of severe public criticism. But they are exceptions. If officials expect to suffer serious consequences for carrying out a decision fully, few will do so.

Differences in the implementation of Supreme Court policies result chiefly from differences in the policy preferences and self-interest of implementers. Police departments tend to resist decisions that limit their powers but follow with alacrity those that expand them. They have carried out *Miranda* more faithfully than limitations on searches because *Miranda* causes them fewer difficulties in practice. The Deep South and the border states responded differently to the *Brown* decision because attitudes toward race and segregation differed between the two regions.

The Court's Authority. In *Singleton v. Norris* (1997), the federal court of appeals for the Eighth Circuit in St. Louis upheld the death sentence in an Arkansas murder case. Judge Gerald Heaney wrote a separate opinion "to add my voice to those who oppose the death penalty as violative of the United States Con-

stitution. My thirty years' experience on this court have compelled me to conclude that the imposition of the death penalty
is arbitrary and capricious." Heaney went on to describe what he
saw as the fundamental problems in the administration of capital punishment, including discrimination on the basis of race
and economic status. Having said all this, Heaney nonetheless
voted to affirm the death sentence in this case. Why would he
cast this vote, one that conflicted with his strongly held view that
the death penalty was unconstitutional? His answer was simple:
"I am compelled to adhere to the law."[36] Almost surely, the law
to which Heaney referred was the Supreme Court's position
that capital punishment is constitutionally acceptable.

Judge Heaney was accepting both the Supreme Court's authority to make authoritative judgments about the law and his
own obligation to comply with the Court's decisions. This acceptance is an important force in the implementation of those
decisions, because it motivates public officials to carry out policies that they view negatively.

The Court's authority is strongest for judges, because they
have been socialized to accept the leadership of higher courts
and because as judges they also benefit from acceptance of judicial authority. But judges may give narrow interpretations to
Court decisions with which they strongly disagree, thereby limiting the impact of those decisions while acknowledging the
Court's authority. And some judges, who resent their subordi-
nation to the Court or who feel that its basic approach to the law
is wrong, accord its decisions less authority.

The Court's authority extends to administrators. Some
school officials eliminate religious observances that they would
prefer to maintain because they accept their duty to follow
Supreme Court rulings.[37] On the whole, however, the Court's
authority is weaker for administrators than it is for judges. Administrative agencies are somewhat removed from the judicial
system and its norm of obedience to higher courts, and relatively few administrators have had the law school training that
supports this norm. As a result, administrative officials find it
somewhat easier to justify deviation from Supreme Court policies than do judges.

The Court's authority tends to decline as organizational distance from the Court increases. Officials at the grass-roots level,

far removed from direct contact with the Court, may not feel obliged to adjust their policies to the Court's decisions. State trial judges typically orient themselves more closely to appellate courts in their state than to the Supreme Court, several steps removed from them in the judicial hierarchy.

The Court's authority is an important motivation for acceptance of its policies. Particularly within the judiciary, the authority attached to Supreme Court decisions reduces noncompliance with those decisions. But the Court's authority is not so powerful that it produces full compliance by officials who have strong reasons not to comply.

Sanctions for Disobedience. More tangible than the Court's authority as a force for compliance is the potential use of sanctions for noncompliance. Judges and administrators might follow the Court's lead in order to avoid those sanctions.

For judges, the most common sanction is reversal. If a judge fails to follow an applicable Supreme Court policy, the losing litigant may appeal the case and secure a reversal of the judge's decision. This sanction is significant, in part because people often evaluate judicial performance by the frequency of reversals. Judges express a variety of attitudes toward reversal, but few are indifferent toward it. "Do I wince when a decision of mine is reversed by an appeals court?" one judge asked. "You bet I do."[38]

The possibility of reversal also encourages lower courts to follow the Court's general line of policy. If the Court begins to adopt more conservative policies in a particular field, the proportion of conservative rulings in the lower courts is likely to increase, as judges shift their positions to reduce the chances of reversal. Indeed, studies indicate that decisional trends in the lower federal courts often move in the same direction as Supreme Court policy.[39]

But reversal has its limits as a sanction. A judge who feels strongly about an issue may be willing to accept a few reversals on that issue as the price of following personal convictions. Judge Stephen Reinhardt of the Ninth Circuit Court of Appeals, one of the most liberal judges in the federal courts, has had several of his decisions reversed by the more conservative Supreme Court. He was asked whether those reversals bothered him. "'Not in the slightest!' he boomed. 'If they want to take away rights, that's their privilege. But I'm not going to help

them do it.'"[40] And failure to follow the Supreme Court's lead
does not always lead to reversal. The losing litigant may not
appeal. Moreover, the great majority of judges are reviewed by
a court other than the Supreme Court, and the reviewing court
may share their opposition to the Court's policies.

For administrators, the most common sanction is a court order that directs compliance with a decision. If a public welfare
agency fails to follow an applicable Supreme Court policy,
someone who is injured by its failure may bring a lawsuit to
compel compliance with the Court's decision. Such a suit in
itself hurts the agency because of the trouble and expense it
entails. A successful suit is even worse, because an order to comply with a Supreme Court rule puts an agency under judicial
scrutiny and may embarrass agency officials. The agency may
also be required to pay monetary damages to the person who
brought the lawsuit.

But this sanction has weaknesses. Most important, it requires
that people bring litigation challenging agency behavior, and
they do not always do so. To take one example, school religious
observances that violate the Supreme Court's rulings have gone
unchallenged in many communities. And if a lawsuit is threatened or actually brought, agencies can usually change their
practices in time to avoid serious costs. Thus the possibility of a
lawsuit, in the abstract, is not always a strong deterrent against
noncompliance.

Still, to follow a policy that conflicts with a Supreme Court
ruling carries risks that most officials prefer to avoid. This attitude helps to account for the frequency with which administrative organizations on their own initiative eliminate practices
prohibited by the Court. And administrators whose actions require court enforcement, such as officials in some regulatory
agencies, have even more reason to avoid noncompliance that
may cost them judicial support.

Police practices in searches and seizures illustrate both the
strength and limitations of this sanction. Under *Mapp*, noncompliance with rules for searches jeopardizes the use of evidence in court. As a result, officers engage in a good deal of
compliance with rules that they would prefer to ignore. On the
other hand, officers seldom receive any personal sanctions for
practices that cause evidence to be thrown out. Moreover, ille-

gal searches may not prevent convictions. Most defendants plead guilty, and by doing so they generally waive their right to challenge the legality of searches. Trial judges often give the benefit of the doubt to police officers on borderline evidentiary questions. And evidence that is ruled illegal may not be necessary for a conviction. Thus police officers have a strong incentive to avoid illegal searches, but not so strong that they always try to follow the applicable rules.

This discussion suggests two conditions that affect the implementation process. First, enforcement of a Supreme Court decision is enhanced when interest groups act to challenge noncompliance. Second, the Court's decisions are easiest to enforce when the affected policy makers are few in number and highly visible. It has been relatively simple for the Court to oversee the fifty state governments that must carry out its decisions on the drawing of legislative districts. It is a far more difficult matter for the Court to oversee the day-to-day activities of the thousands of police officers who investigate crimes.

In general, the sanctions available to the Court are fairly weak. The Court can do relatively little to overcome resistance to its policies. Thus help from Congress and the president can make a great deal of difference when the Court faces widespread noncompliance. In enforcing school desegregation, that help was a necessity.

Summary. The Supreme Court's policies are implemented more effectively in some settings than in others. Judges generally carry out the Court's policies more fully than administrators because communication of decisions to judges is relatively good, most judges accord the Court considerable authority, and their self-interest is less likely to conflict with the implementation of decisions. For some of the same reasons, federal judges and administrators are probably better implementers of decisions than are their state counterparts. The Court's decisions are communicated to them more effectively, and its authority and sanctions affect them more directly.

On the whole, the Court's policies are implemented fairly well, but the gap between the rules of law that the Court establishes and the actions taken by judges and administrators is often considerable. To a degree, this gap reflects the Court's weaknesses as a policy maker, in that it can exert little control

over the implementation process. Most important, the sanctions that it can apply to disobedient officials are relatively weak
compared with those available to Congress or the president. But
more striking than this difference is the similarity in the basic
positions of Court, Congress, and president: each proclaims
policies that have uncertain and often unhappy fates in the implementation process.

Responses by Legislatures and Chief Executives

After the Supreme Court hands down its decisions, Congress,
the president, and their state counterparts can respond in various ways. They may help or hinder the implementation of decisions, they may act to change the Court's interpretations of the
law, and they may attack the Court or its members.

Congress

Statutory Interpretation. Congress is supreme in statutory law:
it can override the Supreme Court's interpretation of a statute
simply by adopting a new statute with different language that
supersedes the Court's reading of the old statute. Congress can
also ratify or extend the Court's interpretation of a statute, but
overrides of statutory decisions are especially significant.

A substantial proportion of statutory decisions receive some
congressional scrutiny, and proposals to override decisions are
common. Most of these proposals fail, for the same reasons that
most bills of any type fail: legislation must navigate successfully
through several decision points at which it can be killed, and
there is usually a presumption in favor of the status quo. Still,
overrides are far from rare. Over the past three decades, on average, more than ten statutory decisions have been overturned
in each two-year Congress. Of the statutory decisions in the
Court's 1978–1989 terms, Congress had overridden more than
five percent by 1996.[41] As Table 6-2 illustrates, overrides range
across a wide array of issues and areas of law. The table also
shows that some overrides follow quickly after a decision, while
others come considerably later.

In most respects, the politics of congressional response to the
Court's statutory decisions resembles congressional politics
generally.[42] The initiative for bills to overturn decisions often
comes from interest groups. Just as groups that fail to achieve

TABLE 6-2
Selected Congressional Legislation Overturning
Supreme Court Statutory Decisions, 1995–1996

Migrant Worker Protection (enacted 1995)
Overturned *Adams Fruit Co. v. Barrett* (1990) by prohibiting migrant farm workers from suing employers for injuries when they could obtain workers' compensation benefits for those injuries.

False Statements Accountability Act of 1996
Overturned *Hubbard v. United States* (1995) by making it a criminal offense to make a false statement in a judicial proceeding.

Federal Courts Improvement Act of 1996
Overturned *Pulliam v. Allen* (1984) by giving judges immunity from lawsuits for injunctive relief and from the payment of costs in lawsuits; also overturned *Primate Protection League v. Administrators of Tulane Educational Fund* (1991) by allowing federal agencies to remove lawsuits against them from state to federal court.

Small Business Job Protection Act of 1996
Partially overturned *John Hancock Mutual Life Insurance v. Harris Trust* (1993) by giving life insurance companies an exemption from federal pension regulations for certain funds until 1999.

their goals in Congress frequently turn to the courts for relief, groups whose interests suffer in the Supreme Court frequently turn to Congress.

The success of efforts to overturn statutory decisions depends on the same broad array of factors that influence the fates of other bills in Congress. The political strength of the groups that favor or oppose overrides is important. Not surprisingly, the federal executive branch enjoys considerable success in getting Congress to overturn unfavorable decisions, while nearly all decisions that work to the detriment of criminal defendants are left standing.[43] When a significant group favors action and organized opposition does not exist, Congress may override a decision quickly and easily. Many successful overrides are enacted not as separate bills but as provisions of broader bills such as appropriations, and members of Congress who vote for those bills are not always aware that they are overriding a Supreme Court decision.

Congress does not always have the last word when it overrides a statute, because the new statute is subject to judicial interpretation. In *Westfall v. Erwin* (1988), the Court held that federal officials could be sued for personal injuries under some circumstances. A few months later Congress overrode *Westfall* by allowing the attorney general to certify that an employee who had been sued was acting as a federal official and thereby substituting the federal government for the employee as a defendant. But in *Gutierrez de Martinez v. Lamagno* (1995), the Court weakened the override by holding that the attorney general's certification could be challenged in court. The Court sometimes goes even further. In *Plaut v. Spendthrift Farm* (1995), it held that a congressional override of a 1991 decision on the statute of limitations in securities fraud cases was unconstitutional because it violated the constitutional separation of powers between the legislative and judicial branches.

Constitutional Interpretation. When the Court interprets the Constitution, the most direct and decisive way to overturn its decision is through a constitutional amendment. But that is a very difficult route, because the amending process is arduous and there is a widespread reluctance to tamper with the Constitution. It is far easier to adopt a new statute, but a constitutional decision cannot be overturned directly by a statute. Under some circumstances, however, a statute can negate or limit the effects of a constitutional decision.

If the Court has nullified or limited a statute on constitutional grounds, Congress can enact a second statute to try to meet the Court's objections. In *United States v. Harriss* (1954), the Court gave a narrow reading to the coverage of the Federal Regulation of Lobbying Act. The Court did so in order to avoid holding that the act's criminal penalties for failure by lobbyists to register with Congress were unconstitutional because of vagueness about who was required to register. But the Court's narrow interpretation greatly weakened the act, because under that interpretation most people who acted as lobbyists did not have to register. More than forty years later, Congress addressed that problem by enacting the Lobbying Disclosure Act of 1995. The new act required a broad range of people to register as lobbyists, but its description of those people was far more precise than the description in the original act.

When the Court holds that a right is not protected by the Constitution, Congress often can protect that right by enacting a statute. Congress has taken that action on issues such as the use of search warrants to gather information from newsrooms. In one recent instance, however, the Court ruled that such congressional action was invalid. In *Employment Division v. Smith* (1990), the Court gave a narrow interpretation to the protections of freedom of religion in the First and Fourteenth Amendments, making it easier for governments to justify rules that treat religion neutrally but that have the effect of putting a burden on a particular religious practice. A broad set of religious groups attacked the decision. In response, Congress enacted the Religious Freedom Restoration Act in 1993 to restore the broader pre-*Smith* standard of protection for religion. But in *City of Boerne v. Flores* (1997), the Court held that the 1993 act was unconstitutional as applied to state and local governments because it went beyond congressional power to enforce the Fourteenth Amendment.

In situations where constitutional decisions cannot be negated by statute, members of Congress often introduce resolutions to overturn them with constitutional amendments. In recent years, resolutions have been submitted on a variety of issues. The range of these issues is suggested by a sampling of resolutions introduced in 1997, shown in Table 6-3.

Not surprisingly, few of these efforts to propose amendments have achieved the necessary two-thirds votes in both houses. Only five times has Congress proposed an amendment that was aimed directly at Supreme Court decisions. And one of these, proposed in 1924 to give Congress the power to regulate child labor, was not ratified by the states. (A few amendments have indirectly negated Supreme Court decisions.) Since the child labor proposal, the only amendment that Congress has proposed in order to overturn a decision was the Twenty-sixth Amendment, adopted in 1971. In *Oregon v. Mitchell* (1970), the Court had ruled that Congress cannot regulate the voting age in elections to state office; Congress acted quickly to propose an amendment overturning the decision, and the states quickly ratified it.

In contrast with the Twenty-sixth Amendment, the most prominent failed campaigns for amendments in recent years were aimed at decisions that increased legal protections for civil liberties. Even highly unpopular decisions, such as prohibitions of school prayer, stood up against efforts to overturn them. In

TABLE 6-3

Selected Resolutions Introduced in Congress for Constitutional Amendments to Overturn Supreme Court Decisions, 1997

Purpose	Decisions that would be overturned
Giving states power to impose term limits on members of Congress	*U.S. Term Limits v. Thornton* (1995)
Giving Congress power to limit campaign spending	*Buckley v. Valeo* (1976), later decisions
Allowing organized prayer in public schools	*Engel v. Vitale* (1962)
Giving federal and state governments power to prohibit flag desecration	*Texas v. Johnson* (1989), *United States v. Eichman* (1990)
Prohibiting abortion under most circumstances	*Roe v. Wade* (1973), *Planned Parenthood v. Casey* (1992), other decisions
Allowing states to reduce prisoners' credits toward early release retroactively	*Lynce v. Mathis* (1997)

these instances, the general reluctance to amend the Constitution was compounded by a special reluctance to limit the protections of rights in the Bill of Rights.

That reluctance is illustrated by the effort to propose an anti-flag-desecration amendment. In *Texas v. Johnson* (1989), the Supreme Court struck down a state statute prohibiting flag burning on the ground that it punished people for political expression. Four months later Congress enacted a federal statute against flag burning, written in an effort to meet the Court's objections to the Texas statute. But in *United States v. Eichman* (1990), the Court held that the new statute was also unconstitutional.

Members of Congress then sought a constitutional amendment to allow prohibition of flag desecration. Its passage seemed inevitable, because a member's vote against the amendment might provide an opponent with a powerful issue in the 1990 election. But the House defeated the amendment by thirty-four votes, the Senate by nine. In the more conservative

Congress that resulted from the 1994 election, an amendment that passed the House by a 312–120 margin in 1995 failed by only three votes in the Senate; an amendment approved by the House in 1997 with a similar majority might win Senate approval.[44] Even so, the lack of an anti-flag-desecration proposal from Congress by 1996 underlines the difficulty of amending the Constitution.

Affecting the Implementation of Decisions. By passing legislation, Congress can influence the implementation of Supreme Court decisions by other institutions. Its most important tool is budgetary. Congress can provide or fail to provide funds to carry out a decision. It can also help the Court by withholding federal funds from state and local governments that refuse to comply with the Court's decisions. Congressional use of the latter power was critical in achieving school desegregation in the Deep South.

Occasionally a Supreme Court decision requires implementation by Congress itself. In these situations Congress generally has accepted its obligation with little resistance. The legislative veto is an exception.[45] In *Immigration and Naturalization Service v. Chadha* (1983), the Court indicated that any statutes allowing Congress or one of its units to "veto" proposed executive branch actions are invalid. After the decision, Congress eliminated legislative veto provisions from several statutes. But it maintained others, and since 1983 it has adopted more than two hundred new legislative veto provisions—most requiring that specific congressional committees approve action by administrative agencies. Agency officials are willing to accept these provisions rather than challenging their legality, in order to maintain good relations with congressional committees and to avoid even more stringent congressional controls. Thus political realities have allowed noncompliance with *Chadha* to continue.

Attacks on the Court and Its Members. When members of Congress are dissatisfied with the Supreme Court's behavior, they may attack the Court or the justices directly. The easiest way to do so is verbal, and members of Congress frequently express their disapproval of the Court by denouncing it publicly. More concretely, Congress can take formal legislative action of several types.

One type of action concerns jurisdiction. The Constitution allows Congress to alter the Court's appellate jurisdiction through legislation, though there is some question about whether Congress can narrow the Court's jurisdiction to prevent it from protecting constitutional rights. Congress has used its power over jurisdiction to control the Court only once, in an unusual situation: in 1869 it withdrew the Court's right to hear appeals in habeas corpus actions in order to prevent it from deciding a pending challenge to the post–Civil War Reconstruction legislation. In *Ex parte McCardle* (1869), the Court ruled that this congressional action was constitutionally acceptable.

In recent years, Congress has considered several bills that would have limited the Court's jurisdiction in areas of civil liberties activism. In 1964, the House did pass a bill to eliminate the jurisdiction of all federal courts over the drawing of state legislative districts, and in 1979 the Senate approved a provision to eliminate federal court jurisdiction over cases that concerned school prayer. Both of these bills died in the other house. Since the early 1980s, bills and amendments have been introduced to limit the Court's jurisdiction over such issues as abortion, school busing, and prayer. But none have passed either house.

The most extreme action that Congress can take against individual justices is to remove them through impeachment. One justice was impeached by the House—though not convicted by the Senate—in 1804, and impeachment has been threatened in several other instances. But impeachment based on disagreement over policy is extremely unlikely.

Congress controls the Court budget, limited only by the constitutional prohibition against reducing the justices' salaries. With a few exceptions, Congress has refrained from using its budget power to attack the Court.[46] But in 1964 Congress singled out the justices when it increased their annual salaries by $4,500—$3,000 less than the raises given to other federal judges. That action was motivated by displeasure with the Court's civil liberties policies. A proposal to provide that $3,000 to the justices was defeated in the House the next year, after a debate in which several members attacked the Court, and one—Robert Dole of Kansas—suggested that the pay increase be contingent on the Court's reversing a legislative districting decision that he disliked.[47]

That attack on the justices through their salaries was perhaps the most serious concrete action that Congress has taken against the Court in the twentieth century; Congress has made little use of its enormous powers over the Court. Why has it been hesitant to employ them, even at times when most members were unhappy about the Court's direction?

To begin with, there are always some members of Congress who agree with the Court's policies and lead its defense. Further, serious forms of attack against the Court, such as impeachment and reducing its jurisdiction, seem illegitimate to many people. Finally, when threatened with serious attack, the Court sometimes retreats to reduce the impetus for congressional action. For these reasons, the congressional bark at the Supreme Court has been a good deal worse than its bite.

The President

Influencing Congressional Response. The president can influence congressional responses to the Supreme Court by taking a position on proposals for action. Sometimes it is the president who first proposes anti-Court action. The most dramatic example in the twentieth century is President Roosevelt's Court-packing plan.

Since the 1960s, conservative presidents have encouraged efforts in Congress to limit or overturn some of the Court's liberal rulings on civil liberties. For instance, George Bush led the effort to overturn the Court's flag-burning decisions in 1989 and 1990.

Bill Clinton has also sought action to reverse the effects of some decisions. One effort came after the Court held in 1995 that a federal statute prohibiting guns in and around schools had gone beyond congressional power to regulate interstate commerce. Clinton said in his radio address three days later that "this Supreme Court decision could condemn more of our children to going to schools where there are guns."[48] Clinton then proposed narrower legislation that was tied more directly to interstate commerce. Ultimately, that legislation was enacted as part of an appropriations bill in 1996. It remains to be seen whether the Supreme Court will find the new statute constitutionally acceptable.

Using Executive Power. As chief executive, the president has a number of means to shape the implementation of Supreme Court decisions. For one thing, presidents can decide whether to support the Court with the power of the federal government when its decisions encounter open resistance from officials with the responsibility to carry them out.

The most coercive form of federal power is deployment of the military. When southern states began to defy *Brown v. Board of Education,* President Eisenhower indicated that he would not use troops to enforce the decision. But in 1957, when a combination of state interference and mob action prevented court-ordered desegregation of the schools in Little Rock, Arkansas, Eisenhower abandoned his earlier position and brought in troops. In 1962 President Kennedy used federal troops to enforce desegregation at the University of Mississippi.

Presidents can also use litigation and their control over federal funds. The Johnson administration's vigorous use of both these mechanisms was directly responsible for breaking down segregated school systems in the Deep South. More recent presidents have differed in their readiness to use federal money and initiate lawsuits in conflicts over school desegregation.

President Reagan's use of his executive powers helped to spur a major change in labor-management relations. In *National Labor Relations Board v. Mackay Radio & Telegraph Company* (1938), the Court ruled that under a federal labor law, companies could hire new employees as permanent replacements for workers who were on strike. For several decades companies made little use of the Court's ruling. But after federal air traffic controllers went on strike in 1982, Reagan ordered the strikers replaced. The strike failed, and this episode encouraged employers to take similar action. By doing so, they accelerated a decline in the power of organized labor.

Bill Clinton sought legislation to override *Mackay;* a bill with that purpose passed the House in 1994 but died with a Senate filibuster. The next year Clinton issued an executive order under which companies receiving substantial amounts of money from federal contracts were prohibited from hiring permanent replacement workers. An effort to override the executive order through legislation failed in Congress, but in 1996 a federal court of appeals ruled that the order violated the statute that the Court had interpreted in *Mackay*.[49]

Presidential Compliance. Occasionally a Supreme Court decision requires compliance by the president, either as a party in the case or—more often—as head of the executive branch. Some presidents and commentators have argued that the president need not obey an order of the Supreme Court, which is a coequal body rather than a legal superior. In any case, presidents would seem sufficiently powerful to disobey the Court with impunity.

But in reality their position is not that strong. The president's political power is based largely on the ability to obtain support from other policy makers. This ability, in turn, depends in part on perceptions of the president's legitimacy. Because disobedience of the Court would threaten this legitimacy, Samuel Krislov argued, presidents "cannot afford to defy the Court."[50]

That conclusion is supported by presidential responses to two highly visible Court orders. In *Youngstown Sheet and Tube Co. v. Sawyer* (1952), the Court ruled that President Truman had acted illegally in seizing steel mills to keep them operating during a wartime strike and ordered that they be released. Truman immediately complied.

Even more striking is *United States v. Nixon* (1974). During investigation of the Watergate scandal, President Nixon withheld recordings of certain conversations in his offices that were sought by special prosecutor Leon Jaworski. In July 1974, the Supreme Court ruled unanimously that Nixon must yield the tapes.

In oral argument before the Court, the president's lawyer had indicated that Nixon might not comply with an adverse decision. Immediately after the decision was handed down, Nixon apparently considered noncompliance. By the end of that day, however, Nixon released a statement indicating that he would comply. At the least, this compliance speeded Nixon's departure from office: he released transcripts of some of the tapes, whose content provided strong evidence of presidential misdeeds, and opposition to impeachment evaporated. Fifteen days after the Court's ruling, Nixon announced his resignation.

In light of that result, why did President Nixon comply with the Court order? He apparently did not realize how damaging the evidence in the tapes actually was. Perhaps more important, noncompliance would have damaged his remaining legitimacy fatally. For many members of Congress noncompliance in itself would have constituted an impeachable offense, one on which there would be no dispute about the evidence. Under the circumstances compliance may have been the better of two unattractive choices.

State Legislatures and Governors

State governments have no direct power over the Supreme Court as an institution. But state legislatures and governors can influence the implementation of the Court's decisions. Most noteworthy are the instances when they seek to limit or overturn such decisions.

Like Congress, state legislatures can rewrite statutes to try to meet the Court's constitutional objections. The Supreme Court struck down the existing death penalty statutes in *Furman v. Georgia* (1972), with some members of the five-justice majority emphasizing the arbitrary element in the use of the penalty. In the next few years, thirty-five states adopted new capital punishment laws that were designed to avoid arbitrary sentencing. In a series of decisions from 1976 on, the Court upheld some of the new statutes and overturned others. States whose laws were rejected by the Court then adopted the forms that the Court had found acceptable. As a result, the impact of *Furman* has nearly been nullified.

Legislatures sometimes adopt statutes that seem clearly to violate the Court's decisions, in order to limit the Court's impact and to express opposition to its rulings. In the decade after *Brown v. Board of Education,* southern states passed a large number of statutes to prevent school desegregation, and some states have enacted laws to restore school religious observances that the Supreme Court invalidated. Often, such statutes are overturned quickly by the federal courts.

In eighteen states the voters can amend the state constitution by adopting initiative measures. After the Supreme Court held in 1995 that the states could not impose term limits on members of Congress, voters in nine states adopted initiatives that would punish any federal or state legislator who did not support specified term limits by putting on the ballot next to that member's name, "DISREGARDED VOTER INSTRUCTION ON TERM LIMITS." The Arkansas Supreme Court ruled that its state's initiative was unconstitutional; in 1997 the U.S. Supreme Court chose not to hear the case.[51]

The states can play two roles in amending the Constitution. When Congress proposes amendments, they must be ratified by three-quarters of the states. In an alternative procedure, the Constitution also allows the states a role in the proposal stage. By submitting petitions, two-thirds of the state legislatures can require Congress to convene a convention to consider proposing amendments. This procedure has never been used successfully, but in the 1960s thirty-three of the necessary thirty-four states petitioned for a convention to consider overturning the Court's decisions on legislative districting.

Like presidents, governors can influence both legislative responses to the Court's decisions and their implementation. Southern governors helped to block school desegregation in the 1950s and 1960s through their efforts to stir up resistance. More recently, governors have been prominent in state controversies over issues such as school prayer and criminal procedure, sometimes supporting and sometimes opposing the Court's decisions.

Legislatures and governors must act to put some Supreme Court decisions into effect. In 1989 the Court ruled that it was illegal for states to tax retirement benefits for federal workers while exempting similar benefits for state and local workers, as twenty-three states did. Several state governments balked at refunding tax money to federal retirees, and the Court had to decide cases from Virginia in 1993 and Georgia in 1994 to make clear that refunds were necessary. Even so, federal retirees in Virginia who refused to settle for partial payments did not receive refunds until the state supreme court ruled that the state government had no choice but to pay the money it owed them.[52]

Gideon v. Wainwright (1963) and later decisions required state and local governments to fund legal services for indigent criminal defendants. The response has been mixed. Government now spends well over $1 billion each year for legal defense of the poor,[53] and low-income defendants are in far better posi-

tion than they were prior to *Gideon*. But funding of counsel
has never been fully adequate, and it has become less adequate
with growth in the number of criminal cases. As a result, according to one federal judge, "perfunctory representation of indigent criminal defendants is the order of the day in American
courts."[54]

State legislatures and governors engage in direct defiance of
the Court's decisions more often than do Congress and the
president. This difference may result chiefly from the sheer
number of states rather than from differences in the behavior
of state and federal officials. Still, it suggests that the Court may
face special difficulties when it seeks to bring about fundamental changes in state policies.

Yet resistance to the Court by state governments should not
be exaggerated. Undoubtedly, their most frequent response
to the Court's decisions is compliance. And much of what governors and legislatures do to limit the Court's impact, such as
their reinstatement of the death penalty, is an effort to maintain the policies they want within the constraints of the Court's
rulings.

Two Policy Areas

Patterns of response to the Court's decisions by the other two
branches of government can be examined more closely with a
look at two areas in which there has been a good deal of interaction between the Court and other policy makers.

Civil Rights Statutes. Beginning in 1957, Congress adopted
a series of statutes that prohibited discrimination along racial
and other lines; the two most important were the Civil Rights
Act of 1964 and the Voting Rights Act of 1965, both amended to
broaden their impact since then. Thousands of cases are
brought under the civil rights statutes each year, and the Supreme Court has issued several major decisions and many minor ones interpreting them.

In some decisions the Burger and Rehnquist Courts have interpreted these statutes broadly, giving them greater impact.
But other decisions—particularly in the late 1980s and early
1990s—have narrowed the meaning of these statutes, sometimes in important ways. Meanwhile, Congress maintained a relatively liberal position on civil rights issues until the mid-1990s,

in part because of effective lobbying by civil rights groups. As a result, at least ten statutes have been adopted to overturn the Court's narrow interpretations.[55]

The Reagan and Bush administrations were more favorable than Congress to the Court's narrow interpretations of the civil rights laws. One bill intended to overturn a Court decision became law only after Congress overrode President Reagan's veto in 1988. The sweeping Civil Rights Act of 1991, which overturned nine Court decisions, became law only after an earlier version had been vetoed by President Bush.

In 1994 the Court ruled that the Civil Rights Act of 1991 does not apply to cases that were pending when it was enacted.[56] Efforts immediately began in Congress to overturn that decision, but they were unsuccessful. With Congress and the Court now closer to each other ideologically than they were up to the early 1990s, overrides of the Court's civil rights decisions are less likely.

Abortion. After the Supreme Court struck down state prohibitions of abortion in *Roe v. Wade* (1973), most states enacted laws to regulate abortion.[57] Many of these laws were neutral regulations that would clearly be acceptable to the Court, such as a requirement that abortions be performed by licensed physicians. But many other state laws were motivated by the goal of limiting the Court's impact by making abortions more difficult to obtain. Some states adopted several different statutes of this type. Rhode Island sought to nullify the Court's decision altogether with a new statute.

Groups that opposed legal restrictions on abortion regularly challenged restrictive state laws. In a series of decisions from 1976 to 1986, the Court struck down a number of these laws as inconsistent with *Roe.* But the Court did uphold federal and state restrictions on the funding of abortion in the Medicaid program for low income people. (Several state courts, however, struck down state funding restrictions on the basis of provisions in state constitutions.)

As new appointments made the Court more conservative, its support for the principles of the *Roe* decision weakened. Many people interpreted the Court's decision in *Webster v. Reproductive Health Services* (1989) to mean that the Court would now allow substantial restrictions on abortion or even overturn *Roe* in an appropriate case. Consequently, legislators and interest groups in nearly every state sought new legislation that heavily restricted abortion. In the two years after *Webster,* the great majority of these efforts failed, but Pennsylvania enacted major restrictions on abortion, and Utah, Louisiana, and Guam prohibited abortions under most circumstances. In contrast, Connecticut and Maryland passed statutes protecting the right to abortion under state law.

The Court's decision in *Planned Parenthood v. Casey* (1992), which reaffirmed *Roe* for the most part, made it clear that the Court would strike down state prohibitions of abortion. But the decision also encouraged states to adopt restrictions that might be consistent with the Court's new rules for regulation of abortion. Since 1992 some states have adopted statutes requiring parental consent or notification for young women unless a judge allows a waiver of that requirement, some have mandated a waiting period between a woman's receiving certain information and obtaining an abortion, and Mississippi in 1996 enacted a substantial set of regulations on abortion. In *Lambert v. Wicklund* (1997) the Court unanimously upheld a parental notification law similar to statutes it had accepted in the past. With that exception, it has said little about what kinds of regulations are acceptable under *Casey.*

At the federal level, the Reagan and Bush administrations established restrictions on the availability of abortion in some areas of federal activity, such as the military. In the early 1990s, Congress took steps to overturn some of these restrictions, but President Bush used the veto power to block these initiatives. One example involved the "gag rule," a set of regulations by the Department of Health and Human Services that broadly prohibited family planning clinics funded by the federal government from engaging in activities that encouraged or facilitated abortion. The Court upheld these regulations in *Rust v. Sullivan* (1991). Later that year Congress passed a bill intended to overturn the regulations, but President Bush vetoed it; he vetoed similar legislation in 1992.

Two days after he became president, Bill Clinton eliminated the regulations of family planning clinics along with several other restrictions on abortion. When the Court ruled in 1993 that abortion clinics could not use a civil rights law to sue those engaged in protests that obstruct access to the clinics, the Clinton administration encouraged Congress to pass a statute aimed at curbing those protests.[58] Congress did so in 1994, allowing criminal prosecutions and civil lawsuits against those engaged in such activities as blockading abortion clinics.

The abortion issue illustrates the importance of legislative responses to the Court's decisions. Even a seemingly definitive ruling in *Roe v. Wade* did not prevent Congress and state legislatures from enacting laws limiting access to abortion, and legislatures have done a great deal to shape the law of abortion within the constraints of the Court's decisions. The issue also underlines the role of chief executives. Governors in some states have encouraged restrictions on abortion, while other governors have prevented their enactment. The difference in the actions of the Bush and Clinton administrations underlines the president's importance in influencing federal responses to the Court's abortion decisions.

Impact on Society

Supreme Court decisions are directed at other public policy makers, establishing legal rules to govern policy decisions within government. But the ultimate significance of those decisions depends primarily on their impact outside government, on American society as a whole. The Court's rulings in labor law are important chiefly because of their potential effects on the relationship between employees and employers. Its decisions on sex discrimination are significant to the extent that they affect the status of women.

People who disapprove of the Supreme Court's policies often depict the Court as a very powerful force in American society. Republican presidential candidate Pat Buchanan said in 1996 that "by redefining individual rights as it wished, the court has centralized control over virtually every moral, political, social and economic issue in this country."[59] One scholar concluded that "clearance rates for violent crime would be several percentage points higher without *Miranda*, with the result that each year police would solve an additional 100,000-plus violent crimes."[60] And the Court's decisions on school religious observances are viewed by many people as having fundamental and highly unfortunate effects. North Carolina senator Jesse Helms said that "I think it is possible to pinpoint when the decline of this country really began"—with "the lawsuit that resulted in the first Supreme Court decision banning prayer. Since that time, America has been on the slippery slope. Morality has been all but forgotten."[61]

By no means does everyone see the Court as holding such enormous power; some commentators argue that it has little capacity to produce significant change in society. In 1991 one scholar advised liberals not to expend energy and resources opposing the confirmation of Clarence Thomas to the Court, because the Court does not have a major effect on achievement of liberal social reform.[62] But interest groups do devote considerable energy to the Court, and the mass media give considerable attention to it. These choices reflect a widely shared belief that the Court's decisions *are* important to American society. To what extent is this belief accurate?

A General View

Any government policy can have a wide range of effects on society, including some that are indirect and quite unexpected. Certainly this is true of Supreme Court decisions. Often it is difficult to distinguish between the Court's impact and that of other forces contributing to the same result. For this reason it is seldom possible to make firm judgments about the effects of the Supreme Court on society.

Still, there is reason to be skeptical about judgments that the Court has a fundamental impact on American society. In reality, the effects of Supreme Court policies on society are constrained a great deal by the context in which those policies operate.

Part of that context is governmental. As we have seen, the impact of decisions is often narrowed by other policy makers who fail to implement them fully or who take other action to limit them. For example, Senator Helms's statement appears to reflect an assumption that public schools ended prayer and Bible-reading exercises after the Supreme Court prohibited those practices, but in fact they remained widespread.

More broadly, the Court is seldom the only government agency that deals with a particular set of issues. Rather, in most areas the Court is one policy maker among many that render decisions and undertake initiatives. In environmental policy, for instance, Congress sets the basic legal rules, administrative agencies elaborate on these rules and apply them to specific cases, and lower courts resolve most disagreements over agency decisions. The Court's participation is limited to resolving a few of the legal questions that arise in the lower courts. The Court can still have considerable impact, but it can hardly determine the character of environmental policy by itself.

The Court's policies also operate within a context of nongovernmental action. Even the direct impact of most decisions depends largely on the responses of people outside government. Especially important are the actions of people and institutions that the Court gives greater freedom. These beneficiaries of the Court's policies may not take full advantage of the freedom that the Court provides them. One reason is that they may not be aware of favorable decisions. But even those who know about such decisions do not always act on them. For example, welfare recipients may not insist on their procedural rights because they do not want to alienate officials who hold power over them. A 1996 decision struck down state prohibitions on advertising of liquor prices,[63] but some store owners may decide against advertising prices because it does not seem profitable to compete on the basis of price.

The broad impact of Supreme Court decisions on society is also limited by nongovernmental forces. Phenomena such as the crime rate and the quality of education are affected by family socialization, the mass media, and the economy. Those forces are likely to exert a much stronger impact on the propensity to commit crimes or the performance of students than does a Supreme Court policy. Moreover, any effects that the Court does have operate within the context of these forces. This limitation is common to all public policies, no matter which branch issues them. But the Supreme Court is in an especially weak position, because it has little control over the behavior of the private sector and because it seldom makes comprehensive policy in a particular area.

Despite all these limitations, Supreme Court decisions can and do have a significant effect on society. Frequently their direct impact is considerable, because they help to determine the scope and content of government action on an issue. The Court plays a part in shaping federal policy on matters ranging from mergers of businesses to criminal justice. By doing so, the Court may have a hand in shaping important social phenomena. To take two examples that were discussed earlier, the effects of the Court's decisions on the hiring of replacement workers for strikers and on government regulation of campaign finance have been quite substantial. The Court's 1995 invalidation of state-imposed term limits for members of Congress will affect the course of national government unless and until term limits are adopted in another fashion, and its 1997 decisions upholding state prohibitions of doctor-assisted suicide are likely to have a fundamental impact on some people's lives. While it would be a mistake to regard the Court as all-important, it would also be a mistake to accept Dr. Jack Kevorkian's judgment that "what the Supreme Court does is irrelevant."[64]

Some Areas of Court Activity

We can gain a better sense of the Court's impact on society and the forces that determine that impact by looking at a few areas of the Court's activity. These examples demonstrate that the Court's impact is complex, highly variable, and sometimes quite difficult to measure.

Abortion. Prior to the Court's 1973 decisions in *Roe v. Wade* and *Doe v. Bolton,* two-thirds of the states allowed abortion only under quite limited circumstances, and all but four states had very substantial restrictions. With its decisions the Court disallowed nearly all significant legal restrictions on abortion. By the best estimates, there are now about 1.5 million legal abortions each year. In light of the sequence of events, it seems reasonable to conclude that the Court is responsible for the performance of large numbers of legal abortions. But the reality is more complicated, and it is impossible to assess the Court's impact with any precision.[65]

As Figure 6-1 shows, the number of legal abortions increased by about 150 percent between 1972 and 1979. This massive change suggests that the Court made a great deal of difference. But the rate of increase was actually greater between 1969 and 1972. That increase reflected changes in state laws before and during that period, as some states relaxed their general prohibitions of abortion and a few eliminated most restrictions. If the

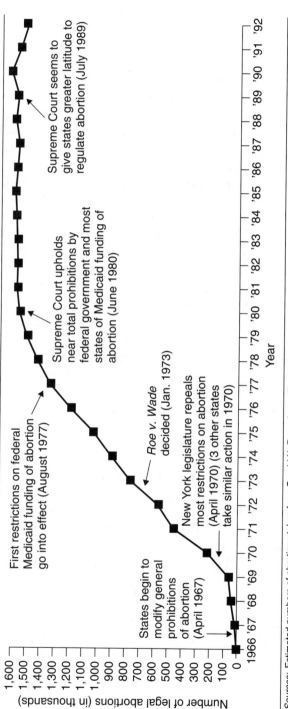

FIGURE 6-1

Estimated Numbers of Legal Abortions and Related Government Policy Actions, 1966–1992

First restrictions on federal Medicaid funding of abortion go into effect (August 1977)

Supreme Court seems to give states greater latitude to regulate abortion (July 1989)

Supreme Court upholds near total prohibitions by federal government and most states of Medicaid funding of abortion (June 1980)

Roe v. Wade decided (Jan. 1973)

New York legislature repeals most restrictions on abortion (April 1970) (3 other states take similar action in 1970)

States begin to modify general prohibitions of abortion (April 1967)

Number of legal abortions (in thousands)

1,600
1,500
1,400
1,300
1,200
1,100
1,000
900
800
700
600
500
400
300
200
100
0

1966 '67 '68 '69 '70 '71 '72 '73 '74 '75 '76 '77 '78 '79 '80 '81 '82 '83 '84 '85 '86 '87 '88 '89 '90 '91 '92

Year

Sources: Estimated numbers of abortions taken from Gerald N. Rosenberg, *The Hollow Hope: Can Courts Bring About Social Change?* (Chicago: University of Chicago Press, 1991), 180 (for 1968–1985); and Stanley K. Henshaw and Jennifer Van Vort, "Abortion Services in the United States, 1991 and 1992," *Family Planning Perspectives* 26 (May–June 1994): 101 (for 1986–1992).

Court had never handed down *Roe v. Wade,* it is likely that the abortion rate would have grown further as a result of increasing numbers of abortions in the states that already allowed it and continuing change in state laws. But it is impossible to know how state laws would have evolved if the Court had not intervened. For that reason, there is need for considerable caution in assessing the Court's effects on the abortion rate.

In this area, as in others, the extent of the Court's impact reflects action by other individuals and institutions. Of course, the number of abortions depends largely on women's choices whether to seek them. But also important is the ability of women who want abortions to obtain them.[66] About two-thirds of all abortions occur in clinics, in part because most hospitals do not perform abortions. Urban areas generally have clinics that perform abortions, but many rural areas lack such clinics. The limited number of facilities that perform abortions in some areas and some states reflects personal beliefs about abortion on the part of potential providers as well as restrictive laws and pressures against providing abortions, ranging from disapproval in the local community to threatened and actual violence. Decisions by the federal government and most states not to fund abortions through Medicaid under most circumstances have affected the availability of abortions to low-income women. These conditions help to explain interstate variation in abortion rates and the absence of further increases in the number of legal abortions since 1979, as indicated in Figure 6-1.

In the 1980s and early 1990s, Presidents Reagan and Bush adopted some new restrictions on abortion and the Court indicated that it was more willing to accept restrictions. Yet the abortion rate remained stable. Actions by the president and Court may have had an effect, but if so that effect was small or counterbalanced by other developments.

Roe v. Wade has had an unexpected and important political impact. The decision greatly strengthened the developing movement against legalized abortion by creating a perceived need for action and a target to attack. By the same token, the groups that had sought legalization of abortion found it difficult to maintain their strength after their major goal had been accomplished. As a result, opponents of legalized abortion had an advantage for several years in influencing elections and legislation. This advantage helped to bring about the array of federal and state restrictions on abortion that followed *Roe*. And the Court at least accelerated the development of a situation in which abortion is a major issue in national politics, one that affects government action on a variety of other issues.

Political Dissent. The Supreme Court often reviews government actions that punish people for making unpopular political statements. The Court has a mixed record in these cases, but over the last four decades it has done much to protect political dissenters from censorship and punishment. In the 1960s it struck down a number of government policies aimed at people with Communist associations. During the Vietnam War it issued several decisions that shielded opponents of official U.S. policy from punishment for their activities. In the past decade it has ruled that people cannot be denied government contracts because they criticized government officials and that they cannot be given criminal penalties for burning the flag as a political statement.

The impact of these decisions is difficult to measure, but undoubtedly the Court has made some difference. For instance, its protection of opponents of the war in Vietnam—particularly its decisions disallowing retaliation by the Selective Service System against antiwar protesters[67]—probably encouraged the open expression of dissent.

Yet there is no evidence that the Court has brought about a massive increase in the level of political dissent in the United States. One reason is the Court's own mixed and incomplete support for political dissent. But also important are conditions that lie primarily in the private sector. For one thing, most people simply do not hold highly unpopular views about political matters that they wish to express; for that reason, their freedom to express such views makes no difference to them.

Further, people realize that the Court cannot prevent all the negative consequences of political dissent. People may refrain from saying what they think because they fear that friends and neighbors will ostracize them, community groups will attack them, customers will withdraw their patronage, or employers will fire them. A player in the National Basketball Association who decided on religious grounds not to stand for the national anthem was suspended by the league until he backed down.[68]

Even worse consequences may befall those who express unpopular views. Opponents of government-sponsored religious activities frequently experience property damage, harassment, and death threats. The black parents and local leaders who fought against inadequate and segregated schools in the South often had to deal with severe economic pressures and violence. It is not surprising that people often choose to remain silent rather than face such consequences. This result underlines the limits on the Court's ability to change basic social realities.

Racial Equality

In debates over the Supreme Court's efficacy, considerable emphasis is given to its impact on racial equality. That emphasis is appropriate in light of the Court's heavy involvement in this field and the central importance of racial equality as an issue in American society.

The Court gave strong and increasing support to racial equality between the 1940s and 1960s. It attacked discrimination in areas such as education and voting, and it also sought to protect the civil rights movement from legal attack in the South. The Court took a more mixed position in the 1970s, but in that decade it endorsed strong remedies for school segregation and upheld the use of affirmative action programs in education and employment.

The implicit goal of these decisions was improvement in the status of black Americans. To what extent have the Court's policies achieved that goal?

Change in Status. The process of effecting change in the situation of black Americans has been complex and ambiguous. Understandably, there is considerable disagreement about how much change has actually occurred. Perhaps the best generalization is that progress has varied among the major areas of racial inequality.

Politically, racial barriers to black voting in the South were overcome. The growth in black voting and changes in racial attitudes have led to large increases in the number of black elected officials—from about 300 in 1965 to 8,000 in 1993.[69] Growth in black political power is also reflected in the growing willingness of white officials to respond to black concerns.

Socially, the segregation of American life has broken down to a limited degree. Segregation of hotels and restaurants, once standard practice in much of the country, is now unusual. Legally segregated school systems no longer exist in the Deep South and the border states, but the level of actual segregation remains substantial and has increased somewhat since the 1970s.[70] Continuing racial segregation in schools reflects the high level of housing segregation, which has declined little since 1970.[71]

Economically, the overall status of black citizens has improved significantly, but there remains considerable inequality. In 1994 the median annual income for black families was 62 percent of the median for whites. In the same year 43 percent of black children lived in poverty, compared with 16 percent for whites.[72] Employment discrimination has declined, probably a great deal, but a 1991 study in Chicago and Washington, D.C., demonstrated vividly that it has not disappeared.[73]

The Court's Role. Because progress toward racial equality has been limited, it is clear that the most optimistic expectations of the Supreme Court have not been realized. Federal judge Robert Carter, who was a lawyer with the NAACP Legal Defense Fund in 1954, recalled that when the Court decided *Brown v. Board of Education*, "I really thought that was it, the end of the civil rights struggle." It did not take long for him to realize that he had been wrong.[74]

Of the progress toward racial equality that *has* occurred, how much can be ascribed to the Supreme Court? Certainly there have been other important sources for the change that has occurred. Particularly during the 1960s, Congress and the federal executive branch made significant contributions to the achievement of equal rights; so have many state and local governments. Nongovernmental forces for change include the mass media and, more important, the civil rights movement itself.

The limits of the Court's own impact are clear in education and voting, the areas in which it has been most active. Despite *Brown v. Board of Education* (1954), school segregation in the Deep South did not break down until the Civil Rights Act of 1964 provided financial inducements for desegregation. The Court's decisions eliminated some barriers to black voting, but those decisions did not bring about full access to the ballot box in the South. That access came after the Voting Rights Act of

1965 created administrative mechanisms for effective enforcement of the right to vote. In both areas the Johnson administration's vigorous use of its enforcement powers under these laws was also important.

Because constitutional protections do not apply directly to private discrimination, the Court could do little by itself to attack discrimination in employment and housing. Instead, the initiative has come primarily from the other branches: Congress passed statutes mandating equal treatment, and the executive branch has enforced them. But the Court has given important interpretations to these laws; until the late 1980s it generally gave them expansive interpretations that enhanced their potential impact. There is evidence that the federal laws against employment discrimination have had a significant impact on the economic status of black citizens; this impact can be ascribed primarily to the executive and legislative branches, but the Court might be given a small degree of responsibility for it.

It is difficult to ascertain whether the Court's early civil rights decisions helped to spur passage of federal legislation in this area and strengthened the civil rights movement. In his careful analysis of this issue, Gerald Rosenberg concluded that the Court's impact in both respects was minimal,[75] but a case can be made that the Court actually had significant impact.

The development of a mass civil rights movement in the South was probably inevitable, and the Supreme Court was hardly the major force contributing to its development. But the Court may have speeded the movement's growth. Its decisions in education and other areas created hope for change and established rights to be vindicated by political action. This is particularly true of the *Brown* decision, which had considerable symbolic importance for some people.[76] The Court's protection of the civil rights movement itself did not eliminate the harassment of civil rights groups in the South or the violence against their members, but the Court helped to ensure that the movement would be able to withstand the pressures placed on it.

The series of civil rights laws adopted from 1957 on also may owe something to the Court. In education and voting, the Court initiated government action against discrimination and helped to create expectations that Congress and the executive branch were pressed to fulfill. It is true that congressional action was most directly responsible for bringing about school desegregation in the Deep South. But if the Court had not issued the *Brown* decision, Congress might have had less impetus to act against segregation at all.

In the last decade, a more conservative Court has been less favorable to the goals of civil rights groups. In a series of decisions it gave narrow interpretations to statutes prohibiting employment discrimination. It has set very high standards for governments that seek to justify affirmative action programs for minority-owned businesses or the design of legislative districts to facilitate the election of black candidates.

It is possible that this new wave of decisions will have a significant impact on the status of black citizens, but such an impact seems unlikely. Congress has overturned many of the Court's narrow interpretations of civil rights statutes. It is uncertain whether legislative districting has much impact on the political power of black citizens. If extended to other areas, the Court's limiting of affirmative action ultimately might have a marked effect, but such an impact is not guaranteed.

An Assessment. The issue of racial equality illustrates both the strengths and limitations of government in achieving societal change. Public policy has helped to bring about significant reductions in the disadvantages of black Americans. But these disadvantages have hardly disappeared, and even a stronger government commitment to equality could not have eliminated them altogether.

For the Supreme Court specifically, the assessment is also mixed. The Court has had little direct impact on discrimination in the private sector. Even in the public sector, it has been weak in the enforcement of rights. But it has helped to initiate and support processes of change, and its members probably can take some credit for progress toward racial equality. If the Court's effects have been far more limited than many people had hoped, the Court has contributed to significant social change.

Conclusion: The Court, Public Policy, and Society

It is now possible to reach some general conclusions about the role of the Supreme Court as a public policy maker. As this chapter and Chapter 5 suggest, that role is fundamentally limited in some respects but still quite important.

The most obvious limitation on the Court's role is that it addresses only a small number of issues. In many policy areas, the Court rarely makes decisions. To take the most important example, the Court is a minor participant in the making of foreign policy. And it plays only a small part in many fields of significant judicial activity, such as contract law and family relations.

Even in its areas of specialization, the Court intervenes in the policy-making process only in limited ways. It makes decisions on a small sample of the issues that affect the rights of criminal defendants or freedom of expression. And the Court has been cautious about substituting its judgment for that of Congress and the president.

When the Court does intervene, its impact is often reduced by the actions of other institutions and individuals. A ruling that public schools must eliminate organized prayers does not guarantee that those observances will disappear. Efforts to broaden freedom of expression may be stymied by conditions in society that the Court cannot influence.

These limitations must be balanced against the Court's considerable strengths. Certainly a great many Supreme Court decisions have significant direct effects. Antitrust decisions determine whether companies can merge. School desegregation decisions determine the schools that students attend. Interpretations of the Voting Rights Act shape the course of local politics. The effects of capital punishment decisions are literally matters of life and death for some people.

The Court also helps to shape political and social change. Its partial opposition to government regulation of private business was ultimately overcome, but the Court slowed a fundamental change in the role of government. If *Roe v. Wade* was not as consequential as most people think, it *has* been the focus of a major national debate and struggle for more than two decades. The Court's decisions have not brought about racial equality, even in conjunction with other forces, but they have helped to spur changes in race relations.

As the examples of abortion and civil rights suggest, the Court is perhaps most important in creating conditions for action by others. Its decisions put issues on the national agenda so that other policy makers and the general public consider them. The Court is not highly effective in enforcing rights, but it often legitimates efforts to achieve them and thus provides the impetus for people to take legal and political action. Its decisions affect the positions of interest groups and social movements, strengthening some and weakening others.

The Supreme Court, then, is neither all-powerful nor insignificant. Rather, it is one of many public and private institutions that shape American society in significant ways. That is a more limited role than some have claimed for the Court. But the role that the Court does play is an extraordinary one for a single small body that possesses little tangible power. In this sense, perhaps more than any other, the Supreme Court is a remarkable institution.

NOTES

1. *Engel v. Vitale* (1962); *Abington School District v. Schempp* (1963).
2. *Jaffree v. Board of School Commissioners*, 554 F. Supp. 1104, 1128 (S.D. Alab. 1983).
3. Edward Keynes, with Randall K. Miller, *The Court vs. Congress: Prayer, Busing, and Abortion* (Durham, N.C.: Duke University Press, 1989), 174–205.
4. William Booth, "Crusade for Prayer in School Wins Converts," *Washington Post*, April 1, 1994, A1, A4; Pamela Coyle, "Prayer Pendulum," *American Bar Association Journal*, January 1995, 62–66.
5. Katharine Q. Seelye, "Religion Amendment is Introduced," *New York Times*, May 9, 1997, A14.
6. *Burden v. Zant*, 126 L. Ed. 2d 611, 614 (1994).
7. Darryl Paulson and Paul Hawkes, "Desegregating the University of Florida Law School: Virgil Hawkins v. The Florida Board of Control," *Florida State University Law Review* 12 (Spring 1984): 59–71; David Margolick, "At the Bar," *New York Times*, February 25, 1994, A19.
8. The case was *Vasquez v. Harris* (1992). See Katherine Bishop, "After Long Night of Legal Battles, California Carries Out Execution," *New York Times*, April 22, 1992, A1, C23.
9. "Harassment Case Heard by High Court is Settled," *New York Times*, February 10, 1995, A25.
10. *Grumet v. Cuomo* (N.Y. Ct. App. 1997); Raymond Hernandez, "Defying Courts, Lawmakers Approve School District for Hasidim," *New York Times*, August 5, 1997, C24.
11. *Biggins v. Hazen Paper Company*, 111 F.3d 205, 206 (1st Cir. 1997).
12. James Brent, "An Agent Serving Two Principals: United States Courts of Appeals Responses to *Employment Division v. Smith* and the Religious Freedom Restoration Act" (Paper presented at the annual meeting of the Midwest Political Science Association, Chicago, April 1997).
13. R. Shep Melnick, *Between the Lines: Interpreting Welfare Rights* (Washington, D.C.: Brookings Institution, 1994), 253–255.

14. See Michael J. Berens, "Punishing the Poor," *Columbus Dispatch,* September 25, 1994, 1A, 2A; Berens, "'Hook 'Em and Book 'Em'," *Columbus Dispatch,* November 18, 1996, 2A.
15. Harrell R. Rodgers, Jr., and Charles S. Bullock III, *Law and Social Change: Civil Rights Laws and Their Consequences* (New York: McGraw-Hill, 1972), 75.
16. *Green v. School Board* (1968); *Alexander v. Holmes County Board of Education* (1969).
17. *Missouri v. Jenkins* (1990); *Spallone v. United States* (1989).
18. Leigh A. Morrissey, "State Courts Reject *Leon* on State Constitutional Grounds: A Defense of Reactive Rulings," *Vanderbilt Law Review* 47 (April 1994): 917–941; *State v. Canelo* (N.H. Sup. Ct. 1995).
19. Richard A. Leo, "The Impact of *Miranda* Revisited," *Journal of Criminal Law and Criminology* 86 (Spring 1996): 652–653. See also Paul G. Cassell and Bret S. Hayman, "Police Interrogation in the 1990s: An Empirical Study of the Effects of *Miranda*," *UCLA Law Review* 43 (February 1996): 887–892.
20. Leo, "Impact of *Miranda* Revisited," 663. See Stephen J. Schulhofer, "*Miranda*'s Practical Effect: Substantial Benefits and Vanishingly Small Social Costs," *Northwestern University Law Review* 90 (Winter 1996): 507–510.
21. Antonio Olivo and Jim Newton, "Suit Says Police Violate Suspects' Miranda Rights," *Los Angeles Times,* December 21, 1995, B3.
22. *Harris v. New York* (1971).
23. Jerome H. Skolnick, *Justice Without Trial: Law Enforcement in Democratic Society,* 3d ed. (New York: Macmillan, 1994), 277 (emphasis in original).
24. Bradley C. Canon, "Is the Exclusionary Rule in Failing Health? Some New Data and a Plea against a Precipitous Conclusion," *Kentucky Law Journal* 62 (1974): 702–725; and Myron W. Orfield, Jr., "The Exclusionary Rule and Deterrence: An Empirical Study of Chicago Narcotics Officers," *University of Chicago Law Review* 54 (Summer 1987): 1024–1049; Craig D. Uchida and Timothy S. Bynum, "Search Warrants, Motions to Suppress and 'Lost Cases': The Effects of the Exclusionary Rule in Seven Jurisdictions," *Journal of Criminal Law and Criminology* 81 (Winter 1991): 1034–1066.
25. Skolnick, *Justice Without Trial,* 279.
26. Thomas Y. Davies, "A Hard Look at What We Know (and Still Need to Learn) about the 'Costs' of the Exclusionary Rule: The NIJ Study and Other Studies of 'Lost' Arrests," *American Bar Foundation Research Journal* (Summer 1983): 611–690.
27. Harold J. Rothwax, *Guilty: The Collapse of Criminal Justice* (New York: Random House, 1996), 41.
28. *United States v. Hollingsworth* (7th Cir. 1994). The Supreme Court decision was *Jacobson v. United States* (1992).
29. Elliot E. Slotnick and Jennifer A. Segal, *Television News and the Supreme Court: All the News That's Fit to Air* (New York: Cambridge University Press, forthcoming).
30. William C. Heffernan and Richard W. Lovely, "Evaluating the Fourth Amendment Exclusionary Rule: The Problem of Police Compliance with the Law," *University of Michigan Journal of Law Reform* 24 (1991): 333.
31. *Matsushita Electric Industrial Co., Ltd. v. Epstein,* 134 L. Ed. 2d 6, 26 (1996). See William Carlsen, "Frontier Justice," *San Francisco Chronicle,* October 6, 1996, Sunday section, 1, 4, 5.

32. Anne Freedman, *Patronage: An American Tradition* (Chicago: Nelson-Hall, 1994). The major decision was *Rutan v. Republican Party of Illinois* (1990).

33. Michael J. Berens, "Holding the Purse Strings," *Columbus Dispatch,* November 19, 1996, 1A, 2A.

34. J.W. Peltason, *Fifty-eight Lonely Men: Southern Federal Judges and School Desegregation* (Urbana: University of Illinois Press, 1971), 9.

35. "Parents Stage Demonstration," *New Orleans Times Picayune,* November 24, 1960, quoted in Robert Coles, *Children of Crisis: A Study of Courage and Fear* (Boston: Little, Brown, 1967), 385 n. 2.

36. *Singleton v. Norris,* 108 F.3d 872, 873–874, 876 (8th Cir. 1997).

37. William K. Muir, Jr., *Prayer in the Public Schools: Law and Attitude Change* (Chicago: University of Chicago Press, 1967); and Richard Johnson, *The Dynamics of Compliance* (Evanston, Ill.: Northwestern University Press, 1967).

38. Robert Satter, *Doing Justice: A Trial Judge at Work* (New York: Simon & Schuster, 1990), 227.

39. See Donald R. Songer and Reginald S. Sheehan, "Supreme Court Impact on Compliance and Outcomes: *Miranda* and *New York Times* in the United States Courts of Appeals," *Western Political Quarterly* 43 (June 1990): 297–316; and Donald R. Songer, Jeffrey A. Segal, and Charles M. Cameron, "The Hierarchy of Justice: Testing a Principal-Agent Model of Supreme Court–Circuit Court Interactions," *American Journal of Political Science* 38 (August 1994): 673–696.

40. David G. Savage, "Crusading Liberal Judge Keeps High Court Busy," *Los Angeles Times,* March 3, 1996, A3.

41. William N. Eskridge, Jr., "Overriding Supreme Court Statutory Interpretation Decisions," *Yale Law Journal* 101 (November 1991): 338; updating through 1996 is from Lori Hausegger and Lawrence Baum, "Behind the Scenes: The Supreme Court and Congress in Statutory Interpretation," in *Great Theater: The American Congress in Action,* ed. Herbert F. Weisberg and Samuel C. Patterson (New York: Cambridge University Press, forthcoming).

42. Beth M. Henschen and Edward I. Sidlow, "The Supreme Court and the Congressional Agenda-Setting Process" (Paper presented at the annual meeting of the Midwest Political Science Association, Chicago, April 1988); Michael E. Solimine and James L. Walker, "The Next Word: Congressional Response to Supreme Court Statutory Decisions," *Temple Law Review* 65 (1992): 425–458; Melnick, *Between the Lines,* 261–264.

43. Eskridge, "Overriding Statutory Decisions," 348, 351, 359–367.

44. Sam Fulwood III, "House Again Approves Ban on Burning American Flag," *Los Angeles Times,* June 13, 1997, A27.

45. Louis Fisher, "The Legislative Veto: Invalidated, It Survives," *Law and Contemporary Problems* 56 (Autumn 1993): 273–292.

46. Dean L. Yarwood and Bradley C. Canon, "On the Supreme Court's Annual Trek to the Capitol," *Judicature* 63 (February 1980): 324.

47. U.S. Congress, House, *Congressional Record,* 89th Cong., 1st sess., 1965, 111, pt. 4, 5275. See John R. Schmidhauser and Larry L. Berg, *The Supreme Court and Congress: Conflict and Interaction, 1945–1968* (New York: Free Press, 1972), 8–12.

48. "The President's Radio Address," *Weekly Compilation of Presidential Documents* 31 (May 8, 1995): 735.

49. *Chamber of Commerce of the United States v. Reich* (D.C. Cir. 1996).
50. Samuel Krislov, *The Supreme Court in the Political Process* (New York: Macmillan, 1965), 140.
51. *Arkansas Term Limits v. Donovan* (1996, 1997).
52. The decisions were, respectively, *Davis v. Michigan Department of Treasury* (1989); *Harper v. Virginia Department of Taxation* (1993); *Reich v. Collins* (1994); and *Harper v. Virginia Department of Taxation* (Va. Sup. Ct. 1995).
53. Bureau of Justice Statistics, *Justice Expenditure and Employment, 1990* (Washington, D.C.: U.S. Department of Justice, 1992), 3.
54. Richard A. Posner, *The Federal Courts: Challenge and Reform* (Cambridge, Mass.: Harvard University Press, 1996), 326.
55. See William N. Eskridge, Jr., "Reneging on History? Playing the Court/Congress/President Civil Rights Game," *California Law Review* 79 (May 1991): 613–684.
56. *Landgraf v. USI Film Products* (1994); *Rivers v. Roadway Express* (1994).
57. Glen A. Halva-Neubauer, "The States after *Roe*: No 'Paper Tigers,'" in *Understanding the New Politics of Abortion,* ed. Malcolm L. Goggin (Newbury Park, Calif.: Sage Publications, 1993), 167–189.
58. The decision was *Bray v. Alexandria Women's Health Clinic* (1993).
59. From remarks at the Heritage Foundation, Washington, D.C., January 29, 1996 (transcript from Federal Document Clearing House).
60. Paul G. Cassell, "True Confessions About *Miranda*'s Legacy," *Legal Times,* July 22, 1996, 21.
61. U.S. Congress, Senate, *Congressional Record,* daily ed., 103d Congress, 2d session, February 3, 1994, S725.
62. Gerald N. Rosenberg, "What the Court Can't Do," *New York Times,* September 22, 1991, 17. See also Rosenberg, *The Hollow Hope: Can Courts Bring about Social Change?* (Chicago: University of Chicago Press, 1991); and Posner, *The Federal Courts,* 325–327.
63. *44 Liquormart, Inc. v. Rhode Island* (1996).
64. "Kevorkian Wants No Part of Supreme Court 'Kooks'," *Washington Post,* January 6, 1997, A6.
65. This discussion of abortion is based in part on Rosenberg, *The Hollow Hope,* 175–201; and Matthew E. Wetstein, "The Abortion Rate Paradox: The Impact of National Policy Change on Abortion Rates," *Social Science Quarterly* 76 (September 1995): 607–618.
66. Information on facilities performing abortions is from Stanley K. Henshaw, "Factors Hindering Access to Abortion Services," *Family Planning Perspectives* 27 (March 1995): 54–59, 87.
67. *Oestereich v. Selective Service System* (1968); *Gutknecht v. United States* (1970).
68. Jack McCallum, "Oh Say Should We Sing?" *Sports Illustrated,* March 25, 1996, 51–52, 54.
69. Gerald David Jaynes and Robin M. Williams, Jr., *A Common Destiny: Blacks and American Society* (Washington, D.C.: National Academy Press, 1989), 238; U.S. Bureau of the Census, *Statistical Abstract of the United States, 1996* (Washington, D.C.: Government Printing Office, 1996), 284.
70. Peter Applebome, "Schools See Re-Emergence of 'Separate but Equal'," *New York Times,* April 8, 1997, A8. See also Gary Orfield, Susan E. Eaton, and the Harvard Project on School Desegregation, *Dismantling Desegregation: The Quiet Reversal of* Brown v. Board of Education (New York: New Press, 1996).

71. Douglas S. Massey and Nancy A. Denton, *American Apartheid: Segregation and the Making of the Underclass* (Cambridge, Mass.: Harvard University Press, 1993).
72. Bureau of the Census, *Statistical Abstract 1996,* 461, 472.
73. Margery Austin Turner, Michael Fix, and Raymond J. Struyk, *Opportunities Denied, Opportunities Diminished: Discrimination in Hiring* (Washington, D.C.: Urban Institute, 1991).
74. Ron Grossman and Charles Leroux, "Brown vs. Segregation: Landmark Case at 40," *Chicago Tribune,* May 15, 1994, sec. 1, 1.
75. Rosenberg, *The Hollow Hope,* 107–156.
76. Jesse H. Choper, *Judicial Review and the National Political Process* (Chicago: University of Chicago Press, 1980), 93–94; and Bradley C. Canon, "The Supreme Court as a Cheerleader in Politico-Moral Disputes," *Journal of Politics* 54 (August 1992): 637–653.

Glossary

Legal Terms Related to the Supreme Court

Affirm. In an appellate court, to reach a decision that agrees with the result reached in the case by the lower court.

Amicus curiae. "Friend of the court." A person, private group or institution, or government agency, not a party to a case, that participates in the case (usually through submission of a brief) at the invitation of the court or on its own initiative.

Appeal. In general, a case brought to a higher court for review. In the Supreme Court, a small number of cases are designated as appeals under federal law; formally, these must be heard by the Court.

Appellant. The party that appeals a lower court decision to a higher court.

Appellee. A party to an appeal who wishes to have the lower court decision upheld and who responds when the case is appealed.

Brief. A document submitted by counsel to a court, setting out the facts of the case and the legal arguments in support of the party represented by the counsel.

Certiorari, writ of. A writ issued by the Supreme Court, at its discretion, to order a lower court to send a case to the Supreme Court for review. Most cases come to the Court as petitions for writs of certiorari.

Civil cases. All legal cases other than criminal cases.

Class action. A lawsuit brought by one person or group on behalf of all persons in similar situations.

Concurring opinion. An opinion by a member of a court that agrees with the result reached by the court in the case but offers its own rationale for the decision.

Dicta. *See* Obiter dictum.

Discretionary jurisdiction. Jurisdiction that a court may accept or reject in particular cases. The Supreme Court has discretionary jurisdiction over most cases that come to it.

Dissenting opinion. An opinion by a member of a court that disagrees with the result reached by the court in the case.

Habeas corpus. "You have the body." A writ issued by a court to inquire whether a person is lawfully imprisoned or detained. The writ demands that the persons holding the prisoner justify the detention or release the prisoner.

Holding. In a majority opinion, the rule of law necessary to decide the case. That rule is binding in future cases.

In forma pauperis. "In the manner of a pauper." In the Supreme Court, cases brought in forma pauperis by indigent persons are exempt from the Court's usual fees and from some formal requirements.

Judicial review. Review of legislation or other governmental action to determine its consistency with the federal or state constitution; includes the power to strike down policies that are inconsistent with a constitutional provision. The Supreme Court reviews government action only under the federal Constitution, not state constitutions.

Jurisdiction. The power of a court to hear a case in question.

Litigants. The parties to a court case.

Majority opinion. An opinion in a case that is subscribed to by a majority of the judges who participated in the decision. Also known as the opinion of the court.

Mandamus. "We command." An order issued by a court that directs a lower court or other authority to perform a particular act.

Mandatory jurisdiction. Jurisdiction that a court must accept. Cases falling under a court's mandatory jurisdiction must be decided officially on their merits, though a court may avoid giving them full consideration.

Modify. In an appellate court, to reach a decision that disagrees in part with the result reached in the case by the lower court.

Moot. A moot case is one that has become hypothetical, so that a court need not decide it.

Obiter dictum. (Also called *dictum* [sing.] or *dicta* [pl.].) A statement in a court opinion that is not necessary to resolve the case before the court. Dicta are not binding in future cases.

Original jurisdiction. Jurisdiction as a trial court.

Per curiam. "By the court." An unsigned opinion of the court, often quite brief.

Petitioner. One who files a petition with a court seeking action or relief, such as a writ of certiorari.

Remand. To send back. When a case is remanded, it is sent back by a higher court to the court from which it came, for further action.

Respondent. The party in opposition to a petitioner or appellant, who answers the claims of that party.

Reverse. In an appellate court, to reach a decision that disagrees with the result reached in the case by the lower court.

Standing. A requirement that the party who files a lawsuit have a legal stake in the outcome.

Stare decisis. "Let the decision stand." The doctrine that principles of law established in earlier judicial decisions should be accepted as authoritative in similar subsequent cases.

Statute. A written law enacted by a legislature.

Stay. To halt or suspend further judicial proceedings. The Supreme Court sometimes issues a stay to suspend action in a lower court while the Supreme Court considers the case.

Vacate. To make void or annul. The Supreme Court sometimes vacates a lower court decision, requiring the lower court to reconsider the case.

Writ. A written court order commanding the designated recipient to perform or not perform acts specified in the order.

Selected Bibliography

The books listed here may be useful to readers who would like to explore further subjects discussed in this book. Books are listed according to the chapters that are most closely related to their subject matter.

Chapter 2: The Justices

Abraham, Henry J. *Justices and Presidents: A Political History of Appointments to the Supreme Court,* 3d ed. New York: Oxford University Press, 1992.

Carter, Stephen L. *The Confirmation Mess: Cleaning Up the Federal Appointments Process.* New York: Basic Books, 1994.

Maltese, John Anthony. *The Selling of Supreme Court Nominees.* Baltimore: Johns Hopkins University Press, 1995.

Massaro, John. *Supremely Political: The Role of Ideology and Presidential Management in Unsuccessful Supreme Court Nominations.* Albany: State University of New York Press, 1990.

Schmidhauser, John R. *Judges and Justices: The Federal Appellate Judiciary.* Boston: Little, Brown, 1979.

Silverstein, Mark. *Judicious Choices: The New Politics of Supreme Court Confirmations.* New York: W. W. Norton, 1994.

Watson, George L., and John A. Stookey. *Shaping America: The Politics of Supreme Court Appointments.* New York: HarperCollins, 1995.

Chapter 3: The Cases

Fried, Charles. *Order and Law: Arguing the Reagan Revolution—A Firsthand Account.* New York: Simon & Schuster, 1991.

Garrow, David J. *Liberty and Sexuality: The Right to Privacy and the Making of* Roe v. Wade. New York: Macmillan, 1994.

Ivers, Gregg. *To Build a Wall: American Jews and the Separation of Church and State.* Charlottesville: University Press of Virginia, 1995.

Kluger, Richard. *Simple Justice: The History of Brown v. Board of Education and Black America's Struggle for Equality.* New York: Alfred A. Knopf, 1976.

Kobylka, Joseph F. *The Politics of Obscenity: Group Litigation in a Time of Legal Change.* Westport, Conn.: Greenwood Press, 1991.

Lawrence, Susan E. *The Poor in Court: The Legal Services Program and Supreme Court Decision Making.* Princeton, N.J.: Princeton University Press, 1990.

McGuire, Kevin T. *The Supreme Court Bar: Legal Elites in the Washington Community.* Charlottesville: University Press of Virginia, 1993.

Perry, H. W., Jr. *Deciding to Decide: Agenda Setting in the United States Supreme Court.* Cambridge, Mass.: Harvard University Press, 1991.

Provine, Doris Marie. *Case Selection in the United States Supreme Court.* Chicago: University of Chicago Press, 1980.

Salokar, Rebecca Mae. *The Solicitor General: The Politics of Law.* Philadelphia: Temple University Press, 1992.

Sorauf, Frank J. *The Wall of Separation: The Constitutional Politics of Church and State.* Princeton, N.J.: Princeton University Press, 1976.

Urofsky, Melvin. *Affirmative Action on Trial: Sex Discrimination in* Johnson v. Santa Clara. Lawrence: University Press of Kansas, 1997.

Walker, Samuel. *In Defense of American Liberties: A History of the ACLU.* New York: Oxford University Press, 1990.

Wasby, Stephen L. *Race Relations Litigation in an Age of Complexity.* Charlottesville: University Press of Virginia, 1995.

Chapter 4: Decision Making

Brenner, Saul, and Harold J. Spaeth. *Stare Indecisis: The Alteration of Precedent on the Supreme Court, 1946–1992.* New York: Cambridge University Press, 1995.

Cooper, Phillip J. *Battles on the Bench: Conflict Inside the Supreme Court*. Lawrence: University Press of Kansas, 1995.

Davis, Sue. *Justice Rehnquist and the Constitution*. Princeton, N.J.: Princeton University Press, 1989.

Epstein, Lee, and Jack Knight. *The Choices Justices Make*. Washington, D.C.: CQ Press, 1998.

Epstein, Lee, and Joseph F. Kobylka. *The Supreme Court and Legal Change: Abortion and the Death Penalty*. Chapel Hill: University of North Carolina Press, 1992.

Lamb, Charles M., and Stephen C. Halpern, eds. *The Burger Court: Political and Judicial Profiles*. Urbana: University of Illinois Press, 1991.

Marshall, Thomas R. *Public Opinion and the Supreme Court*. Winchester, Mass.: Unwin Hyman, 1989.

Murphy, Walter F. *Elements of Judicial Strategy*. Chicago: University of Chicago Press, 1964.

Savage, David G. *Turning Right: The Making of the Rehnquist Supreme Court*. New York: John Wiley & Sons, 1992.

Schwartz, Bernard. *Decision: How the Supreme Court Decides Cases*. New York: Oxford University Press, 1996.

Schwartz, Bernard. *The Unpublished Opinions of the Rehnquist Court*. New York: Oxford University Press, 1996.

Segal, Jeffrey A., and Harold J. Spaeth. *The Supreme Court and the Attitudinal Model*. New York: Cambridge University Press, 1993.

Simon, James F. *The Center Holds: The Power Struggle Inside the Rehnquist Court*. New York: Simon & Schuster, 1995.

Smolla, Rodney A., ed. *A Year in the Life of the Supreme Court*. Durham, N.C.: Duke University Press, 1995.

Chapter 5: Policy Outputs

Gates, John B. *The Supreme Court and Partisan Realignment: A Macro- and Microlevel Perspective*. Boulder, Colo.: Westview Press, 1992.

Leuchtenburg, William E. *The Supreme Court Reborn: The Constitutional Revolution in the Age of Roosevelt*. New York: Oxford University Press, 1995.

McCloskey, Robert G., rev. by Sanford Levinson. *The American Supreme Court*, 2d ed. Chicago: University of Chicago Press, 1994.

Pacelle, Richard L., Jr. *The Transformation of the Supreme Court's Agenda From the New Deal to the Reagan Administration.* Boulder, Colo: Westview Press, 1991.

Scigliano, Robert. *The Supreme Court and the Presidency.* New York: Free Press, 1971.

Shapiro, Martin. *The Supreme Court and Administrative Agencies.* New York: Free Press, 1968.

Wolfe, Christopher. *Judicial Activism: Bulwark of Freedom or Precarious Security?* Pacific Grove, Calif.: Brooks/Cole, 1991.

Chapter 6: The Court's Impact

Bradley, Craig M. *The Failure of the Criminal Procedure Revolution.* Philadelphia: University of Pennsylvania Press, 1993.

Davis, Richard. *Decisions and Images: The Supreme Court and the Press.* Englewood Cliffs, N.J.: Prentice-Hall, 1994.

Johnson, Charles A., and Bradley C. Canon. *Judicial Policies: Implementation and Impact.* Washington, D.C.: CQ Press, 1984.

Keynes, Edward, with Randall K. Miller. *The Court vs. Congress: Prayer, Busing, and Abortion.* Durham, N.C.: Duke University Press, 1989.

Lasser, William. *The Limits of Judicial Power: The Supreme Court in American Politics.* Chapel Hill: University of North Carolina Press, 1988.

Peltason, J. W. *Fifty-Eight Lonely Men: Southern Federal Judges and School Desegregation,* 2d ed. Urbana: University of Illinois Press, 1971.

Rosenberg, Gerald N. *The Hollow Hope: Can Courts Bring About Social Change?* Chicago: University of Chicago Press, 1991.

Case Index

Index